Authority

NOMOS I

Authority

*Edited by CARL J. FRIEDRICH for
The American Society of Political
and Legal Philosophy*

HARVARD UNIVERSITY PRESS
Cambridge, Massachusetts
1958

Library of Congress Catalog Card Number 58-7248
Printed in the United States of America

Preface

The present volume, entitled *Authority,* is the first in what is hoped to become an annual publication of the American Society for Political and Legal Philosophy. This Society was founded in 1955 by a group of friends in the social sciences, law, and philosophy who share an interest in the range of problems traditionally treated within the broad framework of political and legal philosophy. It is our belief that these problems are of vital importance and that they require interdisciplinary exploration, treatment and discussion. One major activity of the Society is the publication of an annual volume dedicated to the topic of the annual meeting and built around the major contributions to the conference.

We are calling the series NOMOS, which is the broadest Greek term for law, because in this term there are also traditionally comprised the notions of a basic political order and of customs and a way of life. It describes reasonably well, and perhaps better than any term of modern English, what must be the focus of a society such as ours, uniting the several social sciences, law, and philosophy.

The volume grew out of the discussions of the meeting held in 1956, but is not simply a collection of the papers there read. Some of the chapters are that (Arendt, Hall, Hendel), but others were developed from briefer invited comments (Friedrich, Jacobson). Still others are elaborations of spontaneous remarks made in the course of the discussion by a participant (Catlin, de Jouvenel, Knight, Kraus, Spiro). Finally, there are some which were contributed by members of the Society who had not participated in the meeting (Easton, Hoebel, Parsons), in order to round out and balance the presentation. The rich variety of discussion is, thus, reflected in the contrasting viewpoints of the papers which state very different positions. Yet there would seem to be a common core which the interested reader will probably identify fairly readily.

The next volume, scheduled for 1958-59, will deal with Community, the subject of our 1957 meeting.

It remains to express our appreciation for the aid given by the Twentieth Century Fund which has made this publication possible. The editor would like also to thank Messrs. August Heckscher and Frederick Mundel Watkins for their help in shaping the volume, and Miss Roberta Hill for her competent editorial assistance.

Contents

viii   Contents

PART THREE. AUTHORITY IN SOCIO-POLITICAL PERSPECTIVE

Authority in General

1. An Exploration of the Nature of Authority

CHARLES W. HENDEL

I. A COMMON STATE OF MIND ABOUT AUTHORITY
AND SOME OF ITS SOURCES

An attitude to authority in government that is characteristic of our nation is derived in part from early experience. In the beginning the colonists were rebellious against the rule of a distant government that regulated their commerce and their lives without their having any proper say in the matter. They complained that they were being denied their birthright of political liberty, the right of representation in government, and that they had to suffer violation, without redress, of the personal rights for which their ancestors had fought the century before. There was, however, considerable controversy among them before they declared a necessity of taking up arms.

Thus, Daniel Leonard, writing as "Massachusettensis," and John Adams as "Novanglus," engaged in weekly debate with each other in the public press, and between them defined the issue precisely as one of authority. Leonard objected to an error in the "first principle" assumed by "many of our politicians . . . in denying that the constitutional authority of parliament extends to the colonies."[1] Adams conceded the need of "some superintending power to draw together all the wills and unite all the strength of the subjects in all the dominions [of the British Empire], in case of war and in the case of

[1] *The Political Writings of John Adams, Representative Selections*, ed. George A. Peek, Jr., The American Heritage Series (1954), p. 33.

trade," and held that "it is equally our interest and duty to continue subject to the authority of parliament in the regulation of our trade as long as she shall leave us to govern our internal policy . . ." [2] Such a reservation, however, Leonard could not abide: "We have only to cease contending with the supreme legislature respecting its authority . . . to dismiss our illegal committees, disband our forces, despise the thraldom of arrogant congresses, and submit to constitutional government to be happy." [3] The "arrogant congresses" referred to the Continental Congress that had met several times since 1774, and the term "arrogant" sounds like a retort to Jefferson's *Summary View of the Rights of British America* (1774), challenging "that authority which the British Parliament would arrogate over us," and declaring "that the British Parliament has no right to exercise authority over us." [4] It was not long before the Americans committed themselves to battle and conferred upon their Continental Congress the "superintending power" and the "authority" needful for the offices of war and peace. But while the Congress of the United States was virtually a successor authority to the British Parliament, those first Americans still regarded authority with a jealous eye, wary and fearful of it in any guise. This general attitude became an ingrained habit of the American character.

So, in our day, this ancient disposition is aroused whenever government appears as a distant and external authority extending its power too much into our internal affairs, our private lives and our business. Given the immensity and complexity of the social economy of our time, government is necessarily involved, be it only in a regulative role, in many things that were until recently left to individual initiative and decision. This is felt to be unwarranted interference and resented, not only as an abuse of authority but because it is an act of authority.

Our attitude to authority is, however, really ambivalent. When we are drawn into war, we grant the authority and power necessary for the exigencies of the situation, and this has involved an extension of the arm of government into many activities previously considered

---

[2] *The Political Writings of John Adams*, pp. 47, 52.
[3] *The Political Writings of John Adams*, p. 72.
[4] *The Political Writings of Thomas Jefferson, Representative Selections*, ed. Edward Dumbauld, The American Heritage Series (1955), pp. 18, 21.

outside its reach. Even restrictions upon the liberty of the press and freedom of speech, about which a free people are and ought to be most sensitive, are accepted, and the authority is not felt to be oppressive. In many peacetime enterprises, it is not regarded as an interference. Whenever we want to get things done, for example, about seaports, roadways, or river systems that serve several states or cities, wherever we must break through habits of jealousy and self-interest and a previously demonstrated inability to agree and get on with needed business, an authority is proposed for its obvious benefits, and the name "authority" is readily employed in designating any such useful agency. That authority which secures for us some particular public good is then entirely acceptable. It still remains true, however, that authority on the whole is not welcomed. We are willing to honor it for whatever clear and present good it accomplishes but will not give it unlimited credit. The recent history of "authoritarian" governments elsewhere strengthens that strong indigenous aversion we have to the authority of the State when it seems likely to become an absolute and total rule.

So we oscillate between two moods with respect to authority, one resentful, one welcoming. When it appears as an unlimited remote power over which we seem to have little or no control ourselves and to which we cannot gain access even to put in our word and register our grievance, we envisage authority as evil. If it is a sort of home rule, an assigned authority for a specific task to be performed and one of general benefit to the nation, we accept such authority without concern or the slightest animus. Our experience is compounded of two different attitudes, or rather of an attitude that is ambivalent, and it is hard to be of one mind or opinion about the phenomenon of political authority.

We are further confused by an uncritical general philosophy unfavorable to authority in any form. The modern ethical image of man is that of a person free and entirely responsible for himself. This idealization has passed into common currency where it has accumulated an additional trait that seriously alters its value for philosophy. The free, responsible, self-governing individual is thought of as self-sufficient. Cherishing this notion, one becomes blind to the need and importance of society for the free individual. The wisdom of Aristotle in the *Politics* is not understood, that man actually lives in society "by choice and by necessity." We fail to realize that man can enjoy the desired freedom and self-sufficiency only in a social order where there is an effective authority. But in the popular philosophy there is no room for this truth.

The mind is also closed to the need and value of authority in society by a long-prevalent optimistic notion of history. The general progress of man is the theme, the advance from barbarism to civilization. The harshness as well as the crudity of primitive human existence is seen happily left behind, and authority is one of the antiquated relics of the past. The world is moving forward in a progressive emancipation from the necessity of any obedience to authority. History is "the story of freedom," and the goal of it is a state of freedom without authority.

2. THE NEED OF A THOROUGHGOING PHILOSOPHY

Thus superficial theory adds to the confusion. While in practice we do accept the exercise of authority when we experience the necessity for it and realize its benefits, we have a negative attitude toward it that derives initially from the past history of our nation and is further sustained by a fatuous progress-theory of the history of man and society. The resulting mixture of sentiments and opinion respecting authority calls for a complete rationale, a thoroughgoing philosophy.

A philosophy that once met the need is scarcely credible nowadays. There used to be a philosophical rationale wherein the Being of God was central to the whole *Weltanschauung*. In accordance with this view, God was manifest in the causality of nature, that is, in the necessary laws of the causal order; and God was manifest also in the free will of man, a causality not subject to the necessity of nature but free; and both this freedom of man and that causal necessity were indefeasibly real together under the ordinance of the Supreme Being. A parallel correlation obtained at a lower level, so to speak, when theistic philosophy envisaged the relation of man and the State. All authority derived from God. The power and righteous will of God were manifested in the authoritative law of the State and were also invested in the personal law of man's conscience as he conducted his life in the State. In this case, too, there was a steady belief that the personal freedom and the public authority were reconcilable in the divine order of creation, so that it was not felt necessary to reject either one or the other as mutually exclusive. Any excess of pretension on one side or the other called forth genuine religious protest. The "divine right" of kings was offensive and rejected on religious as well as on political grounds; but the excess of liberty, as something beyond law or restriction, was equally repugnant. The rational position was this: authority is a great universal fact of creation, with God's will the ultimate originative power, and the freedom of created man is ultimately in accord, with the lawful, authoritative order of the State, so long as both reverently stand under the judgment of God.

Except in traditionally religious circles, this view has virtually disappeared from philosophy. We see now only man and the world, with nothing beyond. Man claims moral and metaphysical freedom, the world exhibits an inexorable necessity, and the system of nature, man-and-the-world, is without a reconciling ground in God. Metaphysics tends to stop at this juncture, wrestling with the problem of man and nature but doing little or nothing about the remainder of human experience.

Whenever philosophy even glances at this question nowadays, it seems to have eyes only for freedom and ignores authority. A metaphysician today will easily install freedom as an ultimate metaphysical property of Being, proper to God, but he scarcely ever thinks of speaking about God in his ancient quality as the fount of authority. The moral philosopher will have no truck whatsoever with authority. For to allow of any possible role for authority in the moral life of man is to take away its properly ethical character, no matter whether the authority be divine or regal, because morality consists in actions of an individual's own authentic choice, choice in the light of his own knowledge, appraisal, and conviction, without any external inducements or sanctions. Since the role of authority interjects such alien motivations, it simply spoils the moral life. It is therefore practically outlawed from ethics.

3. THE PRACTICAL AND PHILOSOPHIC ASPECTS OF AUTHORITY

We shall attempt to make a fresh start in philosophy by examining anew, with the help of the insights of various philosophers, authority as it can be seen at work and about its business in the practical life

of man. Attention will be concentrated on certain essential aspects
of "public" or political authority. These aspects reveal what authority
means in the experience of mankind.

A Saving Power

"The experience of mankind" is used advisedly, for authority is "as
old as creation." It can hardly be dissociated from the notion of the
Author of all being. The metaphor in the term "authority" is of the
word spoken by the Supreme Being declaring the law, the requirement, or the responsibility enjoined upon his creatures here below.
The religious connotation of authority clings to it, even when people
have no conscious theology or philosophy.

"In this our unquiet world" authority is a "necessity," wrote
Richard Hooker in his *Laws of Ecclesiastical Polity,* during the
troublous days after the Reformation in England. Our world is at no
time quiet enough to dispense with authority. Whether society be
primitive or civilized, a tolerable order in it is a perpetual desidera-
tum. It is the very nature of the human animal not to stay confined
to any routine but to err from the set path. Disturbance of the peace
is then a natural occurrence. It is characteristic, certainly, of people
having the intelligence and capacity to develop a civilization also to
take an individual line of personal advantage within the very system
which provides them with their opportunities and their enjoyments.
Though settled ways and regulation by laws are a basic condition for
existence in society, yet within their own social order men will
launch out in enterprises that threaten its stability and even its survival. Self-interest is an explosive centrifugal force that drives men
both apart from each other and out of the bounds of the social order.
Men will always "take liberties," so to speak, and thus authority is
ever necessary in some form to maintain "peace and order" in
civilized society.[5]

The recognition of this need for authority does not depend upon
the instruction of philosophy. Plain folk feel the necessity of some
sustaining power for their community before philosophers offer their
reasonings on behalf of the *res publica* and the common good.
People can have a present sense of the reality of the whole body of

[5] "Of the Origin of Government," *David Hume's Political Essays,* Library of
Liberal Arts (1955), pp. 39, 42.

which each one is a member and naturally react, through a kind of self-preservation, toward anything that disrupts the familiar order and leaves them lost, helpless, and exposed to the terrors of an alien, threatening environment. Thus men look to authority as a saving power in their existence. This welcoming of authority as a means of salvation can happen at any level of social organization and enlightenment, whenever people feel grave insecurity and the threat of the destruction of hearth and home.

There is, besides dire need, a moral reason for authority. Men recognize that society has a claim upon them which must be asserted against the self-assertion of its parts. This public claim is seen by intelligent human beings in the very situation where their own self-interest is rampant, for the inevitable consequences, as Hobbes pointed out so clearly, of the operation of unrestricted liberty in men who are seeking advantage over each other teaches them to appreciate the public interest and to feel its claim upon them.

The public claim differs in quality from the egoistic claims of individuals. It does not compete with the private ones in the same way as men compete with each other, for the object is not the same particular goods each man seeks for his own advantage but some general good that ranks above the particular and in effect puts a ceiling upon the otherwise unlimited selfish competition. When this limit is formally expressed in law, the law then "has authority." Thus authority is a quality which the law possesses in virtue of the fact that it stands for the public claim, a claim on behalf of the whole "republic."

The Investiture of Authority

The mantle of authority naturally falls, however, on whatever serves to represent and uphold the public claim amid the strife of private interests. The established laws are invested with authority, but so are all the particular agents of government who are useful or essential to the maintenance of society. The personages who govern or serve the State are "the authorities"; and indeed, the meaning of authority is sometimes exclusively associated with those eminent figures who have *de facto* rule. They are the visible bearers of the authority of the State whose decisions and actions directly touch the conduct and lives of those governed, whereas the laws are invisible and without the direct impact of force. Nevertheless, people can distinguish between the man who wields power and the quality of authority attached to him by virtue of his office.

The combination of the primitive sense of a "saving power," as we have called it, with the moral respect accorded to the laws and to officers of the State because they represent the public claim imparts to authority a special character of sanctity often alluded to in writings on law and politics. Thus the force applicable by the State through its officers, when there is infraction of law and order, is traditionally called a sanction. But quite apart from such occasions requiring the coercive power of the state, the recognition of the great need for rule, joined with the regard for the dignity of the public office, imparts a partly sacrosanct character to everything invested with authority.

Despite the "divinity that doth hedge a King" and the cement of established custom and tradition, authority is not absolutely fixed or unchangeable in those who are invested with it. Succession to office by a regular procedure has allowed of some continuity in rule. In a period of marked change, as at the advent of the "modern" age, "new" authority comes on the scene. Machiavelli's *Prince* opens: "All states or dominions, past or present, that have held authority over men are or have been either republics or monarchies . . . New ones [monarchies] may be entirely new . . . and they are acquired by the new prince by force of his own arms or those of others as they fall to him by fortune or because of his character and ability." [6] The maxims of Machiavelli were lessons derived from history, showing such "new" authorities the political art of having and holding their power. A break with the old order could thus be made in case of necessity or real advantage. But above all, the new Prince must provide more surely for the safety of the State, the great need for which the very fact of his own recent emergence into power makes apparent. He must take stronger and more effective measures than the government he supersedes in order to give people thenceforward a greater sense of security. Such developments, however, rarely occur without

[6] *The Prince*, trans. Thomas G. Bergin (1947), p. 1.

previous default of authority. A royal line may itself break the glorious spell that holds a nation in fee, either by some egregious failure to protect the body politic, or by long-protracted neglect, or even by violation of the accepted privileges of the subjects who in terms of character and ability are themselves near-competitors of the prince and likely to be able to provide the statesmanship needed. The shift of allegiance can readily occur in such circumstances. Old habits of loyalty are dissolved, the fence of divinity is down, and the people look to new authority with better promise of security, peace, and law.

But change in the location of authority is not so simple an affair as swapping rulers. We must leave the Machiavellian picture for another one presented by Montesquieu who was an equally "realistic" student of political matters. The changes that occur in the offices of government are reflections of alterations in the whole complex of factors determining the manner of life of a nation. These factors range from climatic conditions, the nature of the terrain, and the possible sources of livelihood to moral influences, the morals proper, religion, examples of past greatness or goodness cherished in traditions and art, and aspirations for the future. Certain common ways of life result from these material and spiritual forces, and these ways are the "fundamental" laws of that particular social order. An individual character and unity, too, emerge from the conspiring of all these influences which Montesquieu named "the spirit of the laws," and "the spirit of the nation." [7] All actual governments, no matter how powerful or despotic, operate under these laws, and the spirit of the nation of which the laws themselves are the most noticeable manifestations. Montesquieu was not talking about "mere" ideals but about the realities of historical politics. Changes occur in the form of government and in the investiture of authority even where there is no overt and violent revolution. The extreme cases of change are themselves possible precisely because facts and history on the one hand, and the requirements of obedience to the spirit of the laws on the other, have been too long ignored by those exercising power.

[7] For further discussion see my article, "To Montesquieu: Acknowledgment and Appreciation," in the anniversary number, dedicated to Montesquieu, of *Revue Internationale de Philosophie* (Belgium, November 1955).

The Basic Authority of the Law

That case is especially instructive which is not an affair of one prince unhorsing another and taking over control, but of a people who are able to organize a rebellion and effect a revolution. The "character and ability" of the English people, for example, in the period of the Puritan Revolution was noted carefully by Hume, a very keen and fairly objective student of their politics. "The House of Commons," he commented, "was almost entirely governed by a set of men of the most uncommon capacity and the largest views . . . Nothing can give us a higher idea of the capacity of those men who now guided the Commons and of the great authority which they had acquired than the forming and executing of so judicious and difficult a plan of operations." [8] This plan was to reduce the royal prerogative and assert instead the superior authority of "popular assemblies" represented by Commons. The first step was for the Puritans to declare their grievances in a Petition of Right recalling the Great Charter. And throughout their long-continuing controversy the case rested upon their claim to be vindicating the "ancient common laws" of England. They thus invoked the authority of the traditional laws of the nation. They found in them the criteria for a judgment of the performance of their king, and they then claimed on behalf of the public, the people of England, the necessity of both a restoration of respect for those honored laws and a limitation of the royal power. Authority is not all lodged in a king; higher in authority than the power of any government is law itself, and those who like themselves stand for the law derive more authority from their function than a king who flouts it and abuses his power.

But the king also claimed to be acting on behalf of the public interest and he, too, could speak persuasively about law and authority. The crucial moment came when the victorious party had the king in their power and set up the High Court of Justice to try him. By what authority, he asked, could they justify such a summons? And he appealed to the people and to God. "How the

---

[8] *History of England* (New York, Harper and Brothers, n.d.), vol. V, ch. I, pp. 4–5, and ch. II, p. 33. These passages and additional ones are quoted in *David Hume's Political Essays*, pp. xxxiff.

House of Commons can erect a Court of Judicature which was never itself one (as is well known to all lawyers), I leave to God and the world to judge." [9] We are not passing a judgment upon these competing claims; our concern is with the fact which these citations show, that both parties appealed to the fundamental and ancient law as authoritative in the affair.

This superiority of law is, however, far from being peculiar to the British and the subsequent American tradition. The early modern doctrine of "natural law" bears witness to the prevalence of the idea in western European civilization. The "law of nature" enjoyed a sacred authority as being the law of God. But it also had a secular authority in that it represented the interests of humanity, a universal claim that includes the public interest of each political society. Thus all sovereigns alike stood under "natural law," and there was in the work of Grotius the notion of authoritative "laws of war and peace" that ought to be observed by all states and powers because they were rational and right and in the true interest of all nations. This "international law" was inadequate enough, yet its conception, formulation, and citation by many jurists and political writers testifies to a recognition of a law higher than the sovereignty of the State. In some fashion or other the public claim rides high above the authorities of any nation or of any day or generation in history, and law is supreme in a sense, whether or not there be means to enforce it.

Power-with-Right and Justice

Power is, however, an essential element of authority, and authority is a sustaining power for the whole community. It asserts the claim of the community upon the lives and conduct of those who are part of it, and asserts it on occasion by applying it with force. But we have spoken of international law as lacking force. Often, too, the civil laws need more power behind them than they actually have, and governments may be weak; yet in none of these cases is authority necessarily lacking.

A passage from moral philosophy may be cited where the distinction between power and authority is made. Bishop Butler in

---

[9] *The Constitutional Documents of the Puritan Revolution: 1625–1660*, selected and ed. Samuel Rawson Gardiner (3rd ed. rev. 1951), p. 375.

his *Fifteen Sermons Preached in the Rolls Chapel* (1726) developed
a theory of conscience which he designated more precisely as "the
principle of reflection." Through this reflective principle man has
the capacity to effect order and balance in his life, even allowing
for the powerful and ever-present distorting operation of his self-
interest. As a religious writer, however, Butler could not allow that
man ever has sufficient power to redeem himself without the
Christian dispensation. So he had to admit a defect in conscience
by itself for the ordering of human life. "Had it power as it hath
authority," he sighed, the human scene would be transformed into
a society of good neighbors approximating the Christian ethic. So
it would seem that there can be authority, even with insufficient
force to accomplish its object. This concession is made in the case
of the private "authority," the conscience of the individual.
Conscience goes some way toward sustaining the social and moral
order, but it lacks both the complete reflection and the perfection
of power which it ought to have to that end. The religious man here
turns to the power-and-authority of God. But the secular remedy
is also resorted to in theory for this very same situation, where
public authority supplies both the necessary broad-viewed regulation
of the conduct of men and the force to hold all men to law and
order, thus providing where private conscience fails.

There is a complementary relationship here. Public authority,
though marked by its preponderance of force, is still as authority
something very like conscience, or rather, it is essentially affiliated
with conscience. For authority is connected with the idea of right.
In other words, authority must always be "*rightful* authority."

The controversy already cited between the king and the Parliamen-
tary party offers evidence on this point. When the king gave his reasons for declining the jurisdiction of the High Court of Justice, he
appealed to the world: "How can any free-born subject of England
call life or anything he possesseth his own, if power without right
daily make new, and abrogate the old fundamental laws of the
land which I now take to be the present case?" [10] Power without
right lacks not only legality but also authority.

Nor was this a special doctrine of English philosophy and politics.

---

[10] *Constitutional Documents of the Puritan Revolution,* p. 374.

It was an essential feature of the theory of sovereignty that had established itself in Europe from the sixteenth century onward. Bodin was explicit about this aspect of right for he conducted his argument purposely in opposition to what he believed to be Machiavelli's meaning, that power and authority coincide. For Bodin presented sovereignty in the guise of a property right. The dominion of a prince in the State was analogous to the authority of the proprietor in the "domus" — and political sovereignty was thus by initial conception subject to "natural law" and limited by it, even though it was absolute in other respects. It was the absolute right to make law within a given jurisdiction — a power regarded as supreme and omnicompetent within the State and also entirely independent of any external authority. Yet despite this absoluteness, the entire subsequent argument, as carried on by Grotius and others, during which sovereignty was variously redefined and located, always presupposed that it is a power that has a rightful character and that it acts for and by means of laws. Sovereignty is political authority invested with the character of right, and not simply unjudgeable *de facto* power.

Right and Obedience, Obligation and Responsibility

Of course the meaning and the reality of right itself have constituted one of the most difficult philosophical problems of the ages. Socrates braced himself to solve it many times and sought to demonstrate that right or "justice" is no mere derivative of power. What emerged from the argument of Greek philosophy was summed up in its practical meaning by Aristotle when he concluded: "It is evident, then, that all those governments which have a common good in view are rightly established and strictly just." [11] But while the Greeks attended chiefly to the end in view, the moderns who had learned to regard government and law as institutions which were established by men envisaged the proper origin of government in a social act, a contract or compact. The complicity of the wills of all men is essential to establishing rightful public authority. This was the meaning embodied in Rousseau's theory of the "general will." Sometimes, however, this conception is confused with a crude notion that the will of the people "makes"

[11] *Politics*, Book III, ch. VI (Ellis translation, Everyman).

right or justice, which was not Rousseau's intention, since the
general will is not truly general unless its object is general, namely,
the "general good." Here Rousseau, while formulating a philosophy
of politics congenial to the active temper of modern man, reaffirmed
the principle of the Greek tradition of justice.

However difficult it be to define the meaning of right in theory,
its practical meaning when associated with authority appears in
certain consequences for human behavior. Genuine authority calls
out characteristic attitudes in people, for instance, a spirit of "obedience." Thus Rousseau declared that "the essence of the body politic
is the reconciling of obedience with liberty." [12] The obedience of
the free man is correlated with rightful authority.

The characteristic human response to authority is designated by
several other terms in moral philosophy. Besides the willing obedience of man there are the phenomena of allegiance and obligation,
studied by Hume in his moral and political essays. Of these alternatives it seems that obligation is most comprehensive and of most
penetrating meaning, and indeed Rousseau, and later Kant, dwelt
upon this obligatory quality in the attitude and response of man
towards genuine authority. For authority appearing in the character of right is answered by an internal moral obligation and is
never merely power; nor are the acts of authority ever those only of
an external force. A power graced with the quality of right evokes
man's responsive sense of duty.

There is also a moral counterpart to the obligation of the citizen
in the responsibility of those who have authority. The reciprocal
moral relation between the governing and the governed was the
chief thought conveyed by the old contract theory of government:
both the rulers and the ruled undertake something which it is
their duty to perform. In another respect, however, that metaphor
of contract could well be misleading if it were taken to mean that
the bond of union depended simply and entirely upon the act of
agreement and mutual promise. Both parties must above all be
related to each other through a common allegiance and concern
for the safety, the justice, and the good of the body politic. Thence
arises a common conscience which expresses itself in either their

[12] *Social Contract*, Book III, ch. XIII, "How the Sovereign Authority Maintains
Itself" (G. D. H. Cole translation, Everyman).

individual sense of obligation or sense of responsibility. It is a familiar enough fact that sovereigns, so-called, have departed on many occasions from the common *ethos* of their society and acted contrary to accepted moral principle. They excused this on grounds of a *raison d'état* that required it. In offering such justifying reasons, however, they were still paying obeisance to the moral conscience of their community in making the very claim that it was their responsibility to the state to act as they had done. It seems quite proper to use "responsibility" in their case rather than "obligation," for the latter suggests restraints, while responsibility suits the aspect of initiative, independence, and eminent capacity on the part of those who have authority.

Responsibility, however, has its own entailed meanings which do not accrue to obligation. To have responsibility means to be answerable for one's conduct and oneself, and answerable to another. In its original form the concept had a religious context: those in authority were responsible to God. But the theme was rung in several changes. A king by "divine right" would answer for his rule only before the judgment of God, not render an accounting to anybody, not to Parliament, certainly not to "the people." But that royal opposition to vulgar accountability betrays the fact that the other theory was current and had to be scotched — that the rulers are responsible to the people as well as to God. During the Puritan Revolution this sort of thinking was anathema not only to the harassed king but also to the contemporary philosopher Hobbes, who regarded it as an utter absurdity to seek to limit authority thus and "to control the controllers."

The Coercive Aspect and the Opposition to Liberty

Hobbes returns us to the aspect of authority with which we began; the necessity of some power acting to sustain the community, to protect it as a whole, and to safeguard many things about it which are deemed important for its subsistence. Since men as individuals or even as disciplined groups will not always regulate their own conduct sufficiently to those ends, authority must intervene on the proper occasion to force them to do what they "ought" to do. When persons will take such "liberties" which cannot be allowed in their society, the "authorities" who pass judgment in the case claim the right to prevent or to punish the action, and those who then feel the effects of this coercion have a lively experience of power contrary to their liberty of action. In this situation where authority is coercive it appears in outright opposition to freedom. The two things are then and there mutually exclusive.

Nor is this opposition only occasional. The power to control, once established, is efficacious, in some way, all the time without overt compulsory action. Thus Hume made the observation that "there is a perpetual intestine struggle, open or secret, between authority and liberty, and neither of them can prevail in the contest." [18]

But the philosopher never leaves the matter thus as a mere blind struggle of powers. Having discovered the problem he will try to work out a rationale of its solution. Hume himself represented the task of enlightened men of modern nations to be that of "reconciling" authority and freedom. There are two values which must be realized together, for "liberty is the perfection of human society, but still authority must be acknowledged essential to its very existence." [14] In this connection Rousseau's statement too will be recalled, that the problem is "the reconciling of obedience with liberty." The solution according to Rousseau as well as Kant is a theory of political obligation, showing how it is compatible with freedom. This question of the apparent opposition of authority and freedom has long been the chief concern of political and social philosophy.

The Limits of Authority

But this moral preoccupation can lead to undue neglect of a practical aspect of authority which was noted especially by both Montesquieu and Hume, who in their inquiries kept close to "history and experience," and made wise observations as to practice. They envisaged authority as something normal to human society. It can function quietly and unobtrusively as the representative of the community and the protagonist of its values. Moreover, authority is in fact regulated, indeed even controlled, though not in that anarchic sense which Hobbes so flatly repudiated where a people

[18] *David Hume's Political Essays*, p. 41.
[14] *David Hume's Political Essays*, p. 42.

are conceived to overrule at will their own rulers. But there is nonetheless effective law in society above the laws of a government. Regular procedures of justice are established through custom and general acceptance. Accordingly acts of authority will not be considered justified, and consequently not obeyed, if they are simply arbitrary and peremptory dictates of power. Furthermore, claims and argument are heard when both questions of right and questions of fact must be examined and proven. Such provisions for the exercise of authority according to law, so that things are done "decently and in order," witness a settled respect for the personal liberty of man. Authority that operates otherwise is condemned as not being true authority. It is by its measure of performance that authority is actually judged, respected, or disobeyed.

The concluding lesson of this philosophy is that authority is always a limited right and power and cannot be absolute despite appearances to the contrary. Authority is primitively a means of salvation, and whatever or whoever has it, the law or the government, acquires not only power-with-right but also sanctity. But the law has the more sacred character and the appeal to it can result in revolution and unseat rulers and install other authorities in their place. Whoever serves in that high capacity is then bound to uphold the public claim better and to provide security, observance of law, and such other benefits as appear needful. Moreover, none of these benefits is possible without the willing service of the men who constitute the society and whose manifold initiative and activities create its civilization. Their interest and energy are essential and they must have room for expansion or scope for liberty. Their own "opinion," then, in Hume's words, as to "right" as well as "interest" is what alone supports authority in its public role.[15] Here, too, is a limitation upon the actual power of a governing authority in a given society. It is in consequence of this limitation by opinion that the locus of regard and loyalty of men will shift from time to time according to the general sense or conscience of the community. The claim to absolute fixed authority on anyone's part is ever a complete illusion. In every aspect, then, authority is essentially limited.

[15] "Of the First Principles of Government," *David Hume's Political Essays*, p. 25.

4. AUTHORITY IN ITS AMERICAN PHASE: ITS ORIGINALITY,
AND SOME SPECULATIONS

When Americans first learned through their studies of history
and philosophy how real the limitation of authority is in every
case, they conceived the further idea of setting up in a written
constitution a system of limited powers that would make quite
sure of the new authority for their union as a free people. The
division of the powers of government would be the Americans'
own special guarantee of personal liberty. Besides choosing their
own government from time to time in elections, besides fostering
a good education in principles, they hoped, by their deliberate
artifice of distributing powers, to make some advance upon the
melancholy history of human authority and hold forth a fresh hope
to mankind with their great experiment in "free government."

But there is far more merit in the early American experiment
than this mere device of government. A more careful examination
of the Americans' own thinking about authority reveals a richer
and more balanced view of it than has long been traditional in the
subsequent American ethos. They actually started a theory of
authority which may be more useful to us now than has yet been
realized.

We should recall some well-known phrases of the debates in the
Convention and the *Federalist*. "All authority is derived from the
people." *From* the people, but where is it lodged? First, with
honor and respect, in the Constitution itself, the fundamental law
organizing the government. Then in the government: "The express authority of the people alone could give due validity of the
government." [16] Through the Constitution the authority of the
United States is distributed to the several parts of the federal
government. Furthermore, in cases of conflicts of authority, a recourse to the people, the source of authority, was anticipated: "As
the people are the only legitimate foundation of power, and it is
from them that the Constitutional character is derived . . . to
recur to the same original authority . . . wherever any one of
the departments may commit encroachments on the chartered

[16] James Madison, *The Federalist*, XLIII.

authorities of the others . . ." [17] Thus constitutional amendments needed to be ratified by the people through their states or through special conventions. The obvious features of the early American experiment are, then, that all authority is derived from the people and that it is delegated and distributed in accordance with the law which they have previously authorized in the manner prescribed.

The design of the Constitution of the United States was being drawn up in the light of experience with the previously established constitutions of the states. John Adams had been, for instance, the "principal engineer" of the Constitution of Massachusetts which had been adopted in June 1780 while he was absent in France.

Adams felt obliged in 1786 to devote some time to criticisms by political thinkers of France — Turgot, the Duc de La Rochefoucauld, Condorcet, and others. Turgot had written an open letter to Price in London, who was favorable to the American type of constitution, and he deplored the "imitation of the Constitution of Great Britain." [18] To this Adams replied in his book, *A Defence of the Constitutions of Government of the United States of America* . . . , published in 1787 at the time of the drafting of the federal Constitution.

Why copy the English system of division of powers, the critics asked, when America was a distinct nation with an individual life of its own conditioned by the many different factors which Montesquieu had taught men to take account of in their political arrangements and law-making? The American nation was not one in which the traditional class system of kings and lords and commoners was repeated. It was one nation, and why not conceive of it with power indivisible instead of divided powers which were only necessary where there were already established and traditional parties of interest? Why could it not be sovereign people functioning as a democracy? Why not unified central government without the oft-demonstrated fatal weakness of the federal form?

Adams and his fellow statesmen were taking a distinctively American "line" and were more or less conscious of it. They knew that they had an alternative between the British and the French

---

[17] *The Federalist*, XLIX.
[18] Quoted from the introductory statement by George A. Peek, Jr., in *The Political Writings of John Adams*, pp. 105–106.

conceptions of government. But their alternative theory had to be worked out through laborious argument and debate which on that occasion furnished as good an example of practical philosophy as there ever had been in western history.

The spirit rather than the letter of the British constitution persisted in the American plan of government. That spirit had sounded forth in the triumphant words of John Wildman in the Putney Army Debates of 1647: "Authority hath been broken into pieces." The Puritans and others meant to keep it so, and the British-Americans were like-minded. The detested memory of the government of a single divine-right authority lived long in their traditions, and their lawyers were well schooled in the history of the English revolution and the formation of its constitutional order.[19] The study of that constitution made by Montesquieu in Book XI of the *Spirit of the Laws* was an interpretation of morale and spirit and not simply an account of an artifice of politics to deal with class divisions. The Americans were particularly in sympathy with the English tradition, that while authority derives from God ultimately, it passes not to a king but through the people whence it is delegated to serve them in performing certain appointed functions, legislative, executive, and judicial.

The objection which troubled Adams most in the criticisms of the American Constitution was one which derived from a conjunction of the traditional connotation of sovereignty with the national idea. Turgot, as Adams understood, was for collecting all authority "into one centre, the nation." But what can this mean "when the centre is to be the nation"? All it says is, "the nation will be the authority, and the authority the nation." But why should Adams cavil at that truism . . . are not the people "sovereign"? Yes, Adams concedes, "our people are undoubtedly sovereign," the meaning of which in the context might be more plainly seen if the order were "undoubtedly our people are sovereign," that is, if one insists on talking about sovereignty.[20] But Adams found it "difficult to comprehend" such a proposition as Turgot's, that simply identified "the authority" with "the nation." He went on to make

[19] See Wallace Notestein: *The English People on the Eve of Colonization* (1954), pp. 86ff.
[20] *The Political Writings of John Adams*, pp. 123–124.

his own point that any "collection" of authority (no matter where it be placed, in a center or distributed) must come from the voluntary agreement of individuals "to form themselves into a nation, people, community, or body politic, and to be governed." [21] Thus the authority must be conceived to be a constituted thing, set up for specific purposes of government. It is a resultant of a nation's will — the substantive result, to put it differently, of an action: "we the people authorise. . . ."

Adams was trying to avoid a simple identification of the authority of the people with the sovereignty of the people. One can declare that all authority derives from the people and still not be committed to the alien doctrine that the people themselves act as a sovereign, exercising authority as one body with undivided power, performing all the functions of government. The reason for saying "alien" is that the smell of absoluteness clung to the notion of sovereignty which had been defined by Bodin, Grotius, and many others in that line, as the power to make laws "without the consent of those governed," independently of anybody on earth, either within or without the state, that is, in reality, unlimited power. To substitute the nation for a personal sovereign is not to change the meaning of such sovereign authority. Moreover, if the authority of the people is thought of as always inherent in the whole body politic, then the very significance of the original act of constituting an authority and delegating it is lost. All authority must be determinate and vested in a particular body of officers who are to perform certain duties of government and who are responsible to the nation whence they derive their power and authority. It is possible to think of such responsible government with limited powers without having recourse to the concept of sovereignty which has quite different connotations and implications.

In the days of constitution-making a distinction between authority and sovereignty was scarcely made. During the Constitutional Convention various men versed in politics and philosophy insisted on talking about sovereignty, which seems often to have confused the discussion rather than advanced matters. The resurrection of the sovereignty idea was inevitable when those who were jealous

---

[21] *The Political Writings of John Adams*, p. 124.

of the powers of the separate states sought to bolster their position with the claim to the independent sovereignty of the states. The skill with which Madison and others firmly but diplomatically worked around these diversions to the formation of a genuine union of the people of the United States while retaining a proper authority for the states is one of the exciting pieces not only of political history but of philosophical dialogue in actual affairs. But, in not confronting at that time the difference between authority as they were working with it and sovereignty, the founding fathers left it for the crisis of civil war, and even then no decision was made as to whether Americans thinking about government should develop and apply the concept of authority with which they had begun or should continue to cling to the notion of sovereignty whose "historic conception" was in a Europe of an earlier absolutist phase before freedom and democracy had much meaning.

Nevertheless it is my opinion that there was a silent philosophical "declaration of independence" behind the discussions of the formation of the union of the American states, in the form of a break with the European tradition of sovereignty. Furthermore, guided by their notion of authority, these early statesmen accomplished something which they would have been hopelessly prevented from doing if they had thought only in terms of sovereignty with its special historic connotation. "It is obviously impracticable," wrote Washington as President of the Federal Convention transmitting the new Constitution to the Congress of the United States, "in the federal government of these states, to secure all rights of independent sovereignty to each, and to provide for the safety of all." [22] It was obviously impracticable, too, in the mid-nineteenth century, to survive and endure as a nation if the states were to resume the old claim to independent sovereignty. It will be obviously impracticable in the twentieth century, if the statesmen or delegates of the United States continue to think in archaic terms of the sovereignty of the United States coexisting with similar sovereignty of every other member of the United Nations. It seems that whatever constructive advance has been made in freedom and civilization

[22] Document Illustrative of the Formation of the Union of the American States, ed. Charles C. Tansill (69 Congress, 1 Sess., House Document No. 398, 1927), p. 1003.

within the past two centuries has come about through avoiding the notion of sovereignty, not by challenging it, but by quietly operating with the more useful concept of authority.

It is the proper business of philosophy, however, to challenge, not to be politic, to expose the issues, and to propose a theory of the working principles of the system honored in practice.

The people, according to the early American formula, are the "source of authority." Do they themselves not have as a people that which they can delegate to certain specific bodies of the government? Yes and no. Of course the authority is theirs that issues from them to the agents who are to exercise it according to the law. But only when it is actually issued and effective is it authority; what it is before that actual "emanation" is not properly called "authority." The nation or the people are the "source." The metaphor is significant: a source is like a spring running down a hillside, taking its courses according to the lay of the land. There is power in it, but the power is delivered only through the particular sluices into which it is channeled for purposes of doing work. Authority should thus always be thought of as power vested in a *determinate* agency, either in the law or in the various bodies that perform the functions of government. The people or nation are the great indeterminate reservoir of all the power that is so put to work.

Another image can be used which may wean the philosophic mind from its habit of thinking along the lines of the older notion of sovereignty. The pre-Socratic philosopher Anaximander followed upon Thales who had proposed that the one Being which manifests itself in all the variety of forms of observable reality was water, which was, to speak later language, the substance of things. Anaximander offered another idea — Being is the Boundless, the Indeterminate, and it is actually observable only in the strife of opposition of the particular, determinate beings whose doings make up the scene of the world. There is a tendency for one part of determinate Being to push the others out of existence, but nature never quite allows any such extreme and, drawing upon the boundless, maintains a balance. That norm of equilibrium among the particulars is justice. Hence our analogy is as follows: the people from whom all power is derived are a boundless and indeterminate source of it, the bodies that actually have and use certain powers are possessed of a determinate and limited authority, and each of these bodies is held in restraint essentially by the fact that the people always have powers in reserve to bestow on whatever other determinate body can serve best the cause of justice and preserve the social order.

The cautious wisdom of the Tenth Amendment should be remembered here: "The powers not delegated to the United States by the Constitution, nor prohibited by it to the states, are reserved to the states respectively, or to the people." On one hand, this is a restraint upon unwarranted federal expansion of powers exercised beyond those delegated. On the other hand, "to the people" opens a vision of resources in the people still indeterminate — not specified in any manner in the Constitution, uncommitted, and able to be called into play in the future as the occasion warrants.

Acts to determine authority are required throughout the life and history of the nation. The Constitution provides for a redetermination of the fundamental law through the procedure of amendment, which involves a reference to the people and a requirement of substantial majority ratifying it. Within the activities of government there is redetermination, at frequent and stated intervals, of those especially who shall exercise executive and legislative power. The determinate authority, whether of the law or of the offices of government, is thus only relatively so — one can never be sure in important vital issues which one or whether any of our institutions "has authority." A redetermination of where the authority of the people lies and who is properly acting or speaking in their name is always likely to become a problem of the day. What this means is that "the people" is not merely a substitution for the "sovereign" of the older European tradition, and further that sovereignty in a democratic society is a legendary survival. The sovereignty of the states is an ancient myth resurrected for other than either legal or peace-making reasons. The doctrine, "all authority derives from the people," carries with it the consequence, then, that the original authority is indeterminate, not absolutely fixed on anything, and that it is necessary in every generation, or whenever serious issues arise, to redetermine and redefine what the relevant authority is and in which body it is vested. Authority never settles anything really important, because when matters are very important, we have to settle the authority itself which is to function in the case.

Authority in its American phase, so viewed, abolishes not only divinely authorized royal lineage and perpetual rule but also any absolutely fixed rights and powers of the government. Constitutional, democratic authority requires that the working of such a flexible system of government with shifting of the order of authority within the system shall be carried on by due process of law and not arbitrarily or recklessly. Such a system calls for an incalculable amount of labor on the part of those engaged in the work of the statesman, and others in the work of the education of the nation. For in the end, whatever form authority may take depends upon the kind of knowledge that is the fruit of free discussion and upon the patience and good will that are necessary both to the holding of public discussions, in meetings or in the press or in conventions, and to seeing the decisions through. The nation is always in the making, so is liberty, so is authority.

2. Authority, Reason, and Discretion[1]

CARL J. FRIEDRICH

Ever since the eighteenth-century revolt against the established authorities in church and state, there has been a marked tendency among freedom-loving intellectuals to view "authority" with a jaundiced eye, if not to denounce it. When Charles S. Peirce wrote a generation ago that "when the method of authority prevailed, the truth meant little more than the Catholic faith," [2] he was echoing this intellectual sentiment. Conservatives have maintained that the implication here is that what Peirce called "the method of authority" was some kind of unreasoning superstition, some foolishness which must be superseded by the clear voice of "reason." When the Jacobins erected altars to the Goddess of Reason, they had proudly assumed that they were abandoning authority for reason. Little did they realize how authoritative was their outlook, and how much depended upon their authority for their particular reasoning to prevail.

[1] An earlier attempt at a formulation of the position of this study may be found in an article, "Loyalty and Authority," in *Confluence* (1954), vol. III, pp. 307ff. Cf. Miss Hannah Arendt's challenging article, "Was ist Autorität?" reprinted from an unspecified journal (1955), and Francis G. Wilson's "The Prelude to Authority," in *The American Political Science Review*, 31:12ff. (1937); see also George S. Langrod, "Liberty and Authority," ch. XIV of *Freedom and Authority in Our Time*, ed. Lyman Bryson, Louis Finkelstein, R. M. MacIver, and Richard McKeon (1953); and Sebastian de Grazia, "Authority and Rationality," *Philosophy*, 27 (1952). See also footnote 20, below.

[2] Charles S. Peirce, "How to Make Our Ideas Clear" as reprinted in *Love, Chance and Logic* (1923), p. 55.

In reaction, conservatives since Bonald and de Maistre have made a fetish of authority beyond all reason. The ringing phrases in which de Maistre denounced the rationalism of the enlightenment center upon the issue of authority against reason. He would claim infallibility for the pope in the same phrase in which he would vindicate an unqualified monarchical sovereignty.[3] Because reasoning, *raisonnement,* can lead to the dissolution of all social order, to anarchy and terror, men ought to and are in fact ready to subject themselves to authority without asking the "reasons why." Similar sentiments are frequently expressed in contemporary American conservatism.

But are reasoning and authority so antithetical? Does authority have no basis in reason? The following analysis seeks to elucidate the proposition that authority and reason are closely linked, indeed that authority rests upon the ability to issue communications which are capable of reasoned elaboration.

In common usage, authority is often confused with power or taken to be a synonym of power. In more learned discourse, authority has been defined as a particular kind of power, such as "formal power" or "rightful power." It has been spoken of in relation to persons, as well as to other entities, such as law or the dictionary. The problem of what makes people "accept" authority, by obeying commands or believing a message, has given rise to a variety of interpretations of authority. Authority has been juxtaposed to freedom, or to force, or to reason. It has been praised and condemned in all these contexts, and as a result, the word has been incorporated in a pejorative adjective, "authoritarian," and linked as a general characteristic to "personality" as an objectionable and eradicable trait. In most of these discussions, both on the popular and the learned level, it has been assumed that authority is a peculiar something that can be possessed, and gained or lost, as the case may be. Against such views it has been argued through the ages that there is only power based on some sort of constraint, and that authority is merely a make-belief, based upon religious faith at best.

It is illuminating to cast a glance at the Roman antecedents from

---

[3] "L'infaillibilité dans l'ordre spirituel, et la souveraineté dans l'ordre temporel, sont deux mots parfaitement synonymes." *Du Pape,* Book I, ch. I.

which the word "authority" is derived. *Auctoritas* is, according to Mommsen,[4] not readily definable in its original meaning. It has predominantly the sense related to the verb from which it is derived: *augere,* to augment. *Auctoritas* thus supplements a mere act of the will by adding reasons to it. Such augmentation and confirmation are the results of deliberation by the "old ones." The *patrum auctoritas* is, for that reason, more than advice, yet less than a command. It is, as Mommsen comments, advice which cannot be properly disregarded, such as the expert gives to the layman, the leader in Parliament to his followers. This augmentation or implementation and confirmation had in ancient Rome, as did indeed authority elsewhere, religious overtones. While it was not intended to set limits to the free decision of the community, it was intended to prevent violations of what was sacred in the established order of things. It was believed that because such violations were a crime (*nefas*) against the divine order, they might jeopardize the divine blessing. Thus, the preservation of good auspices probably was the basic idea underlying the *patrum auctoritas,* the authority of the fathers, that is to say, of the Senate. It was a matter of adding wisdom to will, a knowledge of values shared and traditions hallowed, to whatever the people wanted to do. (Later on, the *auctoritas* became a more general notion, and something of what our modern word "author," meaning a maker or originator, suggests.)

Why bother with these ancient verbal connotations? Because they suggest the role of reasoning, they thereby help to get clearly into focus what is probably the central fact to which a great many of the situations refer in which the word "authority" is employed. When there are good reasons for doing or believing something, such action or thought acquires a quality which is otherwise lacking. This has been overlooked by that rather numerous group of writers and phil-

---

[4] Theodor Mommsen, *Römisches Staatsrecht* (2nd ed., 1888), III, 1033ff. I should like to call attention in this connection to the fact that Apollo was the "augmenter." When one considers the symbolism of Apollo as the God of the Sun, of reason and moderation, this serves as a most revealing symbolic *datum.* Cf. W. K. C. Guthrie, *The Greeks and Their Gods* (1950), pp. 183ff. Guthrie writes of "Apollo's primary aspect, his championship of law and order. . . . limit, moderation, obedience to authority, and condemning excess in all its forms" (p. 203). There also are the precepts which this augmenter represented.

osophers who thought they could build law upon power alone. The power of him who willed something was, they thought, what gave someone's decision authority. Hobbes, as well as Rousseau and many others, thought that the sovereign will was the source of all law.[5] Much Anglo-American legal tradition has, by contrast, retained the older notion — a notion that can be traced back through the Middle Ages to the Stoics — that reason, and more especially Coke's "artificial reason of the law" are of decisive importance in providing law with the necessary authority.[6] It is this view which assigns to the judge such a central position in a legal system: he, as a man "learned in the law," is conceived as lending the statutory "decisions" of an elected legislature an additional quality, by relating them to the basic principles of the law and thus making them authoritative. Only by fitting the willed statutory law into such a broader framework of "reason" does it become fully right, that is to say, authoritative.

In his forthright little study on political verbiage, T. D. Weldon makes an effort at clearing away some of the thick underbrush that has grown up around the word "authority." He remarks that until recent times, no clear distinction has been drawn between power and authority, and that it is "too simple to identify 'authority' with 'force rightly or justly applied.'" He differentiates four kinds of authority, ranging from pure force to unquestioning confidence, and hence asserts that "force exercised or capable of being exercised with the general approval of those concerned is what is normally meant by 'authority.'" Thus, if the followers want wickedness, they will obey a wicked authority.[7] And yet, at the start of his analysis, Weldon had pointed out that authority somehow is related to the fact that he who possesses it could produce reasons, if challenged. Such was the case of the Roman Senate, such is the case of the modern judge. To say, as Weldon does, that "the proper use of force is always authoritative" is quite inadmissible, unless this

[5] Hobbes, *Leviathan*, ch. X, vi–viii; Rousseau, *Contrat Social*, book II. For Hobbes the key of "authority" is "the right of doing any act."

[6] Sir Edward Coke, *Reports*, VIII, Bonham's case; see C. J. Friedrich, *Philosophy of Law in Political and Historical Perspective* (University of Chicago Press, 1958), ch. X. Cf. also C. D. Brown, *The Lion and the Throne — The Life and Times of Sir Edward Coke 1552–1634* (1957), pp. 302ff.

[7] T. D. Weldon, *The Vocabulary of Politics* (Pelican Books, 1953), pp. 50–56.

statement is made into a tautology by giving to the adjective
"proper" the meaning of "reasonable," in the sense of possessing
adequate reasons for him to whom the force is applied. What is
more, Weldon himself seems to know this, for he tells us that
when people begin to ask the question, "Why should I obey X,"
X is on the way to losing his authority.

This last observation deserves further exploration. For when such
a question is raised, a number of answers may be given. One answer
would be in terms of hierarchy and status — because he is your
king or your father. Another might be in terms of religion and
faith — because God has commanded you to do so. A third would
be in terms of interest and advantage — because he may make you
his heir and successor. A fourth would be in terms of personal
emotions and loyalties — because he loves you and you are devoted
to him. A fifth would be in terms of law — because article so-and-
so of the civil code requires you to do it. Such a recital, though
incomplete, suggests some of the values and beliefs involved in
reasoning upon authority, and at the same time, it gives a first
hint of the fluid, indeed the fugitive quality of power based on
authority. However, these five answers do not enable us really to
get at the distinctive phenomenon which the augmentation and
confirmation of will by some sort of reasoning accomplishes. The
escape into the psychological concomitants of this datum of political
experience suggests that a crucial aspect belonging to its ontological
core has not yet been laid bare.[8]

We have, in the previous paragraph, spoken of authority in
terms of obedience. This is very commonly done; indeed, in action-
related situations, obedience is the predominant aspect. But there is
another phase of authority which is paramount in such situations
as those involving the teacher, the scholar, and the dictionary. As to
the last, some very interesting special problems are presented by the
authority of nonpersonal entities, such as dictionaries, laws, and
the like. It might be argued that one could bracket these entities
and their "authority," because their authority may be traced back

---

[8] The close relation between the psychological and the nominalist misinterpre-
tation of phenomena like authority is strikingly illustrated in the approach of
Max Weber, who, confusing authority with legitimacy, misses one of the key aspects
of authority, by minimizing its rational aspect.

to the human "authors" who created them. There is, furthermore, often a question as to who were the makers: the fathers at Philadelphia, or the long line of judges who adorned the Supreme and other courts, or yet the presidents and congressmen. From a certain standpoint, it may even be said that the Constitution as it exists today is the work of the entire American people. The problem of the "authority" of impersonal entities will, I believe, become more comprehensible, once the analysis of the rational component of authority has been further advanced.

Leaving aside, then, the authority of such impersonal entities, we return to the situation of the teacher, the scholar, the doctor, or the lawyer. Here authority seems to be related to the fact that the person wielding authority possesses superior knowledge or insight. Frequently — for instance, among scholars accepting each other's authority — the authority of X rests upon the fact that he could give extended reasons for the opinions he expounds.[9] It is not essential for such authority, however, that these opinions are conclusively demonstrable; indeed only where they are not thus demonstrable, the phenomenon of authority in the strict sense is involved. In any case, the authority of the teacher, the scholar, the doctor, and the lawyer is infused with a rational element, and the belief in it includes the belief in superior "reasoning." It is challenged on the part of those who accept it, by asking, not, why should I obey? but, why should I agree?

Before I proceed with this analysis, it might be well to turn to a kind of primordial authority which has been particularly controversial in our time, namely parental authority. In the course of each child's development, the growth of authority may be studied and experienced. It might be remarked in passing that it is in this sphere that misunderstandings about the nature of authority have been most frequent. Along with the teacher-pupil relationship, the parental relationship has been jeopardized by ideas that in the last generation have played havoc with genuine community in the

[9] This aspect of the matter is strikingly illuminated by the role that agreement upon methods of work and modes of demonstration plays among scientists. For an elaboration of this factor, as far as science is concerned, see my paper, "Political Philosophy and Political Science," in the collective volume to be published (1958) by Northwestern University Press under the title *Approaches to the Study of Politics.*

name of "progress." [10] And yet there was much good in these youth
movements and "progressivisms" of our younger days; it was really
the manner of stating the issue, rather than the criticism of out-
moded patterns of living, that was at fault. In a nutshell, it might
be said that these movements challenged "authority" as such,
when they should have asked for the replacement of outworn and
unreal authority by genuine authority. What this means, I should
like to illustrate by the parental problem. In the beginning, the
child is helplessly dependent and in the power of the parents.
Indeed, their power is absolute force to such a degree that the
legislator has seen fit to step in and regulate by law, to control and
limit, the unlimited power of the parents, at least to some extent.
But this absolute power does not continue, as the child grows. A
wise parent will increasingly prefer to explain what needs to be
done and to be believed, to give reasons, thus replacing subjection
by understanding. He will respond to the questions, "why?" and
"wherefore?" and seek to develop in the child an understanding
of, a participation in, the *reasons* which animate the parent in asking for obedience as well as for agreement. It is in this process that
a new relationship, different from that of power and force, comes
into being, and it is this relationship which I should like to designate as authority. Such authority rests upon the fact that the child
increasingly gains insight into parental orders and regulations, into
parental opinions and beliefs. The child learns to relate both to
basic values, and thereby comes to share these values with his
parents. Such insight anticipates the insight into the regulations
and opinions of the larger community, the church, the school, and
eventually the polity. What is important is to realize that all such
discourse provides for participation of the child. By coming to
understand these regulations and beliefs, the child is helped, so to
speak, to shape them into proper possessions, to make them his own.
Thus discipline is transformed into self-discipline. It may well
happen, and often does in fact happen, that this process takes place
only partially and incompletely. Power and force continue to play

[10] This particular pitfall was the crux of the more radical extravaganzas committed in the name of progressive education some years ago. See, for a statement
of the opposing position, my paper, "This Progressive Education" in *The Atlantic
Monthly*, 154: 421ff. (October 1934), which became a stormy petrel of controversy
for a while, but was never really refuted.

their role, often to the point where they create dangerous tensions and frustrations about which modern psychology and psychoanalysis have taught many revealing lessons. For, if the power of parents is wielded without such growing participation and insight on the part of the child, then either the community of the family is destroyed by the rebellion of the child, or the child's personality is destroyed by the imposition of meaningless opinions, rules, and regulations. It is this latter situation which has been the focal point of attack by many thoughtful critics who have written about the "authoritarian personality" and "authoritarian family relations," when actually what they mean is better termed "totalitarian personality," and "totalitarian family." [11] But I do not care, to speak with Locke, about the words, as long as the matter be clearly understood. What seems to me significant about this well-known development within the family is that the phenomenon of authority is associated with "reasoning." And by reasoning I do not mean the absolute rationality alleged to be possessed by mathematics and logic, that is to say, the reasoning which calls no value judgments into play, but rather the reasoning which relates actions to opinions and beliefs, and opinions and beliefs to values, however defined.[12]

It has, I hope, become apparent that I not only reject the use of the word "authority" for the purpose of designating any kind of power, but that when I speak of authority, I wish to say that the communications of a person possessing it exhibit a very particular kind of relationship to reason and reasoning. Such communication, whether opinions or commands, are not demonstrated through rational discourse, but they possess the *potentiality of reasoned elaboration* — they are "worthy of acceptance." [13] Seen in this perspective,

[11] See Theodor W. Adorno, *et al., The Authoritarian Personality* (1951), especially the section written by Adorno himself. See also the discussion on the issue with Else Brunswick, a contributor to *Totalitarianism,* ed. Carl J. Friedrich (1953), pp. 171ff. and 274f.

[12] Cf., for example, Raymond Polin, *La Création des Valeurs* (1945; 2nd ed., 1952), *passim.*

[13] This suggestive term was proposed by Morton White in a discussion of the group mentioned in footnote 20. It makes it clear that authority in its reasoning dimension is primarily a quality of the bearer of authority and of his communications, rather than those subject to it. But while it helps to express the thought I am concerned with, it does not sufficiently stress the rational component to suffice for this purpose.

authority is a *quality* of communication, rather than of persons, and when we speak of the authority of a person, we are using a shorthand expression to indicate that he possesses the capacity to issue authoritative communications. And furthermore, when we say X possesses authority, we thereby propose to suggest that the communications which X addresses to A, B, and C are based upon reasoning that has meaning not only to X, but also to A, B, and C, in the sense of being related to knowledge which they all possess, or to opinions, beliefs, and values which they all share. But we are not concerned with the problem of persuasion; it is not a matter of X's ability to "influence" the thinking or acting of the others, though this usually is involved in the situation. What matters is that this capacity to issue communications which may be elaborated by reasoning is a decisive phenomenon in a great many social and more particularly political relationships. We should like to call it authority but, whatever it is called, this potentiality of reasoned elaboration would appear to play a vital role in situations which involve authority. Perhaps one should be content to call it the "rational factor" in authority.

As far as the opinions, beliefs, and values involved in such reasoned elaboration are concerned, they may be one or many, readily identifiable or highly speculative and abstract. One value, such as truth or justice or health, may predominate, or there may be an infinitely complex array of values[14] such as is represented by a culture or a way of life.[15] What matters is that some propositions, whether judgments or commands, can be elaborated by suitable reasoning in terms of these values, opinions, or beliefs, while others cannot, or only imperfectly. The capacity of men to speak

[14] I do not use the term "system" here, nor in related contexts, although this is now frequently done, because the term should be avoided, unless the actual presence of a system can be demonstrated — which is rarely the case. On system analysis, cf. Ludwig von Bertalanffy, "Problems of General System Theory" in *General System Theory — A New Approach to the Unity of Science,* from *Human Biology* (1951).

[15] I have no objection to anyone wishing to employ the term "authority" for designating some other social phenomenon, such as "rightful power" or "legitimate power" or yet "power based on esteem or respect." But I do insist that in that case some other term will have to be suggested or invented for designating the social reality which I am describing and have labeled "authority," believing this to be its specific meaning.

in meaningful terms, to say the things which may be thus elaborated, varies enormously. This capacity, I think, is implied when we speak of some of them as authorities.

Now it is important that this "reasoning" is not necessarily, nor even usually, employed in fact, though it may be hinted at or suggested by symbols. But it is important that the "potentiality of reasoned elaboration" of the communication exists. In other words, not the psychological concomitant of a *belief* in the capacity of the authority for such reasoned elaboration is decisive, but the actual existence of such a capacity. This does not mean that there could not arise situations wherein the capacity was erroneously believed to exist. Such errors are a common occurrence in relations among men. But such situations are properly and meaningfully described as involving "false" or "faked" authority. Genuine authority, on the other hand, requires that the capacity actually is present. The respect, esteem, or other psychological concomitants, while undoubtedly present as well, are not a distinctive feature of authority. Power, wealth, and a host of other qualities likewise occasion these psychological reactions.

It is evident that the capacity to communicate authoritatively, that is, to be able to enlarge upon what is being communicated in terms meaningful to those who are being addressed, has a vital relation to the phenomena of power. Indeed, there can be no question but that this capacity always gives some power to him who possesses authority, and therefore authority is one of the sources of power. But just as the dagger by which I can kill a man and thus force him to surrender his purse is in any strict sense not power but the source of it, so likewise authority is *not* power, but it may cause it. This explains the undoubted fact that has been the occasion of much political comment, namely the continuance of power without authority, as well as the continuance of authority without power. Nero exercised power without authority, while the Senate of his time possessed authority yet little or no power. In precise terminology, which would speak of authority only when thinking of communications, this is readily comprehensible.[16]

[16] Harold Lasswell and Abraham Kaplan, by contrast, having defined authority as "formal power" (see *Power and Society,* 1950, pp. 133ff.), leave this kind of situation in the dark. For how does it help to describe the situation in which the Senate found itself as "formal power"?

The phenomenon which we have thus identified as a crucial aspect of authority explains why authority is a necessary part of all human relationships and communities. Such relationships are unmanageable without authority, because communication would become impossibly cumbersome. Wife and husband, no less than government and citizen, could not carry on for long if all the reasoning involved in saying what they have to say to each other would have to be stated or reproduced each time a communication were to be made. It is enough that the potentiality of such reasoning, the relating of actions to opinions, and of opinions to values, exists and is readily recognized. Indeed, in complementary relationships, such as that of husband and wife in contemporary American society, or that of fellow scholars or colleagues in related professional pursuits, there occurs what might be called the phenomenon of mutual authority. What I mean by "mutual" authority is that each of the persons in such a relationship is an authority to the other, but in divergent fields of work. This phenomenon is nearly incomprehensible when the relationship is merely seen in terms of power in its various forms.[17]

The foregoing analysis also helps in understanding better the peculiarly fluid quality of power based on authority. Since opinions, values, and beliefs are continually changing, in response to changes in the environment and to creative innovations, whether of a political, aesthetic, or religious nature, it is quite possible, indeed a recurrent experience, that a person may lose his power based on authority, not because the commands he gives or the opinions he utters are less "authoritative" in the sense that they may be elaborated by reasoning, but because such reasoning is related to opinions, beliefs, and values that have lost their validity. When one, in such situations, says that a man has "lost his authority," this is really a shorthand

[17] This proposition provides the clue to the nature of political authority under democratic conditions. Only the mutual respect of the citizens can give meaning to the acceptance of majority decisions, and the difficulty of mass democracy of the great urban concentrations of the present day must be seen as springing from this dissolution of the neighborhood and the disappearance of the respect associated with it. See my *The New Image of the Common Man* (1941 and later) for an exploration of the problems involved here. The contrast to present-day conditions can be seen in such processes as the New England town meeting; for this see John Gould, *New England Town Meeting* (1940), which, while a bit romantic, conveys well the point of mutuality of which I am speaking.

expression; he has lost power because his authority, or rather the authority of his communications, is disintegrating, because this rational component which is crucial is deteriorating.

Another perplexing situation that becomes clearer, it is hoped, as a result of the analysis attempted here is the role of authority in totalitarian societies. If authority is interpreted as some kind of power, whether "formal," or "legal" or "rightful," the role of authority in totalitarian systems remains controversial and indeed obscure. Some say, with reference to a totalitarian regime, if they identify themselves with it and its rulers, that the authority of the ruler is very great. Others, identifying themselves with the subject elements of the population who are coerced into obedience, insist that there is no authority or very little in such a totalitarian society. The rational aspect of authority which we identified as the potentiality for reasoned elaboration of communications, whether they be commands or opinions or beliefs, makes it possible to understand these societies better. In contrast to constitutional societies where authority is diffuse and pluralistic, since authoritative communications issue from many centers of authority, such as churches, schools, trade unions, parties, all kinds of associations, as well as the government, authority in totalitarian societies is strikingly polarized and intensified at the center of the totalitarian movement. Thus the authority of a Lenin, a Stalin, or a Hitler when confronting his followers is very much greater than that of a democratic leader, while at the same time his authority in confronting the rest of the society is very much weaker. To put it another way, governmental authority is both enlarged and reduced: enlarged, when one considers the followers, reduced, when one considers the rest of the people. Authority is not being centralized, or as the National Socialists called it, *gleichgeschaltet,* but it is being concentrated at the center of such a society. The explanation, in terms of our analysis, is not far to seek. The opinions and the commands of a Stalin or a Hitler, oriented to the regime's ideology, to the values and beliefs embodied in *Das Kapital* or *Mein Kampf,* could as a rule be eloborated by extensive reasoning.[18] It is important to bear in mind that such

---

[18] The recent tergiversations of Khrushchev in trying to explain his adherence to the objectives and purposes of Stalin, while rejecting some of his methods, seemed to me a striking illustration of the point here made: by attaching him-

reasoning may well appear wholly "irrational" to anyone outside the particular belief and value system.[19]

Still another phenomenon, and one of paramount importance to democratic constitutional government which our theory of authority is able to elucidate, is that of discretion. Authority interpreted as involving the potential reasoning in interpersonal communications, that is to say as the capacity for reasoned elaboration, provides the clue to the problem of why discretion is both indispensable and manageable in all political and legal systems. In what follows, I shall concentrate on the phenomenon of discretion in constitutional democracies, that is, governments according to law made with popular participation.

It is worth remembering that John Locke discusses the problem of discretion when he comes to consider the prerogative. "This power to act according to discretion for the public good, without the prescription of the law and sometimes even against it, is that which is called prerogative," he writes in the *Second Essay* (160). And further that "the good of society requires that several things should be left to the discretion of him that has the executive power" (*Second Essay*, 159). There is an interesting similarity between Locke's approach and the Chinese tradition of "tsung-tung" or legitimate authority: no authority can be legitimate that fails to fulfill the function for which it was created — the public good.

Discretion may be defined in various ways, but what is always involved is (1) the notion that a choice between several alternatives can, indeed must, be made; and (2) the notion that such a choice is not to be made arbitrarily, wantonly, or carelessly, but in accordance with the requirements of the situation.[20] There is the

---

self to the "reasoning" of Stalin in terms of the communist ideology, he evidently sought to preserve, and if possible, to strengthen his authority, at the same time reducing that of Stalin, whom he shows to have done things which *he could not have justified by reasoned elaboration*. Hence the juxtaposing of Lenin to Stalin.

[19] This instance is particularly worthy of attention, because Hitler's position appears to any outsider to have been that of utter madness. His conduct was not only irrational, but contrary to all common sense and reason. But reason in the general sense and "reasoning" in the sense here suggested, namely, relating to values, opinions, and beliefs, are not the same thing.

[20] The author wishes here to acknowledge his general indebtedness to an informal discussion group of Harvard faculty members, mostly from the Law School, who met during 1956–1957 and explored the general problems of "rule versus discretion" as a problem of legal philosophy. The group owed its existence to the initiative of Lon Fuller.

further notion (usually) that discretion ought to come into play within the framework of rules, implementing them, carrying them through, elaborating them. Thus a court, when using discretion in imposing a penalty, is acting within the framework of the rules of the penal law according to which the criminal has been adjudged guilty, and an administrative body, in fixing a rate, is acting within the framework of the rules of, say, the law of public utilities which fixes the way such utilities should be operated, after defining them and so forth. When a court or a commission or an administrative official acts in accordance with such general standards as "reasonableness" or "good morals," it is supposed to be doing this within the range of rules established by the law.[21]

To put it another way, discretion comes into play whenever no rules (or principles) can be, or have been, formulated, while at the same time, mere whim cannot be allowed. For a concrete example, one might turn to the choice of personnel. A legislative body or other principal may give fairly elaborate rules and establish precise regulations for the selection of personnel, as is done in civil service legislation. There always will remain, in many instances, an element of discretionary choice. The candidates may all be of a certain age, may all have a certain education and experience, come from certain localities, and possess a variety of other specified traits. There will often be candidates who are identical in all these respects, yet a choice has to be made between them. The selection board may have to decide whether to prefer a man from Yale or from Harvard, they may have to assess the precise meaning of words used in letters of recommendation, and so forth. The law will, therefore, give specified persons "discretion" to select the candidate. In doing so, the expectation will be that the person or persons given discretion will use it "to the best of their ability." What this means is that they will give careful thought to all the factors involved.

---

[21] Here we are face to face with the problem of the general clauses which are carried to such disastrous lengths in totalitarian (as indeed in many autocratic) regimes. A German jurist, J. W. Hedemann, stressed the dangers of such a "flight" in the German judicial decisions preceding Hitler's advent to power in his book *Die Flucht in die Generalklauseln* (1933); but the issue is much more pointedly developed by Fritz von Hippel, in *Die Perversion von Rechtsordnungen* (1955), giving many concrete illustrations of how such general clauses (and some not so general) may be carried beyond the limits allowed by the system. These are instances of the abuse of discretion.

They may, to stay with our illustration, evaluate the writers of the letters of recommendation, considering their reliability, their past record of assessing men's ability, and other factors. They may consider that there are already several Harvard men in the organization and that there should be some diversity; or they may, reversely, consider that experience with Yale men has been so good that preference should be given to another Yale man.

At the same time, it will be generally assumed that a person vested with power to exercise discretion will be able to give reasons for what he has done. This aspect is particularly evident where a superior gives a subordinate discretion. He will ordinarily assume that the subordinate will use good sense, experience, stick to established precedent, and so on. But he will also expect the subordinate to be able to "explain," if for any reason he finds that the decision made ought to be subjected to review. The superior will rarely be satisfied with an explanation such as "I just felt that way" or "my instinct told me this was the right man," let alone an explanation which would say "I liked his face" or "she had such a lovely voice."

If one inspects such "reasoned elaboration" or inquires into what is expected under such a heading, he finds that the reasoning involved is both "instrumental" and "valuational," or to put it another way, it proceeds to argue both in terms of means and ends. The personnel man may suggest that the person chosen believes in democracy, or he may insist that the man rejected is possibly a believer in socialism or a fellow traveler. He may say that the candidate is steady and a good family man, or reversely that he is a drunkard and a bachelor. But besides such value judgments, there may be instrumental judgments, dwelling upon the man's ability, his knowledge of foreign languages, or what have you. The discretion as used is, in other words, tied to the opinions, values, and beliefs shared by members of the organization, as well as to the tasks to be performed.

It is by now becoming apparent why discretion is so valuable and indeed also why it is so inescapable an aspect of not only all government and administration, but all human relationships. Philosophers have since time immemorial dwelt upon the fact that rules can never cope with the infinite variety and detail of the concrete.

situations. To cope with the resulting inadequacy of all law, they have at times sought to find persons of exceptional wisdom, to identify as it were a natural elite of persons who would be so wise as to be able to exercise limitless discretion. Plato went perhaps further than any other thinker in this respect, at least the younger Plato of the *Republic*. Nor is it easy to argue against him, once the crucial concession is made that such men can be found by some reliable method. Plato himself took refuge in the hope of some kind of providential coincidence by which the philosopher and the holder of absolute power are brought together. Most of the rest of us have rejected his notion of the philosopher-king, precisely because the problem which he minimized, namely how to find the persons worthy of being entrusted with so much discretion, seems to be the most difficult.[22] For in the choice of personnel, as our humble illustration suggested, some of the most persistent discretionary problems present themselves. But though one rejects Plato's notion of a natural elite, and most of what goes with it, the fact remains that precisely where the novel, the unprecedented situation arises, calling for creative innovation and invention, all rules and regulations break down and discretion comes to the fore. And when such discretion is used in such a way as to benefit society, when, as the ancient verbiage has it, the "general good" is served, then government and administration are most universally acclaimed. Eisenhower deciding to cross the channel, Congress deciding to grant Puerto Rico commonwealth status, Truman deciding to act in Korea — these are recent instances of the exercise of discretion in dramatic situations calling for creative initiative, and utterly removed from the possibility of being handled by precedent or established rule.

Whenever discretion is thus used, whenever the factors relevant

[22] Cf. Plato, *Republic,* especially at 473d. Aristotle, dubious of this doctrine, has an approach to the problem of discretion which is more nearly in keeping with our views, especially in connection with his doctrine of *epieikeia.* Cf. my *Philosophie des Rechts* (1954), ch. II. Note the sage comment of Kant on this doctrine of the limitless discretion of the philosopher-king: "It is not to be expected that kings philosophize or that philosophers become kings, nor is it to be desired because the possession of power corrupts the free judgment of reason inevitably." See my *The Philosophy of Kant* (1949), p. 456, and *Inevitable Peace* (1948), *passim.* The passage on the royal lie, or "noble falsehood" as A. D. Lindsay translates it, is found in *Republic,* 414.

to a decision are obviously numerous and at least in part unfore-
seeable, it will seem to most men that an attempt to limit such
discretion by pre-established rule or regulation would be unwise
and in its consequences probably unjust.[23] But it appears similarly
unwise and unjust to entrust such discretionary power to persons
not qualified to exercise good judgment, that is to say, not acting in
such a way that their reasoning could afterwards be examined and
found defensible. At this point, we are confronting the vital relationship of discretion to responsibility. Irresponsible discretion is
not what is ordinarily wanted. But what constitutes "responsible
discretion"? Essentially it is discretion which is exercised with due
regard to all the considerations that enter into the situation. This
will usually mean that the person exercising such discretion is
duly qualified. He will seem to act responsibly when he acts in accordance with the full knowledge of the particular science, art,
craft, or operation involved in the situation calling for discretion.
That is why the selection of personnel appears as the core of the
problem of how to arrange for the exercise of discretion. (It is,
incidentally, the sound residue in Plato's notion of the philosopher-
king.) And that is why administrative responsibility turns to such
a large extent upon evaluation of the performance in terms of objective standards prevalent in a particular field of work and the
sense of workmanship connected with it.[24]

At this point, the relation of discretion to the rational aspect of
authority we have stressed becomes almost self-evident. When a
person possesses the capacity to act in such a way that his communications concerning his actions possess by implication the
potentiality of being supported by effective reasoning, he would
appear to be eminently suited to occupy a position of discretionary
power. To put this proposition in terms of our previous analysis,

---

[23] This point was especially emphasized by Henry Hart, in the discussions
referred to in footnote 20. The argument has been elaborated from time to time
by various authors. The political thought of writers like Machiavelli and Hegel
is dominated by this problem, and its range overemphasized by them. Much of
the literature of the New Deal in one way or another carries this implication. It
is equally true of British labor thought. For the latter, see the scholarly work of
W. A. Robson, especially his *Justice and Administrative Law* (3rd ed., 1951).

[24] Cf. *Constitutional Government and Democracy* (1951), ch. XIX, and *The New
Belief in the Common Man* (1941), ch. VI, "Responsibility and the Sense of
Workmanship."

it follows that the exercise of discretionary power presupposes the possession of authority. Whenever a person possesses authority, in the sense in which we have here been employing the term, he is capable of using discretion. The fact that his decisions, commands, or other communications could be reinforced by reasoned elaboration relating them to established values and beliefs will lend his acts that "authority" without which discretion becomes arbitrary abuse of power.

If what has just been said is correct, it explains why authority is so often seen in the perspective of its psychological penumbra. For it is important, if authority is to be the source of power, that is, if the potentiality for reasoned elaboration is to manifest itself by people being willing to "go along" without such reasoned elaboration, that those subject to the command, or expected to conform in opinion or belief, recognize this potentiality. It is this undoubted fact which has led many to mistake the respect, esteem, or admiration involved for the very nature of authority. Actually, as already mentioned, these psychological concomitants are unsatisfactory if made the sole or primary criterion for identifying the nature of authority, because they occur in other comparable situations. For example, power generates esteem, and wealth respect, and holiness admiration, so that if these psychological concomitants are made the heart of the matter, authority tends to be confused with any or all of these.

At this point, it might be well to explore further the difficulties resulting from making authority antithetical to reason and truth. There is some ground for this kind of antithesis on an elementary level; for as we saw earlier, authority as defined by us does not come into play when the communication rests upon self-evidence, or the rigid rationality of demonstrable truth. But truth has a wider connotation and embraces many kinds of existential situations.[25] Incidentally, truth is one of the key values to which

[25] Cf. Karl Jaspers, *Von der Wahrheit* (1947), where incidentally a position concerning authority is developed which has some points of contact with that here stated, at least in general. Cf. especially pp. 862ff., where an authority which reason "grasps" (*ergreift*) is contrasted with an authority that is "catholic," and hence transcendent and absolute. Jaspers' notion that such authority may be "grasped" and thus mastered by "reason" underestimates the amount of reason involved in catholic authority, on one hand and the "power of reason" in mastering authority, on the other.

authority in many contexts is vitally linked. It is the sharing of this value which allows scholars to accept each other's authority, where they would not accept that of a journalist or a preacher. We might add that theology is a striking instance of reasoned elaboration of a patently transcendental system of belief. Ecclesiastical authority is vitally related to it. Thus the Catholic faith is just one of numerous possible grounds for reasoned elaboration. Every body of thought — pragmatism and skepticism as well as "the faith" — must build upon some unexplained major premises. Actually, the great *Summa* of Thomas Aquinas is one of the most ambitious efforts at reasoned elaboration ever attempted by the mind of man, and it stands to reason that those who share with Thomas Aquinas his basic opinions, beliefs, and value judgments should look upon anyone who is fairly conversant with his thought as possessed of a certain authority. The case is really not very different when the authority is rooted in a full knowledge of Karl Marx or John Dewey.

But, we are told by thoughtful men, most of the people who accept authority, whether of the church or of the government, have no idea of these elaborate reasonings, would not understand them if they heard them, and do not care to learn about them. This may well be true, up to a point, as it is when we consult a doctor or engineer, but I submit that it is the potentiality of such reasoned elaboration that matters. The communications are intrinsically "worthy of acceptance." Much institutionalized authority is maintained without the persons involved being able to elaborate. Here are the points where the "interlarding" of authority and power is most frequent. Hence these institutionalized situations are the most fertile source of the confusion between authority and power. For there is always a considerable number of people around who are obeying, believing, or conforming, because they submit to power in its various forms, including physical violence, but talk about it as obeying authority. Far be it from me to insist that all obedience and other kinds of conformity are the result of authority, since I incline toward the view that this is the error involved in the views on authority I am questioning — views which confound authority with power. All I really insist upon is that the potentiality for reasoned elaboration of communications, that is, the potentiality of supporting communications by valuational and instrumental reasoning, since it usually elicits belief, provides a potent ground for maintaining conformity in matters of action, opinion, and belief where a community exists. It is a fundamental aspect of social and more particularly of political relations. Without it no community or society can function, because no discretionary power can for long be exercised, and hence all creative, innovating, inventive activity would cease. It seems to me that this fundamental potentiality of reasoned elaboration is the differentiating characteristic of what men have talked about since the days of the *auctoritas* of the fathers of the Roman Senate, when they have spoken of authority as contrasted with power. It is related to truth as much as to any other value about which men can and do reason. It is related to freedom, because without it there can be no discretion, and without discretion there can be no freedom, in private or public life. It is the result of the fact that man, endowed with reason, is yet a finite being, whose reason is likewise finite and enclosed within definite limits. An extravagant belief in human reason is apt to lead (as it has led in the past) to extravagant claims on behalf of authority. But the reach of authority is forever confined to the reach of reasoning. There can be no absolute, no total authority, because there does not exist any absolute truth or total reason. The belief in such absolute truth is associated with a claim to absolute authority, transcending the analysis here given, as faith transcends science.

What then is "false" authority? It is that phantom which recurs in human society when men issue communications as authoritative which are believed to allow for reasoned elaboration when actually they do not. That is why the psychological interpretation of authority leads astray; for people may well *believe* that communications could be effectively elaborated and are therefore worthy of acceptance when no such potentiality exists. The falseness of such authority is revealed the moment the pretended potentiality has to be actualized. There is nothing subtle or surprising in these observations: "genuine" and "false" are terms which customarily refer to the possibility that the appearance may be deceptive. In a remarkable study on the influence of authority in matters of opinion, a nineteenth-century liberal concluded that "in the present state of the civilized world, the progress of society will depend in part upon legislative improvements, and upon those measures which a government can command or influence; but it will depend still more upon the substitution of competent for incompetent guides of public opinion; upon the continued extension of their influence; and upon the consequent organization of a sound authority in all the departments of theory and practice." [26] Cast into the less hopeful mood of our skeptical age, one might say instead that the maintenance of a measure of civilized existence depends upon the continued operation of authority as outlined in this essay. As long as we can maintain a measure of authority, that is to say, as long as those who wield power recognize their responsibility for discretionary acts in the sense of an obligation to retain the regard for the potentiality of reasoned elaboration, a constitutional order can be maintained. Once this regard is lost — and it may be lost by man at large no longer accepting reason as a guide — the night of meaningless violence is upon us. In conclusion, I should like to quote a little-known passage from an *Address to the King* by Edmund Burke which was written at the time certain members of Parliament who had opposed the measures of the government in the contest between Britain and the American colonies thought of seceding from that venerable body. "We have been too early instructed, and too long habituated to believe, that the only firm seat of all authority is in the minds, affections, and interests of the people, to change our opinions . . . for the convenience of a mere temporary arrangement of state." [27] Only when what is commanded and maintained can be thus reasoned upon and defended is authority secure. Only then can the five answers given above to the question, "why should I agree or obey?" be stated in a manner worthy of acceptance in the eyes of those who give as well as those who receive them.

[26] See George Cornwall Lewis, *An Essay on the Influence of Authority in Matters of Opinion* (London, 1849). Lewis, in a striking sentence, lends support to the position here developed: "He who believes upon authority, entertains the opinion simply because it is entertained by a *person* who appears to him *likely to think correctly on the subject.*" He defines the "principle of authority" as that of "adopting the belief of others, on a matter of opinion, without reference to the particular grounds on which that belief may rest" (pp. 6–7), where the stress is on the *particular*.

[27] Edmund Burke, *Works* (Boston, 1839), vol. V, p. 135.

3. Authority, Values, and Policy

HERBERT J. SPIRO

Students of politics have in recent years devoted much effort to studying the processes by which policy is made. Now, in dealing with authority, they are studying the reasons why policy is accepted. To make policy means to make decisions about the handling of problems which stand between oneself and one's goals or the realization of one's values. In our mobile environment of ever-changing problems, the need for making policy is ceaseless and inescapable, for both individuals and the groups to which they belong. Decisions have to be made about the recognition of problems which deserve to be dealt with, and the order of priority in which they should be handled; about the manner in which the issues about these problems should be formulated, and the way in which one's stand on these issues should be justified; about the issues themselves and the implementation of resulting policy. This continuous flow of policy is complex and hard to analyze, because of the changing character of the institutions within which, and the problems over which, it flows. The goals or values, towards which decisions are directed, are less subject to change and can be studied more easily. The same is true of authority, which provides reasons for the acceptance of policy.

The goals towards which an individual or a group is moving may also be a part of policy and, along with problems and institutions, subject to change. However, at least at the rock-bottom level, these goals do not change as fast or as frequently. Fundamental values are those in terms of which arguments about more superficial values are justified. They are the most stable. In any case, most policy is concerned with the means designed to reach some end, not with the goal itself. The nature of these values is, therefore, less ephemeral than any single decision. The acceptance of policy as "right" by those who will be affected by its consequences may also be the result of a decision. But in most cases once a method of making policy or a maker of policy is accepted as right, the attachment of authority is likely to continue. This is so because authority is concentrated at those points where the dominant values of a group or society are reflected in the most representative fashion. These are the points where decisions are made which are accepted by those who will be affected by their consequences.

Much of what happens to human beings is not due to decisions at all, but the outcome of a "concourse of natural causes." And much of what happens to men as a result of human decisions is not the direct product of their own decisions, but of the decisions of others. Authority is a kind of "additive" which leads us to accept policies about our fate, even though these policies are made by others. What is it that lends authority to policy?

If we ask this question first about different types of policy as they affect different kinds of individuals in our society, we find a variety of answers. A child accepts decisions made about his fate by his parents, at first because the alternative of nonacceptance does not occur to him, later perhaps simply because the parents are older. This kind of authority based upon seniority may be due to the greater resources for implementing decisions which the older person controls. As the child grows older, authority is more likely to be based also on his recognition of the knowledge and experience of his parents. Thus, there is a combination of factors which lends authority to parental policy towards children, and the center of gravity in this combination changes over time. The same also applies to teachers' policies towards their students. Initially, these are accepted for reasons similar to those lending authority to parental decisions. Then, as the child becomes aware of the specialized goals of his education, the center of gravity will shift towards such factors as the teacher's training, experience, and demonstrated competence in his subject, in addition to his general competence in dealing with students. As the student's own reasoning capacities are developed, the center of gravity in the combination of factors lending authority to policy will shift further in the direction of the way in which the policy was made, and away from the individual who made it and his qualities, that is, from substance to method.

Stockholders of a business corporation accept the policies of its president because of a still different combination of factors: the procedures by which the president got that job, his past performance, and the means by which he can be held accountable in the future. Chances are that the man became president of the corporation because of his experience, training, demonstrated ability, "personality," and possibly also wealth, which may be the tangible proof of the preceding qualities. If he made a good profit during his past tenure, this will give additional authority to the policies which he is making for the future. If he has brought the corporation a loss or has been the cause of poor labor relations, his new policies are likely to carry little authority, and that little only because he can, under the by-laws, be removed.

Somewhat similar factors lend authority to the policies made by a local party boss, which affect among others his loyal followers. He, too, has experience and training and would not hold his present position if he did not have "what it takes" — say a combination of shrewdness, ruthlessness, perseverance, good luck, and corruption. He has won votes and elections for the organization in the past, so that the local hacks have reason to rely upon his judgment when he makes new policy. A college president has authority for another set of reasons, perhaps a very similar set, again with a different center of gravity or point of emphasis. The policies which he puts into effect will be accepted by alumni, among others, because of the president's background and experience, including perhaps a successful career as a scholar, and because of the method by which he was appointed to his position. Beyond all this, however, his policies have authority also because the president stands for the traditions of the college, that is, for the values which have helped to shape its life.

An unarmed bobby in England — not necessarily a bigger man than I — can tell me what to do in a traffic snarl, not because the government which appointed him is accountable to me, or because he is older than I am — he may be younger. His decisions about me in this situation carry authority because of his manner and because of his uniform. There are, of course, more exalted examples of the authority derived from external symbols, such as uniforms, rings, crowns, crosses, and even the cut of ordinary civilian clothes. The policies of a parish priest have authority, partly because of his symbols of office, partly because of reasons cited in connection with the more mundane officers above, and partly because of the religious faith of the affected parishioners.

Different occupants of the same office may bear authority for different reasons, beyond those which are functions of personality differences. For example, President Washington had authority — among other reasons — because he had been associated with the founding of the United States. President Eisenhower had nothing to do with this founding, but was elected in accordance with procedures which were laid down in the founding, and this fact enhances the authority of his policies.

Usually, a great deal of authority will attach to some, and very little authority to other decisions affecting others, though these decisions are made by one and the same individual. President Truman was considered authoritative by a majority of Americans when he decided to have the first atom bombs dropped on Japan. But no one thought that he spoke with authority about a music critic who did not think as highly of his daughter's singing as he did. Dr. Paul Dudley White made decisions about the life of President Eisenhower which were accepted as completely authoritative by the President and many other people. But if Dr. White had tried to make similar decisions or even to offer opinions about American foreign policy, he would not have gotten very far. Several scientists have discovered to their dismay that the authority with which they can speak on nuclear production capabilities or fall-out does not carry over to defense and foreign policy.

There are thus many different sources of authority for policy and for the makers of policy. The emphasis varies, depending on the group for which the policy is made and on the function of particular policies. These functional variations in the source of authority are particularly marked in the case of specialized activities, the purpose of which is clearly recognized. Medicine, engineering, business are cases in point. The patient turns to the physician in order to be healed — as Plato put it rather too often. The city turns to the engineer to construct a bridge according to specifications laid down by the city council. The board of directors appoints a successful manager to pull one of the corporation's divisions out of the red. The decisions made by physician, engineer, and manager have authority, because these men are experts in their fields. Their decisions will affect those who hired them, or those on whose behalf they were hired. They will be accepted as right because of the specialized qualifications of the men who made them.

In the case of policies whose goal cannot be so clearly recognized and which are generalized rather than specialized, the source of authority varies less according to function, and more according to the dominant values of the group for which policy is made. This applies particularly to those policies which are the product of "politics" in the popular meaning of the term, and for the same reason which made the ancient Greeks call politics the "master science." There are many possible sources of authority for non-specialized policy. We have already mentioned several. They seem to fall into two major categories: those sources which may be called substantive, because they are like qualities which are attached to, or possessed by, a policy or its maker; and sources which may be called procedural, because they refer to the procedures which produced the policy or according to which policy-makers are selected. Among substantive sources of authority, we can think of age, experience, training, study, foundation, wealth, tradition, beauty, inherited titles, symbols, strength, religion. Among procedural sources of authority, there are methods of election or appointment, systems of accountability, participation and use of information in policy-making, means of publicizing policy. These two main categories of sources, substantive and procedural, are not mutually exclusive. Mr. Dulles has authority because of both his background and the methods by which he was appointed and according to which he operates. But for his job as Secretary of State, in our society today, the procedural sources of his authority are more important than the substantive ones, as becomes evident whenever his policies run into domestic trouble.

Political systems and other organizations could be classified according to prevailing sources of authority. In many business organizations, for example, wealth is the dominant value, so that the wealthiest member is considered most authoritative. In some academic organizations, on the other hand, capacity for dialectic, analysis, criticism, and reflection is valued most highly. Those members who excel in these skills — not those who have published the heaviest volumes — wield the greatest authority. In common-law countries, verdicts that are the outcome of flawless procedures are often accepted as authoritative, even by those who disagree violently with their substance. In continental European jurisdictions, the reverse is more often true.

In western political systems, a shift of emphasis from substantive to procedural sources of authority seems often to have occurred in the course of time. It also takes place for each individual as he matures. For the growing individual, there is a clear relation between changes in his dominant values and changes in his conceptions of authority. As he becomes more rational, substantive sources of authority are slowly, and never completely, replaced by procedural sources. Changing American concepts of authority illustrate this shift in a political system. When the colonies declared their independence from Great Britain, they eliminated tradition as a useful source of authority. The founders of the Massachusetts Bay Colony had, with the name of "our dread Sovereign Lord King James," invoked all the tradition of monarchy, in an act whose religious motivation is well known. The founding fathers of the republic, by contrast, were rejecting not only the tradition of the monarchy of George III, but a great many other traditions as well. They had to seek some substitute for these lost sources of authority in order to build a new authority of their own. They found this substitute in reason, and in the consent of the governed. The whole system of government which they created, almost from scratch, was a construction of self-conscious and relatively self-confident human reason. As a result, and because those affected by the Declaration of Independence and later the Constitution had given their consent, these documents had authority.

The Constitution may be viewed as a device designed to facilitate rational participation by those capable of it, in the selection of policies and personnel of government. In this sense, reason gave authority to the Constitution itself and continues to give authority to the governments that operate under the Constitution. This did not eliminate foundation and tradition as sources of authority. During the first few decades of the republic, the founding fathers carried great authority. As their generation died, tradition became the more important of these two sources. All the time, down to our own day, however, both foundation and tradition have been intimately linked with reason. As our dominant values have become more rationalistic and individualistic, individual reason as a source of authority has also become more important.

Expressed in concrete terms, individualism and rationalism have meant growth of the belief that the individual is largely responsible for his own fate. Within certain limits, recognized more or less clearly in different periods, he has been believed capable of rationally deciding what he wants to make of himself. But much of what happens to him is due to the fate of the groups to which he belongs, especially the nation. He should therefore have opportunities to contribute to shaping the fate of the nation. The individual has such opportunities as a member of the electorate and of the "constituent power." This is the main source of the government's authority. Since it is derived from them, citizens are generally assumed to share in this authority. Indeed, the active and respected citizen often appears as the bearer of authority outside of politics proper, simply because he is known to hold political authority. In the United States today, no government would have authority unless it operated within the framework of the Constitution and with the consent of the citizenry. The Constitution is assumed to be a document devised by human reason, and the basis of political processes which operate rationally. The consent of the citizenry, supplied through these processes, is also assumed to be the product of reason, as it operates, for instance, when voters make choices. Tradition also plays a role in creating authority for government in the United States, much of it in connection with the founding fathers. But, as we know from such constitutional controversies as those about states' rights, tradition may be pleaded on any side of an argument. In deciding which argument from tradition to accept, people once more rely at least in part on their powers of ratiocination. Such decisions derive authority especially from the procedures according to which they were made.

This trend towards procedural rather than substantive sources of authority seems to be fairly widespread and reflects a similar shift of emphasis in dominant values. Many philosophies, whatever substantive disagreements they may have with one another, would agree on

the fundamental norm of individual responsibility.[1] These philosophies place great value upon the individual's *efforts* to become responsible for his own fate. He makes such efforts by using the
resources which are at his disposal, by choosing among alternative
courses of action, and by doing so on the basis of the best knowledge
available about the consequences of his decisions. But these philosophies are fully conscious of the restrictions on human resources,
limits on human choices, and imperfections in human knowledge.
Therefore, they are prepared to accept undesirable consequences of
decisions, so long as responsible procedures were used in arriving at
the decisions. Responsible procedures are used when policies are
made by governments which are accountable to the people who will
be affected by the consequences of these policies. Thus, the "pursuit
of happiness," according to the recognized rules of the game, is
coming to be valued at least as highly as the achievement of happiness, the feasibility of which has become increasingly doubtful in
recent decades in any case. As an index of this trend we may take
the high prestige, and the important role in generalized policy-
making, of lawyers and other technicians of procedure, at least in
the West. In the Soviet world, by contrast, substantive values are
relatively more important. Emphases on sources of authority in these
two great areas differ accordingly.

Still, there are wide variations on this count within the West.
Thus, the authority of a leader, who wields power as the result of
a rational process of selection and within a framework of constitutional accountability, may be enhanced from several different
sources: founding associations (Adenauer, de Gasperi), traditional
associations (Churchill), or even their very opposite, for which the
recent election of an immigrant from India to the United States
Congress may serve as a dramatic illustration. Again, in continental
Europe, the possession of specialized knowledge, as evidenced by
academic degrees (Germany) or literary distinction (France) may
serve as a source of political authority. In the Old World, old age
often provides the kind of authority which, in the New World, goes
with youth.

As dominant values vary from one political system to another, so

[1] See the author's "Responsibility in Citizenship, Government, and Administration,"
in *Public Policy*, IV (1953).

does the content of authority. There are even greater variations in policies and the processes by which they are made. Within separate political systems, policies sometimes change rapidly and radically. Values and sources of authority are usually much more stable. Totalitarian systems seem to be the only exception to this generalization, for there values have on occasion been changed overnight. But this exception may not be valid. Thus, studies of concentration camps have suggested that, while power resides in the commandant, authority often resides in one or more of the "elders" among the inmates, and that this authority is recognized even by some of the guards. The true fundamental values of these camps, and of totalitarian systems as well, are different from the pseudo-values which can be changed overnight. The true values, and the sources of authority which they provide, are more stable than policies, even under totalitarianism. The student of politics, therefore, who is looking for relatively stable patterns, which underlie the instability of policies and institutions, will do well to study values, policy, and authority together.

4. Authority and the Law

JEROME HALL

Authority is a high-level abstraction, and any thorough inquiry into its roles, types, conditions, and functions is no less than a quest for an inclusive philosophy and science of law and politics.[1] The extant literature ranges from realist interpretations of the "essence" of authority to the positivist dismissal of questions concerning authority as meaningless. Even such significant discussions of authority as that by Max Weber suggest the need for more narrowly defined problems and probings. In the present state of the literature, it must be confessed, it is difficult to know precisely what questions should be asked about authority and what the significant problems are concerning it. The following represents an effort to clarify familiar usages and to suggest some perspectives by reference to which a more definite formulation of problems seems possible.

Authority is often said to be "legitimate power" but, although it is very important to distinguish "naked" power from "recognized" power and "right" power, the above usage raises rather than answers many questions, especially the question of whether "legitimate" means legal, and if so, in what sense? Does it also, or instead, imply the recognition of a moral duty to obey a law or to obey "right law"? Again, the authority of certain persons implies that they give commands, and that concerns action by the subjects. This brings the problem of freedom and coercion into focus, and that, in turn, in-

[1] See, generally, *Freedom and Authority in Our Time,* ed. Lyman Bryson, Louis Finkelstein, R. M. MacIver, and Richard McKeon (1953).

volves responsibility. Authority is thus a relational idea and an operative fact that cannot be understood apart from a context in which various reciprocal or correlative notions participate.

Especially important is the relation of authority to order in at least two senses: order as a command, and order as organization; and it is agreed that every group has or is an order. But there are different types and degrees of order and the methods of maintaining it also differ. Moreover, what is order from one viewpoint may be disorder from another. Order is thus both a fact exhibited in patterns and a value that is never sufficiently realized in human society — it borders on ideal harmony. Mussolini substituted "Authority, Order, Justice" for the revolutionary French triad, "Liberty, Equality, Fraternity" and the sequence of his terms suggests his perspective and value-orientation. In an early work, Radbruch said, "The existence of a legal order is more important than its justice and expediency . . ." and quoted Goethe in support.[2] One might certainly hold another opinion regarding this statement; in any case, it seems less controversial to say that freedom and justice depend on order, and the latter implies authority. But order is also a condition of effective authority. Nothing seems to be gained by asserting actual priorities; but preferences are more or less defensible in the realm of values.

"Authority" in the literature of jurisprudence sometimes means the mere existence of a legal rule or that one legal rule is consistent with a higher legal rule. Again, it may mean internal pressure to conform to the moral principle embodied in a rule of law or the recognized power of an official who adheres to valid norms. It may refer to the imperative significance of law as distinguished from its rational and descriptive meanings. It has been given still other meanings, for example, in institutional or integrative contexts where conduct and actual processes are stressed.

Some organization of the many diverse interpretations of authority can be achieved by classifying them with reference to the relatively few perspectives which they represent. For example, there are practical and theoretical approaches. In the natural-law perspective the

[2] *The Legal Philosophies of Lask, Radbruch, and Dabin,* Twentieth-Century Legal Philosophy Series, vol. IV (1950), p. 108. Goethe's quotation is on p. 118. Radbruch sharply modified his legal philosophy in later work, written after his experience with the Nazi regime.

primary question concerning authority is a practical one — is there a moral obligation to obey a particular government or command? In this view, authority is dependent upon the giving of commands which are morally binding. Indeed, authority and the bindingness or "compulsion" of morality are so closely intertwined as to be often identified.

This practical problem has also been treated from the perspective, not of the subject of a state, as above, but from that of the ideal ruler or philosopher-king. Plato's philosophy is the classical exposition of the purposes of authority from the viewpoint of the ruler who conforms to natural law. Since the citizens of a democracy are both rulers and subjects, the democratic perspective consists largely of the union, indeed the planned ambivalence, of these roles.

The perspective of empirical science reflects a theoretical approach in which the enforcement of the norms, the facts of obedience, and the observable manifestations of authority and conformity in institutions are central. But it should be noted that the natural-law perspective is not lacking in emphasis upon objective data and criteria — factual and ideal — which are relevant to the validity of laws and the authenticity (competence) of the officials who make and interpret them. By reference to these objective determinants it is appropriate to speak of decision-*finding* as opposed to decision-*making*. It is also clear that in the empirical perspective, excepting the extreme behavioristic one, authority and obedience involve more than attitudes and movements. In case studies, for instance, where the position taken is that of participation in problem-solving, the bindingness of authority is also interpreted on grounds deemed objectively valid, although for a theoretical rather than a practical purpose — to understand rather than to influence.

The legal positivist view of authority is a practical one in that it is defined by reference to the interests of litigants and the desire to maintain order. On the other hand, the formalism of legal positivism suggests the model of pure or rational science. But, although the current positivist school avowedly excludes the sociology and psychology of law from the orbit of legal science, it insists on the need to recognize the efficacy of law, the factuality of legal sanctions, and the substance of the *Grundnorm*. The resulting interpretations of authority are not compatible with the avowed theory. If, however, the definitions are taken at face value without any attempt to reconcile them, a statement concerning authority is to be taken as merely the equivalent of the statement that a relevant law exists. So, too, the validity of authority is distinguished from its efficacy. Thus, a statement concerning the efficacy of a law is not a statement regarding a legal rule; it is "a statement about actual behavior." [3] And this efficacy is said to be a "condition" of the validity of a law, not an element or attribute of it. These distinctions may be very significant in the perspective of "lawyers' law," that is, where a litigant wishes to know what the authorities may do to him. But from an institutional or integrative viewpoint, behavior does not fortuitously conform to the idea of law. Instead, there is an intelligible connection between the significance of laws and behavior. "Efficacy of law" in this perspective includes an actual process in which the ideational aspect of law, that is, "pure" law, participates. [4]

It may be possible to come to closer grips with our problem by considering some uses of "authority" in certain more definite legal contexts. In one sense of the term, an "authority" is an expert, and one so qualified may give his opinion in court. Authority here substitutes for inquiry and explanation, although it is presupposed that the authority has made the necessary investigation and that his opinion reflects an established body of knowledge. In fact, it is customary to ask an expert witness to state his reasons, but his opinion is not a reason. He stands back of his opinion in a personal, dogmatic way, if only because the application of his knowledge to the precise problem in hand cannot be fully communicated.

A second use of "authority" is found in the law of agency and in that of corporate transactions where *ultra vires* acts are in issue. A salesman can bind his employer, can place him under a legal obligation to other persons even if he exceeds his instructions. His authority is or has power, within limits defined in law, to change legal relations among certain persons. Thus, the agent participates in a type of interpersonal legislation.

The term used both to designate and limit the authority of courts

[3] Hans Kelsen, *General Theory of Law and State,* Twentieth-Century Legal Philosophy Series, vol. I (1945), p. 40; see also pp. 30, 37, 39–40, 42.
[4] Jerome Hall, "Integrative Jurisprudence," in *Interpretations of Modern Legal Philosophies,* ed. P. L. Sayre (1947), p. 313.

is "jurisdiction." The jurisdiction of a court is fixed by statutes and constitutions, especially those sections which determine who is a judge and, once that is settled, the subject of his official duties, the territory where his authority operates, and the persons who are bound by his decisions. There has been some criticism of Holmes' remark that "the foundation of jurisdiction is physical power";[5] attention has been called to the acquisition of jurisdiction by consent of the litigants, the recognition of mailing as valid personal service, and the rendering of declaratory judgments. These criticisms raise pertinent questions regarding the incidence and scope of physical power in adjudication. But, although one may immediately agree that it is fallacious to rest jurisdiction solely upon physical power, it seems equally untenable to eliminate it altogether. In each of the above instances relied upon by Holmes' critics, physical power, though limited in its spheres of spatial and temporal operation, is nonetheless present — at least in threat and in the stage of enforcement.

Another important meaning of "authority" is the authority of legal precedent. It is the holding, interpreted in relation to the "material" facts, which must be followed, not the reasons given in support of the holding. The position of a particular tribunal in the hierarchy of tribunals determines whose holdings are authority for whom. Judges are said to be bound to follow relevant precedents. But if a judge does not follow them, there are no laws to compel him to do so, nor may legal sanctions be imposed for his failure, even his refusal, to conform — except, perhaps, in extreme situations where a question of impeachment might be raised. Moreover, it is always possible to appear to be following precedent by distinguishing facts. Thus, judges are not legally bound to obey the law. Their obligation is a moral one.

An important function of authority is shown in the doctrine *ignorantia legis neminem excusat.*[6] This doctrine does not rest upon the absurd presumption that everyone can know the law or that anyone does know all of it. Instead, it is a regulatory postulate that is essential to the operation of a legal system. Every legal rule, however clear and distinct its core may be, is vague at its periphery — a

---

[5] *McDonald* v. *Mabee, 243 U. S. 91 (1915).*
[6] Jerome Hall, *General Principles of Criminal Law* (1947), ch. 11.

quality shared with all descriptive language. Accordingly, in the determination of specific meanings, opinions differ. The problem is solved by the doctrine of *ignorantia legis,* that is, only the meanings declared by "competent" officials are authoritative. Since the advice of a lawyer, even though he be among the most eminent in the land, is no defense, while a "competent" judge may be a very incompetent lawyer, it is evident that "competence" does not mean wisdom or knowledge of the law.

Certain characteristics of the authority of an expert, the authority of an agent, the authority of precedent, and the authority of "competent" officials have been indicated above. From some viewpoints, there are important differences among these authorities, for example, in regard to the nature of sanctions and the unavoidable subjection to, and operation of, legal sanctions. There are also obvious differences between the authority of an abstraction and the authority of a human being. Accordingly, in any research it would be necessary to employ terms which maintained these and other distinctions.

But are there any common features which account for the use of the term in such apparently different contexts? First, unique attributes set persons who function as authorities apart from other persons. In a court, an expert witness is one who is specifically qualified and technically "recognized" as an authority. An agent has been selected by his employer. Legal precedent is found only in "official" reports, and "competent" officials are designated by reference to the conformity of certain behavior (voting, appointment) with certain laws. Thus, authority is readily identified.

Second, authority implies the acknowledgment of it, whether that turns on respect for scholarship, reliance upon representations and legal powers, acceptance of a moral obligation, or recognition of the legality of a command. This correlative or counterpart of authority in public attitudes is manifested in appropriate conduct.

Third, there is a common negative attribute: authority does not reveal itself as reason or science. An expert need not give his reasons; indeed, when he gives his reasons he is not functioning as an authority. He functions as an authority when he states his *ipse dixit*. Nor do the powers of agents and the jurisdiction of officials depend upon their dialectical skill or their erudition. And, as noted, what is binding in precedents is not the reason for them.

Fourth, authority is expressed as an act of volition. Intentions, decisions, judgments, and obviously commands represent something in addition to the functioning of intelligence. They include so-called determinations of the will. This may seem dubious in regard to the expression of opinions by experts who are not "competent" officials. But the opinion of an expert witness implies a decision regarding what should or should not be done. Indeed, any authoritative opinion has in it a degree of finality or arbitrary termination of inquiry, as of that date, which at least enjoins the direction of others' studies. Of course, if "authority" is limited by stipulating the availability of physical sanctions, a scholar is not an authority.

Fifth, although authority is not an expression of reason, it presupposes, at least in a democracy, that reason and science have been put to the maximum use to solve the problem in hand. This has been discussed in a very perceptive essay by Professor Fuller, in terms of the antinomy of reason and fiat in rules of law and the judicial process.[7] He makes it clear that "fiat" has no objectionable connotation in that context. A particular problem requires a specific solution. After reason and investigation have run their full course, several equally valid solutions become available or the conclusions reached fall short of the necessary specificity. Authority fills the gap, and the solution includes an inevitable degree of arbitrariness. By its relation to the indicated reasoning and investigation this sort of fiat is distinguishable from the indefensibly arbitrary decree of an administrator who has not investigated the facts. It is a fiat which is necessitated by the contingencies of practical knowledge,[8] the availability of equally rational solutions while the objective is organized social action, and the characteristics of specific problem-solving. It is a fiat that is also defensible by reference to the inquiries which determined the boundaries of the area within which authority must function in the given situation. Accordingly, when it is urged that the exercise of authority is or may be rational, the above distinction should be borne in mind. Authority is rational in the sense that it is collaterally supported by relevant knowledge and investigation. But it is not itself an act of reason in any of the recognized principal meanings

[7] L. L. Fuller, *Reason and Fiat in Case Law* (1943); reprinted in *Harvard Law Review*, 59:376 (1945).
[8] Yves Simon, *Nature and Functions of Authority* (1940).

of "reason," such as correct means-end functioning, recognition of universals among discrete phenomena, logical implication, and so on.

With reference to this phase of the problem, it will be recalled that in Plato's *Statesman* the premise is that perfect reason, unfettered by law, can discover the precisely correct solution of specific problems.[9] In the realm of theory and in eternity, this may be incontestable, while in regard to the solution of practical problems here and now, the use of authority is a necessity. Recognition of the theory, however, encourages challenges of existing assumptions that the exercise of authority in any given area is sound. For example, is it actually just as defensible to require motorists to drive on the right as it is to order them to drive on the left? Certainly the specificity of any judicial or administrative decision is not *ipso facto* an assurance that it is the best possible solution. On the contrary, it is always possible on rational-empirical grounds to challenge authority in any specific area.

Finally, if law is viewed as an institution, it includes the various attributes of authority noted above, as well as that of implementation by physical sanctions and their unavoidable incidence. That legal authority is, in part, traditional[10] is manifested in numerous substantive rules: those concerning primogeniture and the disabilities of married women or, to cite modern instances, those governing the conveyance of real estate, the execution of wills, and the age of minority. In procedure, the traditional element is even more evident: trial by jury and the forms of action. That legal authority also tends to be charismatic is indicated in the deference paid the judge even when he is outside the courtroom and clad in ordinary attire. The rationality of legal authority is shown, for example, in its conformity with the evidence and in its implementation of existing, though not necessarily the latest, knowledge. What Weber said regarding the interpenetration of the various types of authority clearly applies to the legal institution.

From a democratic perspective, questions concerning authority must be formulated in relation to problem-solving by discussion and

---

[9] Jerome Hall, "Plato's Legal Philosophy," *Indiana Law Journal*, 31: 184–186 (1956).

[10] Max Weber, *The Theory of Social and Economic Organization*, trans. A. H. Henderson and T. Parsons (1947), pp. 324ff.

the paramount value of self-rule. The objective is the maximization of rational processes and the restriction of authority to minimal requirements. But conformity is far from being purely rational, and if the robes, flags, and insignia of office make authority more effective, due allowance must be made. The assumption, however, is that it is always possible to challenge official authority and to be supported in that effort by other, legal authority.

5. Authority and the Free Society

FRANK H. KNIGHT

The more one thinks about a brief general essay on authority, and "essays" production of one, the more forbidding the task appears.

The word "authority" is used in such a range of meanings, with the things it stands for playing a similar variety of roles, that a definite meaning or list of meanings can hardly be given. In several contexts "authority" is synonymous with "power," which is closely related to freedom, and this must be defined by antithesis with coercion or, in the metaphysical sense, with causality — all highly ambiguous terms with a complicated history. Again, throughout most of human history, authority in society has rested in part on naked power, but in part on belief in supernatural command and sanctions, and this is still the case in a lingering sort of way; hence the treatment would lead into the field of religion, or superstition, as well as other strands of cultural history. Men both hate authority and love it, in their own possession and in that of others; they often appeal to any convenient and plausible authority to evade responsibility. Finally, authority, particularly in our modern form of society, is largely "authorized," as was alleged in the case of spokesmen for the supernatural — and that takes one into the field of the agency relations which permeate our social order. Primary fields of authority in society are the family and the state, each represented in action by a functioning head or body of officials; but the same principle applies in some form and degree to any of the innumerable groups which have some unity in action, ranging in size from two persons up to half the world. This essay will suggest that the issues raised by our concept can be largely brought under two heads, "law" and "leadership." Both must be viewed in historical terms, and they will here be considered with reference to "democratic" society, in its secular and chiefly its politico-legal relations.

A natural way to begin is to consult the dictionary, an "authority" on the use of words to stand for concepts. *Webster's New International* gives as the first definition of authority, "legal or rightful power." The definition is obviously too narrow to indicate the actual use of the word; for it may refer to power without right, legal or moral, or to right without power, or even to an impersonal cause influencing thought or action, which does not involve either law or morals or the use of power. Here we must note that in our context power means that which is exercised by one person over another, or between groups; it is coercive power, not causality in any other sense. As its derivation shows (from French *pouvoir,* Latin *potere*), power originally meant an attribute of purposive beings, beings who "can" (the Germanic homologue), implying choice between action and refraining from action.

Any more than a superficial inquiry into authority and all these related terms would require recognizing that the meaning of each is a stratified deposit accumulated during culture history. "Truth," for example, originally meant fidelity rather than verity — as in German *Treue* — as we speak of a "true" friend, follower, and so on. The difficulty is that such words have kept their "primitive," "animistic" and more or less moralistic meanings, and also have added new ones, causing ambiguity and confusion. "Action," again, ought logically to be restricted to purposive behavior or conduct; but it has been carried over to describe relations of physical causality, an essentially modern concept, for which we have no other convenient name. In the case of "authority," we must think of the root word "author," which applies to supernatural authority, and perhaps remotely or figuratively to that of parents over their own children. But authority now has no such implication (and we hardly need to trace "author" back to its origin in the Latin *augere,* to augment). An author may not be an authority except for what he has said or meant, a trivial point unless this carries authority only because he has said it. Our modern minds have come to make two explicit distinctions — first, between nonpurposive causality and motivation, and second, between two forms of the latter: personal or subjective desire and the "cognitive values" of moral and aesthetic judgments. A change equally fundamental for our analysis occurred with the (very recent) development of the democratic idea and ideal. In our liberal system of thinking and valuation, all exercise of power, by persons over persons, is more or less "wrong" or contrary to the ideal. It is "right" only where necessary, as in the relations between parents and children, who are not in the full sense persons, or between "society" and criminal or defective adults, who also are treated as outside of the community or not fully members of it.

Society, however, acts only through personal agents, as does any human group which acts as a unit at all or in any way. This principle might be followed out by considering any of the infinitely complex congeries of "societies" that make up "society," which, *par excellence,* means political society acting through officials constituting a "government." The term, that is, especially refers to "sovereign" state, though sovereignty is a vague term in both directions. On the one hand, groups of states, up through the civilized world, form groups with varying degrees of unity in action; on the other hand, any state is (as noted) a complex of groups, partly in a hierarchical order going down to the family as a second basic unit. Any real group exercises more or less power over its members, acting through agents who have some personal or "discretionary" power; and any such group exemplifies the principle of sovereignty in various degrees and ways. However, this, to repeat, is contrary to the ultimate democratic ideal, and "authority" ought surely to be distinguished from power, even where legally or rightfully used. In the ideal democracy, power pertains to the group as a whole, with equal participation in its decisions by all its members. In a group of any size and permanence, this must mean acting in accord with *law,* which is the immediate subject of group decisions. The group, then, in the familiar expression, is governed by laws and not by men — and insofar as it is ideally democratic, the authority of its agents is the delegated authority of the law. In strict logic, laws do not command or rule, and men do not "obey" law, but act in conformity with it; but the former is the way in which we must use words. Linguistic usage is in a sense the ultimate type of law, hence of authority, in human society; and these laws can be said to be "made" democratically in the ultimate meaning of that word — or one ultimate meaning. Again the authority of the dictionary comes to mind. Insofar as authority is personal, its essence is superior knowledge, or judgment, and ultimately all knowledge is of this character, is knowledge of law in some of its various meanings, which is the "real" authority. This applies to the authority of the expert, connoisseur, or specialist in art, science, and logic as well as to that of the lawyer or judge. It is not, or ought not to be, "arbitrary."

As we look into history, however, we see that genetically the opposite of all this has been the case, in large part, down to modern times and in western civilization. The evolutionary origin of man as a social being, and of human society, is largely unknown and doubtless must remain a mystery. We do indeed find "leadership" of a sort in animal societies, implying authority of a sort. But we do not know the kind of animal society in which and out of which human society evolved. Animal behavior, in the higher species, is usually attributed to "instinct," which is assumed to operate mechanically and to be produced mechanically in the individual by gene inheritance, changing only through mutations and selective survival. The great mystery of human evolution is the indubitable fact that instincts became so attenuated into vague "drives" as no longer to fit the concept, biological inheritance and evolution being largely replaced by social or cultural. But social inheritance and cultural change could be as mechanistic as the biological sequence — the one a matter of "conditioned response" and the other a matter of "historical law," such as seems to determine linguistic growth and change. And this may have been the case in the beginning, and for ages, before purposive activity in any sense, involving feeling and intelligence, began to affect institutional behavior. We do not know and probably can never learn. If this was the course of evolution, either leadership or law, recognized and felt as imperative, may have been prior in time to the other. Certainly we must recognize leadership, even in the extreme form of which it can be said that the will of the leader is law, as a reality in known human societies, with this arbitrary will gradually becoming limited by and subject to group will and to law.

But in society in general, as known to history and anthropology and inferred for prehistory, the opposite is predominantly the case, down to a few generations ago. Social order was based on law as custom, which has grown, without deliberate action or even awareness on the part of the people concerned. The role of the "authority" or authorities that exist is to know and declare the law "as it is," being in fact regarded as sacred, supernaturally ordained, eternal, and immutable. Of course this never works out in pure accord with the belief, since primitive laws do change, both by "drift" in the manner of language change, and by "prophets" who convert the society to different ideas and norms, generally by first converting the secular leader or ruler. The division in the function of maintaining "law and order" between secular and religious offices (though both were sacred, like the law itself) is one of the mysterious but vital facts of history; and the relation between the two "authorities" is especially noteworthy in our western culture history since, from conversion to ecclesiastical Christianity more or less down to the present. The outstanding exception to the historical predominance of law over leadership is organization for war, with the hunting of the larger animals as somewhat akin. The modern state seems to have evolved primarily out of the leadership in war, rather than from the Church or any more or less specialized judicial functionary. Democracy arose out of political absolutism through increasing subjection to public opinion, formalization and unification of the law, and finally the establishment of the right of the people to change the law at will by legislation.

It is impossible here to take up at length the complex and subtle relation between law and liberty. There is an inherent conflict between order and individual freedom in the literal meaning, including the right of associating by mutual agreement among the parties directly concerned. The effective freedom of the individual in any society acting under law — necessarily interpreted and enforced by some agent with a good deal of arbitrary discretion, that is, power more or less precisely defined and limited by law — is finally limited by his freedom, or actual ability, to leave the organization. This freedom is least in relation to the sovereign state defined by terri-

torial boundaries, and its sovereignty is distinctive in that sense. At
the opposite extreme is the individual freedom from law and
authority in the economic organization of free enterprise. With individual freedom as the fundamental human value — the distinctive
philosophy of modern liberalism — the system of markets and prices
is morally ideal and required wherever it will "work," that is, where
there is not a sufficient reason for replacing it by some politico-legal
alternative which necessarily involves much more compulsion. The
qualification sets the main problem of policy in a society "dedicated
to liberty." Of course it is a sweeping qualification; there are many
compelling reasons for governmental action that interferes with
market relations in economic life — in fact to a rapidly increasing
extent — and for outright replacement by political action in more
and more fields. Of course, too, the enterprise organization cannot
possibly operate without an authoritative legal order, to secure a
fair approximation to the "free competition" of the theoretically ideal
market, as well as to qualify its operation or substitute political action where this will actually be "better" in terms of all the values
involved in civilized life. Prior to freedom, or to "justice," or even to
truth, the primary and virtually absolute requirement is order, which
must mean the existing order, until it can be replaced by a better,
through orderly procedure and without excessive cost.

The "ideal" market is ideally free; the individual has equally good
alternatives open, hence no one can exercise power over anyone else.
(It should not be described as "competitive," since rivalry is contrary
to economic motivation; there is rivalry, but so is there in all social
relations, in fact far more in politics than in business, though it is
equally "irrational," in the instrumental sense. How far rivalry is a
"bad" motive is a question beyond the scope of this discussion, but
any intelligent judgment passed on the enterprise system must rest
on a comparison of business with politics, realistically viewed, and
many of the alleged evils of the one will be seen to hold for the
other also.) The market system enables people to cooperate within
wide limits, without agreeing on their values or arguing about them;
each can choose both his own role in production and what he will
consume. Economic life does, however, become more and more a
phenomenon of organizations rather than individuals, and these
involve more and more personal authority. As production and distri-

bution become more specialized and the enterprise larger and more complex, the individual has less "effective" freedom to leave one organization for another, especially as a worker, by getting another job. Consequently, the individual needs more and more "authoritative" assistance in securing effective freedom and other fundamental rights; again, this is especially the worker, but it is also true of the owner of shares in large-scale enterprise.

Viewed as a whole, the transition from preliberal society to liberalism or individualism, with cultural and economic freedom and democratic government, involved several revolutionary changes. Most fundamental was the freeing of the mind, involving a radical change in the conception of truth. In primitive society the compulsion to conform to custom in behavior was associated with compulsion to "believe" in the ancestral myths and to participate in the rituals by which they were dramatized and enforced. The myths took the place filled in liberal society by both science and history, and the obligation to believe was moral and religious rather than intellectual, or one of good taste. In this fundamental respect — social order being based on a moral and supernaturally sanctioned duty to believe an established dogma and practice an established ritual — Western European medieval society was of the primitive pattern. A main obligation of the individual was to work out his lot in the station of life in which he was born, on the assumption that he was divinely ordained or "called" to this destiny. The first great impulse in the disruption of the medieval order appeared in a religious revolt, of an essentially reactionary character, but reinforced by an upsurge of new political and economic interests. And the first result was displacement of the supreme authority of the Church by that of new national states, which in theory were no more "liberal"; they were governed by dynasties claiming "divine right," that is, divine authority. But the political order has historically been less hostile to change than the religious, and circumstances — especially military competition — compelled these governments to tolerate and foster the scientific movement and the revival of trade, which were already under way, and presently led to their democratization with religious, cultural, and economic liberation. Through technology the scientific and economic interests worked together to generate the revolutionary idea of progress in both fields. This is most evident in the teaching of

Francis Bacon in England, in the early seventeenth century, with Galileo in northern Italy a slightly later contemporary and a more effective contributor.

The main result appeared a few generations later, in the period of the Enlightenment, and the following nineteenth century. The heart of it is that truth is no longer viewed as revealed and known once for all time as eternally unchanging, but the opposite in these respects. First of all, truth is recognized as provisional, subject to revision or replacement in the light of new evidence or insight, to be secured by free inquiry and verified through free discussion. The new view first became effective in natural science, the field of man's knowledge of his environment. Not far behind was the conception of the social order and laws as subject to indefinite improvement — through "reason," but to the men of the Enlightenment this hardly meant critical analysis and discussion. That issue of course involves morals — or as I would prefer to say, "ethics," to have some term to distinguish ideals for the guidance of change from the *mores,* regarded as sacred and unalterable. Finally, the notion of the progressive nature of truth, as to be pursued rather than finally possessed, has been extended to include "truth about" all the values, moral, aesthetic, and philosophical as well as intellectual, especially in the narrow sense of "science." This applies even to religion, in the view of "religious liberals" distinguished by this attitude. The official spokesmen of religion and their more pious followers, organized in the older "authoritarian" churches, have of course fought this change, even in science — witness their reception of Galileo and of Darwin.

The new idea spread rather slowly into the field of man and society, and has given rise to much controversy, even among those who accept in principle progress through free inquiry, with truth so found as the one final authority. In this field the important truths have to do with values rather than facts or empirical generalizations, hence are not subject to manipulative experimental testing or sensory discrimination, in the meaning of natural science. One result is much disagreement about the application of "scientific method" in this grand division of knowledge. "Justice" has undergone a change in meaning as radical as has "truth." It is no longer defined by existing law, moral or jural; instead, liberal society confronts the problem of the justice of the law itself, in comparison with possible alternatives. This repudiation of all absolutes works in various ways to make the problem of social order very hard, besides adding that of social change, and is blamed by many for the supposed crisis of western civilization on which so much is said and written. Proposals for turning the clock of history back and re-establishing the absolutes that have recently lost their "authority" seem to make little sense, and the prospect of getting new ones accepted is hardly either inviting or feasible. The hope for the permanence and progress of any high civilization seems to lie in the direction here indicated, the way of freedom. It means that the masses, who now have the power in society, must accept the provisional norms as authoritative, and acquire the intelligence and good will required to work in terms of them. Good will must also be redefined in "ethical" terms of progress through freedom, in place of the "morality" of personal relations in a given institutional order, calling for conformity to tradition and obedience to authorities deriving their status from some mixture of tradition with coercive power or more or less pious pretense. The doctrine that possession of power proves its rightfulness, identifying power with authority — whether inferred from theistic or from dialectical-historical premises — is hardly likely to be acceptable in the future, at least to the peoples that have known freedom. Such statements, of course, are in the realm of historical prediction, which is always precarious.

At the present juncture, the situation of free society is indeed serious. If truth, or the validity of values, is to be the authority that maintains order as the primary necessity, fairly general agreement must somehow be reached on the content of the values, especially on an acceptable working ideal of justice between individuals, replacing that based on inherited status. Unequal inheritance of position and opportunity is unfair by individualistic standards, but it can only be more or less minimized, not abolished. The start in life and chances for advancement for the children of each generation will inevitably be determined in considerable part by the position of their parents, which clearly cannot be equalized. Too much emphasis is commonly placed on the inheritance of property, which is only one element in the situation, and there are limits to the reduction of even that by social authority or power. More real and more important for economic justice is the distribution of income, which depends on the whole at least as much on personal earning power as on ownership of property. In free society both are determined by an unanalyzable mixture of biological and cultural inheritance, along with individual effort, competence, and foresight. The differences in moral significance of these factors and in their amenability to control by social action are questions too complex to go into here, but public understanding of these difficult matters is a *sine qua non* of intelligent action in the interest of more ideal justice. Also indispensable, and as difficult, is agreement on an authoritative meaning of justice itself. In economic distribution, freedom involves division of the social product in accord with productive contribution, which has strong moral claims in the individual's right to the fruits of his own acts, including the right to pass these on to heirs, while sheer necessity requires its implementation in large measure. But division of products is subject to limitations by necessity and by other ideals, such as sacrifice, need, and equality; and the right of transmission beyond the individual life particularly requires restricting. Yet any action looking toward more justice both violates economic freedom and in addition transfers functions and responsibilities from the family to the state, and tends progressively to undermine the former sacrosanct institution; indeed, family life is the most inviolable sphere of freedom. The connection with economic relations is obvious. More general reasons making it dangerous to go too far with economic reform, however appealing on some idealistic grounds, have been indicated earlier and cannot be further argued here. It is no accident of history that free enterprise, democratic government, and religious and cultural freedom grew up together; it is certain that they are mutually interdependent. An exception might be scientific research, as its devotees are unlikely to be numerous or politically ambitious and powerful. But extreme regimentation of economic life — or religion, and perhaps art — would require a totalitarian dictatorship. Argument on general grounds is confirmed by the case of Soviet Russia.

Particularly in point among hard and finally unescapable problems is the relation between population and resources, with "eugenics" also in the background. And finally, a political society confronts the increasingly menacing problem of its relations with other societies, those of order, freedom, justice, and progress in the world as a whole.

These hard problems must be dealt with by democratic process. Agreement on action is to be reached through a mixture of direct and indirect methods, since men vote partly on issues, partly on candidates for office, forming their opinions on both through free discussion. But this itself is limited, as it must be orderly, hence conducted under the "authority" of existing laws and institutions. The final ideal authority is truth and right, valid values; but the proximate locus is in individuals, who must be chosen for superior knowledge and judgment, and for trustworthiness, which in turn are appraised by the citizens as electors. Free society is largely a tissue of agency relations, in politics and in other spheres; hence the fitness of leaders for responsibility is a main problem for liberal ethics. Moreover, human nature being what it is — well-meaning on the whole, but ignorant and prejudiced — the intermediate authority of leaders must be backed up by power, to preserve order and to improve it, especially in the "sovereign" sphere of politics and the law.

Our discussion of authority has barely scratched the surface of the problems it presents in and for free society, problems theoretical and practical, intellectual and moral or ethical, and also cultural. A crying need of our time is for the public to have a better understanding of their nature, to realize their complexity and difficulty, and to have reasonable expectations from the social order. To preserve freedom and civilization itself, the people must cherish freedom; but they must outgrow the romantic oversimplifications of the doctrinaire liberalism of the Enlightenment and the nineteenth century, of which J. S. Mill was the leading apostle. Freedom, correctly defined as the negative concept of noninterference (in economics called "laissez faire"), relying on the innate rationality and good intentions of men, is not the sole or absolute value, and is no panacea for dealing with all social problems. It is necessary for the masses to learn to avoid wishful thinking, to know and face the facts of life. Especially they must recognize the necessity of authority for civilization, and see that complete justice is impossible, and the ideal final authority of truth, right, and good taste has to be expressed in laws, interpreted and enforced by human agents with power.

PART TWO

Authority in Historical Perspective

6. What Was Authority?

HANNAH ARENDT

It is my contention (the reasons for which I tried to outline in another context[1]) that authority has vanished from the modern world, and that if we raise the question what authority is, we can no longer fall back upon authentic and undisputable experiences common to all. The very term has become clouded by controversy and confusion. Little about its nature appears self-evident and comprehensible to everybody, except that the political scientist knows that this concept was once fundamental to political theory and that a constant, ever-widening and deepening crisis of authority is a naked fact. This crisis, apparent since the inception of the century, is political in origin and nature, but it has spread — and this is perhaps the most significant symptom of its depth and seriousness — to such prepolitical areas as child-rearing and education, where authority in the widest sense has always been accepted as a natural necessity. We shall see later that the earliest (Greek) attempts to define authority were based exclusively on experiences made not in the public-political, but in the private realm of the household, where children are brought up and educated, and that they appealed to this natural necessity of authority implied in the relations between parents and children, teachers and pupils. Thus, the fact that the crisis or the loss of authority has spread to these prepolitical areas signifies that all the old time-honored metaphors and models for

[1] Under the title "Authority in the Twentieth Century," *Review of Politics,* vol. 18, no. 4 (October 1956).

authoritarian relations have lost their plausibility. Practically as well as theoretically, we are no longer in a position to know what authority really *is*.

In the following reflections, I shall assume that the answer to this question cannot possibly lie in a definition of the nature or essence of "authority in general." The authority we have lost in the modern world is no such "authority in general," but rather a very specific form which had once been valid throughout the western world over a long period of time. I therefore propose to reconsider what authority was historically and the sources of its strength and meaning. Yet, in view of the present confusion, it seems that even this limited and tentative approach must be preceded by a few remarks on what authority never was, in order to avoid the more common misunderstandings and make sure that we visualize and consider the same phenomenon and not any number of connected or unconnected issues.

Since authority always demands obedience, it is commonly mistaken for some form of power or violence. Yet, authority precludes the use of external means of coercion; where force is used, authority itself has failed. Authority, on the other hand, is incompatible with persuasion, which presupposes equality and works through a process of argumentation. Where arguments are used, authority is left in abeyance. Against the egalitarian order of persuasion stands the authoritarian order which is always hierarchical. If authority is to be defined at all, then, it must be in contradistinction to both coercion by force and persuasion through arguments. (The authoritarian relation between the one who commands and the one who obeys rests neither on common reason nor on the power of the one who commands; what they have in common is the hierarchy itself, whose rightness and legitimacy both recognize and where both have their predetermined stable place.) This point is of historical importance; one aspect of our concept of authority is Platonic in origin, and when Plato began to consider the introduction of authority into the handling of public affairs in the *polis,* he knew he was seeking an alternative to the common Greek way of handling domestic affairs, which was persuasion (*peithein*); as well as to the common way of handling foreign affairs, which was force and violence (*bia*).

Closely connected with these negative characteristics is the issue of legitimacy, which plays such an enormous role in all truly authoritarian thought. Those who are not only in power but in authority are aware that their (authoritarian) power depends upon its legitimacy, which is assumed and "proven" by invocation of a source beyond or above the ruler. Historically, we know of a variety of sources to which authoritarian rulers could appeal in order to justify their power: it could be the law of nature, or the commands of God, or the Platonic ideas, or ancient customs sanctified by tradition, or one great event in the past, such as the foundation of the body politic. In all these cases, legitimacy derives from something outside the range of human deeds; it is either not man-made at all, like natural or divine law, or has at least not been made by those who happen to be in power.

Another familiar misunderstanding arises from the frequent antithesis of authority and freedom, upon which is based the liberal theory postulating that each loss of authority is compensated by a newly won measure of freedom. The simple fact that, for some time now, we have been living in a world where progressive loss of authority is accompanied by at least an equal threat to freedom, should make us suspect some oversimplification. It seems rather as though traditionally the political concepts of freedom and authority are so intimately interconnected and dependent upon each other that the validity and understanding of the idea of freedom become gravely compromised once the validity of authority has been lost. Historically, at any rate, authoritarian forms of rule did not wish to abolish, but to limit freedom, and these limitations were felt to be necessary to protect and safeguard liberty. An authoritarian structure, therefore, loses its essential substance, its *raison d'être,* if it does away with freedom altogether. Whenever this happens, it is no longer authoritarian but tyrannical. And a tyranny is no less anti-authoritarian than certain extreme types of democracy or anarchy. There is perhaps no clearer symptom of the confusion of our political vocabulary than the almost unanimous habit of calling Soviet Russia or Nazi Germany authoritarian, while these forms of domination in fact arose out of a catastrophic breakdown of all legitimate authority. But this confusion is neither merely semantic nor theoretical; it arises directly out of the modern world, where, outside of certain islands and some circumscribed, not very important areas, it is almost impossible to have a genuine experience of what authority is, or rather was.

It is in the light of this present situation that I propose to raise the following questions: What were the political experiences that corresponded to the concept of authority and from which it sprang? What is the nature of a public-political world constituted by authority? Is it true that the Platonic-Aristotelian statement that every well-ordered community is constituted of those who rule and those who are ruled, was always valid prior to the modern age? Or to put it differently: what kind of a world has come to an end after the modern age has not only challenged one or another form of authority in different spheres of life, but has caused the whole concept of authority to lose its validity altogether?

Authority as the one, if not *the* decisive factor in human communities did not always exist, though it can look back on a long history, and the experiences on which this concept is based are not necessarily present in all bodies politic. The word and the concept are Roman in origin. Neither the Greek language nor the varied political experiences of Greek history show any knowledge of authority and the kind of rule it implies.[2] This is expressed most clearly in the philosophy of Plato and Aristotle, who, in quite different ways but from the same political experiences, tried to introduce something akin to authority into the public life of the Greek *polis*.

There existed two kinds of rule on which they could fall back and from which they derived their political philosophy, the one known to them from the public-political realm, and the other from the private sphere of Greek household and family life. With the *polis*, absolute rule was known as tyranny, and the chief characteristics of the tyrant were that he ruled by sheer violence, had to be protected

[2] This was already noticed by the Greek historian Dio Cassius, who, when writing a history of Rome, found it impossible to translate the word *auctoritas*: *"hellenisai auto kathapax adynaton esti."* Quoted from T. Mommsen, *Römisches Staatsrecht* (3rd ed., 1888), vol. III, p. 952, n. 4. Moreover, one need only compare the Roman Senate, the republic's specifically authoritarian institution, with Plato's nocturnal council in the *Laws*, which, being composed of the ten oldest guardians for the constant supervision of the state, superficially resembles it, to become aware of the impossibility of finding a true alternative for coercion and persuasion within the framework of Greek political experience.

from the people by a bodyguard, and insisted that his subjects mind their own business and leave to him the care for the public realm altogether. The last characteristic, in Greek public opinion, signified that he destroyed the public realm of the *polis* altogether and thereby deprived the citizens of that political faculty which they felt was the very essence of freedom. Another political experience of the need for command and obedience might have been provided by the experience in warfare, where danger and the necessity to make and carry out decisions quickly seem to constitute an inherent reason for the establishment of authority. Neither of these political models, however, could possibly serve the purpose. The tyrant remained, for Plato as for Aristotle, the "wolf in human shape," and the military commander was too obviously connected with a temporary emergency to be able to serve as model for a permanent institution.

Because of this absence of valid political experience on which to base a claim to authoritarian rule, both Plato and Aristotle, albeit in very different ways, had to rely on examples of human relations drawn from Greek household and family life, where the head of the household ruled as a *despótes,* in uncontested mastery over the members of his family and the slaves of the household. The despot, unlike the king, the *basileús,* who had been the leader of household heads and as such *primus inter pares,* was by definition vested with the power to coerce. Yet it was precisely this characteristic that made the despot unfit for political purposes; his power to coerce was incompatible with the freedom of any other person. Wherever he ruled there was only one relation, that between master and slaves. When Plato, therefore, in his old age hoped to find in the *Laws* some quality which would make them undisputable rulers over the whole public realm, he not only construed this rule in an obviously despotic manner, but was even led to apply the terms of private household affairs to the affairs of the *polis* and to say, probably in a variation of Pindar's *nomos basileus pantón* ("a law is king over everything"), *nómos despótes tôn archontôn, hoi de árchontes douloi tou nómou* ("the law is the despot of the rulers, and the rulers are the slaves of the law").[3] In Plato, the despotism originating in the household and

---

[3] *Laws,* 715.

its concomitant destruction of the political realm as antiquity understood it remained utopian. But it is interesting to note that when the
destruction became a reality in the last centuries of the Roman
Empire, the change was introduced by the application to public rule
of the term *dominus,* which in Latin had the same meaning as the
Greek *despótes.* Caligula was the first Roman Emperor who con-
sented to be called *dominus,* that is, to be given a name "which
Augustus and Tiberius still had rejected like a malediction and an
injury," [4] precisely because it implied a despotism unknown in the
political realm, although only all too familiar in the private, household realm.

The political philosophies of Plato and Aristotle have dominated
all subsequent political thought, even when their concepts have been
superimposed upon such greatly different political experiences as
those of the Romans. If we wish not only to comprehend the actual
political experiences behind the concept of authority — which, at
least in its positive aspect, is exclusively Roman — but also to understand authority as the Romans themselves already understood it
theoretically and made it part of the political tradition of the West,
we shall have to concern ourselves briefly with those features of
Greek political philosophy which have so decisively influenced its
shaping.

Nowhere else has Greek thinking so closely approached the concept of authority as in Plato's *Republic,* wherein he confronted the
reality of the *polis* with a utopian rule of reason in the person of the
philosopher-king. The motive for establishing reason as ruler in the
realm of politics was exclusively political, although the consequences
of expecting reason to develop into an instrument of coercion perhaps have been no less decisive for the tradition of western philosophy than for the tradition of western politics. The fatal resemblance
between Plato's philosopher-king and the Greek tyrant, as well as
the potential harm to the political realm that his rule would imply,

---

[4] H. Wallon, *Histoire de l'Esclavage dans l'Antiquité* (1847), vol. III, where one
still finds the best description of the gradual loss of Roman liberty under the
Empire caused by the constant increase of power of the imperial household. Since
it was the imperial household and not the Emperor who gained in power, the
"despotism" which always had been characteristic of the private household and
family life began to dominate the public realm.

seems to have been recognized by Aristotle;[5] but that this combination of reason and rule implied a danger to philosophy as well has been pointed out, as far as I know, only in Kant's reply to Plato: "It is not to be expected that kings philosophize or that philosophers become kings, nor is it to be desired, because the possession of power corrupts the free judgment of reason inevitably," [6] although even this reply does not go to the root of the matter.

The reason why Plato wanted the philosophers to become the rulers of the city lay in the conflict between the philosopher and the *polis*, or in the hostility of the *polis* toward philosophy, which probably had lain dormant for some time before it showed its immediate threat to the life of the philosopher in the trial and death of Socrates. Politically, Plato's philosophy shows the rebellion of the philosopher against the *polis*. The philosopher announces his claim to rule, but not so much for the sake of the *polis* and politics (although patriotic motivation cannot be denied in Plato and distinguishes his philosophy from those of his followers in antiquity), as for the sake of philosophy and the safety of the philosopher.

It was after Socrates' death that Plato began to discount persuasion

[5] A fragment from the lost dialogue *On Kingship* states that "it was not only not necessary for a king to become a philosopher, but actually a hindrance to his work; that, however, it was necessary [for a good king] to listen to the true philosopher and to be agreeable to their advice." See Kurt von Fritz, *The Constitution of Athens, and Related Texts* (1950). In Aristotelian terms, both Plato's philosopher-king and the Greek tyrant rule for the sake of their own interest, and this was for Aristotle, though not for Plato, an outstanding characteristic of tyrants. Plato was not aware of the resemblance, because for him as for Greek current opinion, the principal characteristic of the tyrant was that he deprived the citizen of access to a public realm, to a "market place" where he could show himself, see and be seen, hear and be heard, that he prohibited the *agoreuein* and *politeuein*, confined the citizens to the privacy of their households, and demanded to be the only one in charge of public affairs. He would not have ceased to be a tyrant if he had used his power solely in the interests of his subjects — as indeed some of the tyrants undoubtedly did. According to the Greeks, to be banished to the privacy of household life was tantamount to being deprived of the specifically human potentialities of life. In other words, the very features which so convincingly demonstrate to us the tyrannical character of Plato's republic — the almost complete elimination of privacy and the omnipresence of political organs and institutions — presumably prevented Plato from recognizing its tyrannical character. To him, it would have been a contradiction in terms to brand as tyranny a constitution which not only did not relegate the citizen to his household but on the contrary, did not leave him a shred of private life whatsoever.

[6] "Eternal Peace," *The Philosophy of Kant*, ed. and trans. C. J. Friedrich (Modern Library Edition, 1949), p. 456.

as insufficient for the guidance of men and to seek for something liable to compel them without using external means of violence. Very early in his search, he must have discovered that Truth, namely, the truths we call self-evident, compel the mind, and that this coercion, though it needs no violence to be effective, is stronger than persuasion and argument. The trouble with coercion through reason, however, is that only the few are subject to it, so that the problem arises how to assure that the many, the people who in their very multitude compose the body politic, can be submitted to the same truth. Here, to be sure, other means of coercion must be found, and here again coercion through violence must be avoided if political life as the Greeks understood it is not to be destroyed.[7] This is the central predicament of Plato's political philosophy and has remained a predicament of all attempts to establish a tyranny of reason. In the *Republic,* the problem is solved through the concluding myth of rewards and punishments in the hereafter, a myth which Plato himself obviously neither believed nor wanted the philosophers to believe. What the allegory of the cave story in the middle of the *Republic* is for the few or for the philosopher, the myth of hell at the end is for the many who are not capable of philosophical truth. In the *Laws,* Plato deals with the same perplexity, but in the opposite way; here he proposes a substitute for persuasion, the introduction to the laws in which their intent and purpose are to be explained to the citizens.

In his attempts to find a legitimate principle of coercion, Plato was originally guided by a great number of models of existing relations, such as that between the shepherd and his sheep, between the helmsman of a ship and the passengers, between the physician and the patient, or between the master and the slave. In all these instances, either expert knowledge commands confidence so that neither force nor persuasion are necessary to obtain compliance, or the ruler and the ruled belong to two altogether different categories of beings who already are by implication subject one to the other, as in the cases of the shepherd and sheep and the master and slave. All these examples

[7] Von Fritz rightly insists on Plato's aversion to violence, "also revealed by the fact that, wherever he did make an attempt to bring about a change of political institutions in the direction of his political ideals, he addressed himself to men already in power."

are taken from what to the Greeks was the private sphere of life, and they occur time and again in all the great political dialogues, the *Republic,* the *Statesman* and the *Laws.* Nevertheless, it is obvious that the relation between master and slave has a special significance. The master, according to the discussion in the *Statesman,* knows what should be done and gives his orders, while the slave executes them and obeys, so that knowing what to do and actual doing become separate and mutually exclusive functions. In the *Republic,* they are the political characteristics of two different classes of men. The plausibility of these examples lies in the natural inequality prevailing between the ruling and the ruled, most apparent in the example of the shepherd, where Plato himself ironically concludes that no man, only a god, could relate to human beings as the shepherd relates to his sheep. Although it is obvious that Plato himself was not satisfied with these models for his purpose, to establish the "authority" of the philosopher over the *polis,* he returned to them time and again, because only in these instances of glaring inequality could rule be exerted without seizure of power and the possession of the means of violence. What he was looking for was a relationship in which the compelling element lies in the relationship itself and is prior to the actual issuance of commands; the patient became subject to the physician's authority when he fell ill and the slave came under the command of his master when he became a slave.

It is important to bear these examples in mind in order to realize what kind of coercion Plato expected reason to exert in the hands of the king-philosopher. Here, it is true, the compelling power does not lie in the person or in inequality as such, but in the ideas which are perceived by the philosopher. These ideas can be used as measures of human behavior because they transcend the sphere of human affairs in the same way that a yardstick transcends, is outside and beyond, all things whose length it can measure. In the parable of the cave in the *Republic,* the sky of ideas stretches above the cave of human existence, and therefore can become its standard. But the philosopher who leaves the cave for the pure sky of ideas does not originally do so in order to acquire those standards and learn the "art of measurement" [8] but to contemplate the true essence of Being. The basically

---

[8] Werner Jaeger's statement in *Paideia* (1945), vol. III, p. 416n: "The idea that there is a supreme art of measurement and that the philosopher's knowledge of

authoritative element of the ideas, that is, the quality which enables
them to rule and compel, is therefore not at all a matter of course.
The ideas become measures only after the philosopher has left the
bright sky of ideas and returned to the dark cave of human existence.
In this part of the story, Plato touches upon the deepest reason for
the conflict between the philosopher and the *polis*.[9] He tells of the
philosopher's loss of orientation in human affairs, of the blindness
striking the eyes, of the predicament of not being able to communicate what he has seen, and of the actual danger to his life which
thereby arises. It is in this predicament that the philosopher resorts
to what he has seen, the ideas, as standards and measures, and
finally, in fear of his life, uses them as instruments of domination.

For the transformation of the ideas into measures, Plato is helped
by an analogy from practical life, where it appears that all arts and
crafts are also guided by "ideas," that is, by the "shapes" of objects,
visualized by the inner eye of the craftsman who then reproduces
them in reality through imitation.[10] This analogy enables him to
understand the transcendent character of the ideas in the same manner as he does the transcendent existence of the model, which lives
beyond the fabrication process it guides and therefore can eventually
become the standard for its success or failure. The ideas become the
unwavering, "absolute" standards for political and moral behavior
and judgment in the same sense that the "idea" of a bed in general is
the standard for making and judging the fitness of all particular
manufactured beds.

It is only in this context that the ideas relate to the varied multitude of things concrete in the same way as one yardstick related to
the varied multitude of things measurable, or as the rule of reason or
common sense relates to the varied multitude of concrete events
which can be subsumed under it. This aspect of Plato's doctrine of
ideas had the greatest influence on the western tradition, and even
Kant, though he had a very different and considerably deeper con-

---

values (*phronésis*) is the ability to measure, runs through all Plato's work right
down to the end" is true only for Plato's political philosophy. The very word
phronésis characterizes in Plato and Aristotle the insight of the statesman rather
than the vision of the philosopher.

[9] *Republic*, Book VII, 516–517.

[10] See especially *Timaeus*, 31, where the divine Demiurge makes the universe
in accordance with a *paradigma*.

cept of human judgment, still occasionally mentions this capacity for subsuming as its essential function. Likewise, the essential characteristic of specifically authoritarian forms of government — that the source of their authority, which legitimates the exercise of power, must be beyond the sphere of power and, like the law of nature or the commands of God, must not be man-made — goes back to this applicability of the ideas in Plato's political philosophy.

At the same time the analogy relating to fabrication and the arts and crafts offers a welcome opportunity to justify the otherwise very dubious use of examples and instances taken from activities in which some expert knowledge and specialization are required. Here, the concept of the expert enters the realm of political action for the first time, and the statesman is understood to be competent to deal with human affairs in the same sense as the carpenter is competent to make furniture or the physician to heal the sick. Closely connected with this choice of examples and analogies is the element of violence, which is so glaringly evident in Plato's utopian republic and actually constantly defeats his great concern for assuring voluntary obedience, that is, for establishing a sound foundation for what, since the Romans, we call authority. There is no great difference between using the ideas as models and using them, in a somewhat cruder fashion, as actual yardsticks of behavior, and Aristotle in his earliest dialogue, written under the direct influence of Plato, already compares "the most perfect law," that is, the law which is the closest possible approximation to the idea, with "the plummet, the rule, and the compass . . . [which] are outstanding among all tools." [11]

It is of greater relevance in our context, however, that an element of violence is inevitably inherent in all activities of making, fabricating, and producing, that is, in all activities by which men confront nature directly, as distinguished from those activities, like action and speech, which are primarily directed toward human beings. The building of the human artifice always involves some violence done to nature — we must kill a tree in order to have lumber, and we must violate this material in order to build a table. In the few instances where Plato shows a dangerous preference for the tyrannical form of government, he is carried to this extreme by his own analogies. This, obviously, is most tempting when he speaks about the right

[11] In *Protrepticus,* quoted from von Fritz.

way to found new communities, because this foundation can be easily seen in the light of another "making" process. If the republic is to be made by somebody who is the political equivalent of a craftsman or artist, in accordance with an established *techné* and the rules and measurements valid in this particular "art," the tyrant is indeed in the best position to achieve the purpose.[12]

We have seen that in the parable of the cave, the philosopher leaves the cave in search of the true essence of Being without a second thought to the possible practicality of what he is going to find. Only later, when he finds himself again confined to the darkness and uncertainty of human affairs and encounters the hostility of his fellow human beings, does he begin to think of his "truth" in terms of standards applicable to the behavior of other people. This discrepancy between the ideas as true essences to be contemplated and as measures to be applied [13] is manifest in the two entirely different ideas which represent the highest idea, the one to which all others owe their existence. We find in Plato that this first idea is either that of the beautiful, described in the *Symposion* and elsewhere as *ekphanestaton* (that which shines forth most), or the idea of the good, as in the *Republic*.[14] Obviously, Plato's choice was based on the current ideal of the *kalon-kagathón,* but it is striking that the idea of the good is found only in the strictly political context of the *Republic*. If we were to analyze the original philosophical experiences underlying the doctrine of ideas (which we cannot do here), it would appear that the idea of the beautiful as the highest idea reflected these ex-

---

[12] *Laws,* 710–711.

[13] This presentation is indebted to Martin Heidegger's great interpretation of the cave parable in *Platons Lehre von der Wahrheit* (1947). Heidegger demonstrates how Plato transformed the concept of truth (*alétheia*) until it became identical with correct statements (*orthotés*). Correctness indeed, and not truth, would be required if the philosopher's knowledge is the ability to measure. Although he explicitly mentions the risks the philosopher runs when he is forced to return to the cave, Heidegger is not aware of the political context in which the parable appears. According to him, the transformation comes to pass because the subjective act of vision (the *idein* and the *idea* in the mind of the philosopher) takes precedence over objective truth (*aletheia*), which, according to Heidegger, signifies *Unverborgenheit,* unveiling or revelation (from *a-lanthano,* unveil).

[14] The word *ekphanestaton* is used in *Phaedrus,* 250, to mean the chief quality of beauty. In the *Republic,* 518, a similar quality is stated for the idea of the good, which is called *phanotaton.* Both words derive from *phainesthai,* to appear and shine forth, and in both cases the superlative is used.

periences far more adequately than the idea of the good. Even in the
first books of the *Republic*,[15] the philosopher is still defined as a
lover of beauty, not of goodness, and only in the sixth book is the
idea of good as the highest idea introduced. For the original function
of the ideas was not to rule or otherwise determine the chaos of
human affairs, but, in "shining brightness," to illuminate their darkness. As such, the ideas have nothing whatever to do with politics,
political experience, and the problem of action, but pertain exclusively to philosophy, the experience of contemplation, and the quest
for the "true being of things." It is precisely ruling, measuring, subsuming, and regulating that are entirely alien to the experiences underlying the doctrine of ideas in its original conception. It seems that
Plato was the first to take exception to the political "irrelevance" of
his new teaching, and he tried to modify the doctrine of ideas so that
it would become useful for a theory of politics. But usefulness could
be saved only by the idea of the good, since "good" in the Greek
vocabulary always means "good for" or "fit." If the highest idea, in
which all other ideas must partake in order to be ideas at all, is that
of fitness, then the ideas are applicable by definition, and in the
hands of the philosopher, the expert in ideas, they can become rules
and standards or, as later in the *Laws*, they can become laws. (The
difference is negligible. What in the *Republic* is still the philosopher's, the philosopher-king's direct personal claim to rule, has become reason's impersonal claim to domination in the *Laws*.) The
actual consequence of this political interpretation of the doctrine of
ideas would be that neither man nor a god is the measure of all
things, but the good itself — a consequence which apparently
Aristotle, not Plato, had drawn in one of his earlier dialogues.[16]

For our purposes it is essential to remember that the element of

---

[15] *Republic*, 475–476. In the tradition of philosophy, the result of this Platonic
repudiation of the beautiful has been that it was omitted from the so called
transcendentals or universals, that is, those qualities possessed by everything that is,
and which were enumerated in medieval philosophy as *unum, alter, ens*, and *bonum*.
Jacques Maritain, in his wonderful book, *Creative Intuition in Art and Poetry*
(Bollingen Series XXXV, 1, 1953), is aware of this omission and insists that Beauty
be included in the realm of transcendentals, for "Beauty is the radiance of all
transcendentals united" (p. 162).

[16] In the dialogue *Politicus*: "for the most exact measure of all things is the good"
(quoted from von Fritz). The notion must have been that only through the concept
of the good do things become comparable and hence measurable.

rule, as reflected in our present concept of authority so tremendously
influenced by Platonic thinking, can be traced to a conflict between
philosophy and politics, but not to specifically political experiences.
That is, experiences immediately derived from the realm of human
affairs. One cannot understand Plato without bearing in mind both
his repeated emphatic insistence on the philosophic irrelevance of
this realm, which he always warned should not be taken too seriously, and the fact that he himself, in distinction to nearly all philosophers who came after him, still took human affairs so seriously that
he changed the very center of his thought to make it applicable to
politics. But the rule of the philosopher-king and the domination of
human affairs by something outside its own realm are demanded
precisely because, from the standpoint of philosophy as well as the
philosopher, under no circumstances must they acquire a dignity of
their own.

In the political philosophy of Aristotle, we find the second attempt
to establish a concept of authority in terms of rulers and the ruled; it
was equally important for the development of the tradition of political thought, although Aristotle took a basically different approach.
For him, reason has neither dictatorial nor tyrannical features, and
there is no philosopher-king to regulate human affairs once and for
all. His reason for maintaining that "each body politic is composed
of those who rule and those who are ruled" does not derive from
the superiority of the expert over the layman, and he is too conscious
of the difference between acting and making to draw his examples
from the sphere of fabrication. Aristotle, as far as I can see, was the
first to appeal, for the purpose of establishing rule in the handling of
human affairs, to "nature," which "established the difference . . .
between the younger and the older ones, destined the ones to be
ruled and the others to rule." [17]

The simplicity of this argument is all the more deceptive since
centuries of repetition have degraded it into a platitude. This may be
why one usually overlooks its flagrant contradiction of Aristotle's
own definition of the *polis* as also given in *Politics*: "The *polis* is a
community of equals for the sake of a life which is potentially the

[17] *Politics*, 1332b12 and 1332b36. The distinction between the younger and older
ones goes back to Plato; see *Republic*, 412, and *Laws*, 690 and 714. The appeal to
nature is Aristotelian.

best." [18] Obviously, the notion of rule in the *polis* was for Aristotle himself so far from convincing that he, one of the most consistent and least self-contradictory great thinkers, did not feel particularly bound by his own argument. We therefore need not be surprised when we read at the beginning of the *Economics* (a pseudo-Aristotelian treatise, but written by one of his closest disciples) that the essential difference between a political community (the *polis*) and a private household (the *oikia*) is that the *oikia* constitutes a "monarchy," a one-man rule, while the *polis,* on the contrary, "is composed of many rulers." [19] In order to understand this character-ization, we must remember first that the words "monarchy" and "tyranny" were used synonymously and in clear contradistinction to kingship; second, the character of the *polis* as "composed of many rulers" has nothing to do with the various forms of government that usually are opposed to one-man rule, such as oligarchy, aristocracy, or democracy. The "many rulers" in this context are the household heads, who have established themselves as "monarchs" at home be-fore they join to constitute the public-political realm of the city. Ruling itself, and the distinction between rulers and ruled, belong to a sphere which precedes the political realm, and what distin-guishes it from the "economic" sphere of the household is that the *polis* is based upon the principle of equality and knows no differ-entiation between rulers and ruled.

In this distinction between what we would today call the private and the public spheres, Aristotle only articulates current Greek public opinion, according to which "every citizen belongs to two orders of existence" because "the polis gives each individual . . . besides his private life a sort of second life, his *bios politikos.*" [20] (The latter, Aristotle called the "good life," and redefined its con-tent; only this definition, not the differentiation itself, conflicted with common Greek opinion.) Both orders were forms of human living-together, but only the household community was concerned with keeping alive as such and coping with the physical necessities in-volved in maintaining individual life and guaranteeing the survival of the species. It was in the *polis* that man appeared as an individual

[18] *Politics,* 1328b35.
[19] *Economics,* 1343a1–4.
[20] Jaeger, vol. I, p. 111.

personality, as we would say today.[21] As living beings, concerned with the preservation of life, men are confronted with and driven by necessity. Necessity must be mastered before the political "good life" can begin, and it can be mastered only through domination. Hence the freedom of the "good life" rests on the domination of necessity.

The mastery of necessity then has as its goal the controlling of the necessities of life, which coerce men and hold them in their power. But such domination can be accomplished only by controlling and doing violence to others, who as slaves relieve free men from themselves being coerced by necessity. The free man, the citizen of a *polis,* is neither coerced by the physical necessities of life nor subject to the man-made domination of others. He not only must not be a slave, he must own and rule over slaves. The freedom of the political realm begins after all elementary necessities of sheer living have been mastered by rule, so that domination and subjection, command and obedience, ruling and being ruled, are preconditions for establishing the political realm precisely because they are not its content.

There can be no question that Aristotle, like Plato before him, meant to introduce a kind of authority into the handling of public affairs and the life of the *polis,* and no doubt for very good political reasons. Yet, he too had to resort to a kind of makeshift solution in order to make plausible the introduction into the political realm of a distinction between rulers and ruled, between those who command and those who obey. And he too could take his examples and models only from a prepolitical sphere, from the private realm of the household and the experiences of a slave economy. This leads him into glaringly contradictory statements, insofar as he superimposes on the actions and life in the *polis* those standards which, as he explains elsewhere, are valid only for the behavior and life in the household community. The inconsistency of his enterprise is apparent even if we consider only the famous example from the *Politics* mentioned above, in which the differentiation between rulers and ruled is derived from the natural difference between the younger and the elder. For this example is in itself eminently unsuitable to prove Aristotle's argument. The relation between old and young is educa-

[21] *Economics,* 1343b24.

tional in essence, and in this education no more is involved than the training of the future rulers by the present rulers. If rule is at all involved here, it is entirely different from political forms of rule, not only because it is limited in time and intent, but because it happens between people who are potentially equals. Yet, substitution of education for rule had the most far-reaching consequences. On its grounds, rulers have posed as educators and educators have been accused of ruling. Then, as well as now, nothing is more questionable than the political relevance of examples drawn from the field of education. In the political realm we deal always with adults who are past the age of education, properly speaking, and politics or the right to participate in the management of public affairs begins precisely where education has come to an end. (Adult education, individual or communal, may be of great relevance for the formation of personality, its full development or greater enrichment, but is politically irrelevant unless its purpose is to make up for the education, somehow not acquired in youth, needed for participation in public affairs.) In education, conversely, we always deal with people who cannot yet be admitted to politics and equality because they are being prepared. Aristotle's example is nevertheless of great relevance because it is true that the necessity for "authority" is more plausible and evident in child-rearing and education than anywhere else. That is why it is so characteristic of our own time to want to eradicate even this extremely limited and politically irrelevant form of authority.

Politically, authority can acquire an educational character only if we presume with the Romans that under all circumstances ancestors represent the example of greatness for each successive generation, that they are the *maiores,* the greater ones, by definition. Wherever the model of education through authority, without this fundamental conviction, was superimposed on the realm of politics (and this has happened often enough and still is a mainstay of conservative argument), it served primarily to obscure real or coveted claims to rule and pretended to educate while in reality it wanted to dominate.

The grandiose attempts of Greek philosophy to find a concept of authority which would prevent deterioration of the *polis* and safeguard the life of the philosopher foundered on the fact that in the realm of Greek political life there was no awareness of authority based on immediate political experience. Hence all prototypes by which subsequent generations understood the content of authority were drawn from specifically unpolitical experiences, stemming either from the sphere of "making" and the arts where there must be experts and where fitness is the highest criterion, or from the private household community. It is precisely in this politically determined aspect that the philosophy of the Socratic school has exerted its greatest impact upon our tradition. Even today we believe that Aristotle defined man primarily as a political being endowed with speech or reason, which he did only in a political context, or that Plato exposed the original meaning of his doctrine of ideas in the *Republic,* whereas on the contrary he changed it for political reasons. In spite of the grandeur of Greek political philosophy, it may be doubted that it would have lost its inherent utopian character, if the Romans, in their indefatigable search for tradition and authority, had not decided to take it over and acknowledge it as their highest authority in all matters of theory and thought. But they were able to accomplish this integration only because both authority and tradition had already played a decisive role in the political life of the Roman republic.

At the heart of Roman politics, from the beginning of the republic until virtually the end of the imperial era, stands the conviction of the sacredness of foundation, in the sense that once something has been founded it remains binding for all future generations. To be engaged in politics meant first and foremost to preserve the founding of the city of Rome. This is why the Romans were unable to repeat the founding of their first *polis* in the settlement of colonies but were capable of adding to the original foundation until the whole of Italy and, eventually, the whole of the western world was united and administered by Rome, as though the whole world were nothing but Roman hinterland. From beginning to end, the Romans were bound to the specific locality of this one city, and unlike the Greeks, they could not say, in times of emergency or overpopulation, go and found a new city, for wherever you are you will always be a *polis*. Not the Greeks, but the Romans were really rooted in the soil, and the word *patria* derives its full meaning from Roman history. The foundation of a new body politic — to the

Greek an almost commonplace experience — became to the Roman the central, decisive, unrepeatable beginning of his whole history, a unique event.

The founding of Rome — *tanta molis erat Romanam condere gentem* ("so great was the effort and toil to found the Roman people"), as Virgil sums up the ever-present theme of the *Aeneid*, that all wandering and suffering reach their end and their goal *dum conderet urbem* ("that he may found the city") — this foundation and the equally un-Greek experience of the sanctity of house and hearth, as though Homerically speaking the spirit of Hector had survived the fall of Troy and been resurrected on Italian soil, form the deeply political content of Roman religion. In contrast to Greece, where piety depended upon the immediate revealed presence of the gods, here religion literally meant re-ligare:[22] to be tied back, obligated, to the enormous, almost super-human and hence always legendary effort to lay the foundations, to build the cornerstone, to found for eternity.[23] To be religious meant to be tied to the past, and Livy, the great recorder of past events, could therefore say: *Mihi vetustas res scribenti nescio quo pacto antiquus fit animus et quaedam religio tenet,* "while I write down these ancient events, I do not know through what connection my mind grows old and some *religio* holds (me)."[24] Thus religious and political activity could be considered as almost identical, and Cicero could say: "In no other realm does human excellence ap-proach so closely the paths of the gods (*numen*) as it does in the founding of new and in the preservation of already founded com-munities."[25] The binding power of the foundation itself was re-ligious, for the city also offered the gods of the people a permanent home — again unlike the Greek gods, who protected the cities of the mortals and occasionally dwelt in them, but who had their own home, far from the abode of men, on Mount Olympus.

It is in this context that word and concept of authority originally appeared. The word *auctoritas* derives from the verb "augment,"

---

[22] The derivation of *religio* from *religare* occurs in Cicero. Since we deal here only with the political self-interpretation of the Romans, the question whether this deriva-tion is etymologically correct is irrelevant.

[23] See Cicero, *De Re Publica*, III, 23.

[24] *Annals,* Book 43, ch. 13.

[25] *De Re Publica*, I, 7.

and what authority or those in authority constantly augment is the foundation. Those endowed with authority were the elders, the Senate or the *patres,* who had obtained it by descent and by transmission (tradition) from those who had laid the foundations for all things to come, the ancestors, whom the Romans therefore called the *maiores.* The authority of the living was always derivative, depending upon the *auctores imperii Romani conditoresque,* as Pliny puts it, upon the authority of the founders who no longer were among the living. It is of some importance that the word *auctores* can be used as the very opposite of the *artifices,* the actual builders and makers, and this precisely when the word *auctor* signifies the same thing as our "author." Who, asks Pliny at the occasion of a new theater, should be more admired, the maker or the author, the inventor or the invention, meaning, of course, the latter in both instances. The author in this case is not the builder but the one who inspired the whole enterprise and whose spirit, therefore, much more than the spirit of the actual builder, is represented in the building itself. In distinction to the *artifex* who only made it, he is the actual author of the building, because with it he has become an "augmenter" of the city.

However, the relation between *auctor* and *artifex* is by no means the (Platonic) relation between the master who gives orders and the servant who executes them. The most conspicuous characteristic of those in authority is that they do not have power. *Cum potestas in populo auctoritas in senatu sit,* "while power resides in the people, authority rests with the Senate." [26] Because the "authority," the augmentation which the Senate must add to political decisions, seems to us so curiously elusive and intangible, Mommsen called it "more than advice and less than a command, an advice which one may not safely ignore," whereby it is assumed that "the will and the actions of the people like those of children are exposed to error and mistakes and therefore need 'augmentation' and confirmation through the council of elders." [27] The authoritative character of the "augmentation" of the elders lies in its being a

---

[26] Cicero, *De legibus,* 3, 12, 38.

[27] Mommsen, pp. 1034, 1038–1039. I am very grateful to Professor Carl J. Friedrich, who drew my attention to the important discussion of authority in Mommsen's *Römisches Staatsrecht.*

mere advice, needing neither the form of command nor external coercion to make itself heard.[28]

The binding force of this authority is closely connected with the religiously binding force of the *auspices,* which, unlike the Greek oracle, does not hint at the objective course of future events but reveals merely divine approval or disapproval of decisions made by men.[29] The gods, too, have authority among, rather than power over men; they "augment" and confirm human actions but do not guide them. And just as "all *auspices* were traced back to the great sign by which the gods gave Romulus the authority to found the city," [30] so all authority derives from this foundation, binding every act back to the sacred beginning of Roman history, adding, as it were, to every single moment the whole weight of the past.

Thus, precedents, the deeds of the ancestors and the usage that grew out of them, are always binding.[31] Anything that has happened is transformed into an example, and the *auctoritas maiorum* is identical with authoritative models for actual behavior, is the moral political standard as such. This is also why old age, as distinguished from mere adulthood, was felt by the Romans to contain the very climax of human life; not so much because of accumulated wisdom and experience as because the old man had grown closer to the ancestors and the past. Contrary to our concept of growth, where one grows into the future, the Romans felt that growth was directed toward the past. If one wants to relate this attitude to the hierarchical order established by authority and to visualize this hierarchy in the familiar image of the pyramid, it is as though the peak of the pyramid did not reach into the

[28] This interpretation is further supported by the idiomatic Latin use of *alicui auctorem esse* for "giving advice to somebody."

[29] See Mommsen (2nd ed.), vol. I, pp. 73ff. The Latin word *numen,* which is nearly untranslatable, meaning "divine command" as well as the divine modes of acting, derives from *nuere,* to nod in affirmation. Thus, the commands of the gods and all their interference in human affairs are restricted to approval or disapproval of human actions.

[30] Mommsen (2nd ed.), vol. I, p. 87.

[31] See also the various Latin idioms such as *auctores habere* for having predecessors or examples; *auctoritas maiorum,* signifying the authoritative example of the ancestors; *usus et auctoritas* as used in Roman law for property rights which come from usage. An excellent presentation of this Roman spirit as well as a very useful collection of the more important source materials are to be found in Victor Poeschl, *Römischer Staat und Griechisches Staatsdenken bei Cicero* (1936), especially pp. 101ff.

height of a sky above (or, as in Christianity, beyond) the earth, but into the depth of an earthly past.

It is in this primarily political context that the past was sanctified through tradition. Tradition preserved the past by handing down from one generation to the next the testimony of the ancestors, who first had witnessed and created the sacred founding and then augmented it by their authority throughout the centuries. As long as this tradition was uninterrupted, authority was inviolate; and to act without authority and tradition, without accepted, time-honored standards and models, without the help of the wisdom of the founding fathers, was inconceivable. The notion of a spiritual tradition and of authority in matters of thought and ideas is here derived from the political realm and therefore essentially derivative — just as Plato's conception of the role of reason and ideas in politics was derived from the philosophical realm and became derivative in the realm of human affairs. But the historically all-important fact is that the Romans felt they needed founding fathers and authoritative examples in matters of thought and ideas as well, and accepted the great "ancestors" in Greece as their authorities for theory, philosophy, and poetry. The great Greek authors became authorities in the hands of the Romans, not of the Greeks. The way Plato and others before and after him treated Homer, "the educator of all Hellas," was inconceivable in Rome, nor would a Roman philosopher have dared "to raise his hand against his [spiritual] father" as Plato said of himself (in the *Sophistes*) when he broke with the teaching of Parmenides.

Just as the derivative character of the applicability of the ideas to politics did not prevent Platonic political thought from becoming the origin of western political theory, so the derivative character of authority and tradition in spiritual matters did not prevent them from becoming the dominant features of western philosophic thought for the longer part of our history. In both instances, the political origin and the political experiences underlying the theories were forgotten, the original conflict between politics and philosophy, between the citizen and the philosopher, no less than the experience of foundation in which the Roman trinity of religion, authority, and tradition had its legitimate source. The strength of this trinity lay in the binding force of an authoritative beginning to which "religious" bonds tied men back through tradition. The Roman trinity survived not only the transformation of the republic into the empire but penetrated wherever the *pax romana* created western civilization on Roman foundations.

The extraordinary strength and endurance of this Roman spirit — or the extraordinary reliability of the founding principle for the creation of bodies politic — were subjected to a decisive test and proved themselves, conspicuously after the decline of the Roman empire, when Rome's political and spiritual heritage passed to the Christian Church. Confronted with this very real mundane task, the Church became so "Roman" and adapted itself so thoroughly to Roman thinking in matters of politics that it made the death and resurrection of Christ the cornerstone of a new foundation, erecting on it a new human institution of tremendous durability. Thus, after Constantine the Great had called upon the Church to secure for the declining empire the protection of the "most powerful God," the Church was eventually able to overcome the antipolitical and anti-institutional tendencies of the Christian faith which had caused so much trouble in earlier centuries, and which are so manifest in the New Testament and in early Christian writings and seemingly so insurmountable. The victory of the Roman spirit is really almost a miracle; in any event, it alone enabled the Church "to offer men in the membership of the Church the sense of citizenship which neither Rome nor municipality could any longer offer them." [32] Yet, just as Plato's politicalization of the ideas changed western philosophy and determined the philosophic concept of reason, so the politicalization of the Church changed the Christian religion. The basis of the Church as a community of believers and a public institution was now no longer the Christian faith in resurrection (though this faith remained its content) nor the Hebrew obedience to the commands of God, but rather the testimony of the life, of the birth, death, and resurrection, of Jesus of Nazareth as a historically recorded event. [33] As witnesses to this

---

[32] R. H. Barrow, *The Romans* (1949), p. 194.

[33] A similar amalgamation of Roman imperial political sentiment with Christianity is discussed by Erik Peterson, *Der Monotheismus als politiches Problem* (1935), in connection with Orosius who related the Roman emperor Augustus to Christ. "Dabei ist deutlich, dass Augustus auf diese Weise christianisiert und Christus zum *civis romanus* wird, romanisiert worden ist" (p. 92).

event the apostles could become the "founding fathers" of the Church, from whom she would derive her own authority, as long as she would hand down their testimony by way of tradition from generation to generation. This transformation was to a large extent accomplished by Augustine, the only great philosopher, one is tempted to think, the Romans ever had. For the mainstay of his philosophy: *sedis animi est in memoria* ("the seat of the mind is in memory") is precisely that conceptual articulation of the specifically Roman experience which the Romans themselves, overwhelmed as they were by Greek philosophy and concepts, never achieved.

Thanks to the fact that the foundation of the city of Rome was repeated in the foundation of the Catholic Church, though, of course, with a radically different content, the Roman trinity of religion, authority, and tradition could be taken over by the Christian era, with the result that the miracle of permanence, too, repeated itself; for within the framework of our history, the durability and continuity of the Church as a public institution can only be compared with the thousand years of Roman history in antiquity.

It is true that Roman political thought at a very early date began to use Platonic concepts in order to understand and interpret the specifically Roman political experiences. Yet, it seems as though it was only in the Christian era that Plato's invisible, spiritual yardsticks, by which the visible, concrete affairs of men are to be measured and judged, were unfolding their full political effectiveness. Precisely those parts of Christian doctrine which would have had great difficulty in fitting in and being assimilated to the Roman political structure — namely, the revealed commandments and truths of a genuinely transcendent authority which, unlike Plato's, did not stretch above but were beyond the earthly realm — could be integrated into the Roman foundation legend via Plato. God's revelation could now be interpreted politically as if the standards for human conduct and the principle of political communities, intuitively anticipated by Plato, had been finally revealed directly, so that in the words of a modern Platonist it appeared as though Plato's early "orientation toward the unseen measure was now confirmed through the revelation of the measure itself." [34] To

[34] Eric Voeglin, *A New Science of Politics* (1952), p. 78.

the extent that the Catholic Church incorporated Greek philosophy into the structure of its doctrines and dogmatic beliefs, it amalgamated the Roman political concept of authority, which inevitably was based on a beginning, a founding in the past, with the Greek notion of transcending measurements and rules. General and transcendent standards under which the particular and immanent could be subsumed were now required for any political order, moral rules for all interhuman behavior and rational measurements for the guidance of all individual judgment. There is scarcely anything that eventually was to assert itself with greater authority and more far-reaching consequences than the amalgamation itself.

Since then it has turned out, and this fact speaks for the stability of the amalgamation, that wherever one of the elements of the Roman trinity, religion or authority or tradition, was doubted or eliminated, the remaining two were no longer secure. Thus, it was Luther's error to think that his challenge of the temporal authority of the Church and his appeal to unguided individual judgment would leave tradition and religion intact. So it was the error of Hobbes and the political theorists of the seventeenth century to hope that authority and religion could be saved without tradition. So, too, was it finally the error of the humanists to think it would be possible to remain within an unbroken tradition of western civilization without religion and without authority.

One thing, however, is particularly striking in this context: while all the models, prototypes, and examples for authoritarian relationships — such as the statesman as healer and physician, as expert, as helmsman, as the master who knows, as educator, as the wise man — all Greek in origin, have been faithfully preserved and further articulated until they became empty platitudes, the one political experience which brought authority as word, concept, and reality into our history — the Roman experience of foundation — seems to have been entirely lost and forgotten. And this to such an extent that the moment we begin to talk and think about authority, after all one of the central concepts of political thought, it is as though we were caught in a maze of abstractions, metaphors, and figures of speech in which everything can be taken and mistaken for something else, because we have no reality, either in history or in everyday experience, to which we can unanimously appeal. This, among other things, indicates what could also be proved otherwise, namely that the Greek concepts, once they had been sanctified by the Romans through tradition and authority, simply eliminated from historical consciousness all political experiences which could not be fitted into their framework.

However, this statement is not entirely true. There exists in our political history one type of event for which the notion of founding is decisive, and there is in our history of thought one political thinker in whose work the concept of foundation is central, if not paramount. The events are the revolutions of the modern age, and the thinker is Machiavelli, who stood at the threshold of this age and, though he never used the word, was the first to conceive of a revolution.

Machiavelli's unique position in the history of political thought has little to do with his often praised but by no means unarguable realism, and he was certainly not the father of political science, a role now frequently attributed to him.[35] His unconcern with moral judgments and his freedom from prejudice are astonishing enough, but they do not strike the core of the matter; they have contributed more to his fame than to the understanding of his works, because most of his readers, then as today, were too shocked even to read him properly. When he insists that in the public-political realm men "should learn how not to be good,"[36] he of course never meant that they should learn how to be evil. After all, there is scarcely another political thinker who has spoken with such vehement contempt of "methods [by which] one may indeed gain power but not glory."[37] True, it is only that he opposed both concepts of the good which we find in our tradition: the Platonic concept of the "good for" or fitness, and the Christian concept of an absolute goodness which is not of this world. Both concepts in his opinion were valid, but only in the private sphere of human life; in the public realm of politics they had no more place than

[35] If one understands by political science political theory, its father certainly is Plato rather than Machiavelli. If one stresses the scientific character of political science, it is hardly possible to date its birth earlier than the rise of all modern science, that is, in the sixteenth and seventeenth centuries. In my opinion, the scientific character of Machiavelli's theories is often greatly exaggerated.

[36] Prince, ch. 15.

[37] Prince, ch. 8.

their opposites, unfitness or incompetence and evil. The *virtù*, on the other hand, which according to Machiavelli is the specifically political human quality, has neither the connotation of moral character like the Roman *virtus*, nor that of excellence like the Greek *arete*. *Virtù* has much closer relation to the world; it is man's response to the constellation of *fortuna* in which the world presents and offers itself to him, to his *virtù*. There is no *virtù* without *fortuna* and no *fortuna* without *virtù;* the interplay between them indicates a harmony between man and world — playing with each other and succeeding together — which is as remote from the wisdom of the statesman as from the competence of experts.

His experiences in the struggles of his time taught Machiavelli a deep contempt for all traditions, Christian and Greek, as presented, nurtured, and reinterpreted by the Church. His contempt was leveled at a corrupt Church which had corrupted the political life of Italy, but such corruption, he argued, was inevitable because of the Christian character of the Church. What he witnessed, after all, was not only corruption but also the reaction against it, the deeply religious and sincere revival emanating from the Franciscans and Dominicans, culminating in the fanaticism of Savonarola, whom he held in considerable respect. Respect for these religious forces and contempt for the Church together led him to certain conclusions about a basic discrepancy between the Christian faith and politics that is oddly reminiscent of the first centuries of our era. His point was that every contact between religion and politics must corrupt both, and that a noncorrupt Church, though considerably more respectable, would be even more destructive to the public realm than its present corruption.[38] What he did not, and perhaps in his time could not see was the Roman influence on the Catholic Church which, indeed, was much less noticeable than its Christian content and its Greek theoretical framework of reference.

It was more than patriotism and more than the current revival of interest in antiquity that sent Machiavelli to search for the central political experiences of the Romans as they had originally been presented, equally removed from Christian piety and Greek philosophy. The greatness of his rediscovery lies in that he could not simply revive or resort to an articulate conceptual tradition, but

[38] See especially the *Discourses*, Book III, ch. 1.

had himself to articulate those experiences which the Romans had
not conceptualized but rather expressed in terms of Greek philosophy vulgarized for this purpose.[39] He saw that the whole of
Roman history and mentality depended upon the experience of
foundation, and he believed it should be possible to repeat the
Roman experience through the foundation of a unified Italy which
was to become the same sacred cornerstone for an "eternal" body
politic for the Italian nation as the founding of the Eternal City
had been for the Italic people. The fact that he was aware of the
contemporary beginnings of the birth of nations and the need for
a new body politic, for which he therefore used the hitherto unknown term *lo stato,* has caused him to be commonly and rightfully
identified as the father of the modern nation-state and its notion
of a "reason of state." What is even more striking, though less
well known, is that Machiavelli and Robespierre so often seem to
speak the same language. When Robespierre justifies terror,
"the despotism of liberty against tyranny," he sounds at times as
if he were repeating almost word for word Machiavelli's famous
statements on the necessity of violence for the founding of new
political bodies, the refounding of corrupt ones.

This resemblance is all the more startling since both Machiavelli
and Robespierre in this respect go beyond what the Romans themselves had to say about foundation. To be sure, the connection
between foundation and dictatorship could be learned from the
Romans themselves, and Cicero, for instance, appeals explicitly to
Scipio to become *dictator rei publicae constituendae,* to seize the
dictatorship in order to restore the republic.[40] Like the Romans,
Machiavelli and Robespierre felt founding was the central political
action, the one great deed that established the public-political realm
and made politics possible; but unlike the Romans, to whom this
was an event of the past, they felt that for this supreme "end"
all "means," and chiefly the means of violence, were justified.
They understood the act of founding entirely in the image of
making; the question to them was literally how to "make" a
unified Italy or a French Republic, and their justification of violence

[39] It is curious to see how carefully Machiavelli avoided in his interpretations of
Roman history any reference to Cicero.
[40] *De Re Publica,* VI, 12.

was guided by and received its inherent plausibility from the underlying argument: You cannot make a table without killing trees, you cannot make a republic without killing people. In this respect, which was to become so fateful for the history of revolutions, Machiavelli and Robespierre were not Romans and the authority to which they could have appealed would have been rather Plato who also recommended tyranny as the government where "change is likely to be easiest and most rapid." [41]

It is precisely in this double respect, because of his rediscovery of the foundation experience and his reinterpretations of it in terms of the justification of (violent) means for a supreme end, that Machiavelli may be regarded as the ancestor of modern revolutions, all of which can be characterized by Marx's remark that the French Revolution appeared on the stage of history in Roman costume. Unless it is recognized that the Roman pathos for foundation inspired them, it seems to me that neither the grandeur nor the tragedy of western revolutions in the modern age can be properly understood. Of these, only one, the American Revolution, has been successful: the founding fathers as, characteristically enough, we still call them, founded a completely new body politic without violence and with the help of a constitution. And this body politic has at least endured to the present day, in spite of the fact that the specifically modern character of the modern world has nowhere else produced such extreme expressions in all nonpolitical spheres of life as it has in the United States.

This is not the place to discuss the reasons for the surprising stability of a political structure under the onslaught of the most vehement and shattering social instability. It seems certain that the relatively nonviolent character of the American Revolution, where violence was more or less restricted to regular warfare, is an important factor in this success. It may also be that the founding fathers, because they had escaped the European development of the nation-state, had remained closer to the original Roman spirit. More important, perhaps, was that the act of foundation, namely the colonization of the American continent, had preceded the Declaration of Independence, so that the framing of the Constitution, falling back on existing charters and agreements, confirmed

[41] *Laws,* 711a.

and legalized an already existing body politic rather than made it anew.[42] Thus, the actors in the American Revolution were spared the effort of "initiating a new order of things" altogether; that is, they were spared the one action of which Machiavelli once said that "there is nothing more difficult to carry out, nor more doubtful of success, nor more dangerous to handle." [43] And Machiavelli surely must have known, for he, like Robespierre and Lenin and all the great revolutionaries whose ancestor he was, wished nothing more passionately than to initiate a new order of things.

However that may be, revolutions, which we commonly regard as radical breaks with tradition, appear in our context as events in which the actions of men are still inspired by and derive their greatest strength from the origins of this tradition. They seem to be the only salvation which this Roman-western tradition has provided for emergencies. The fact that not only the various revolutions of the twentieth century, but all revolutions since the French have gone wrong, ending in either restoration or tyranny, seems to indicate that even these last means of salvation provided by tradition have become inadequate. Authority as we once knew it, which grew out of the Roman experience of foundation and was understood in the light of Greek political philosophy, has nowhere been re-established, neither through revolutions nor through the even less promising means of restoration, and least of all through the conservative moods and trends which occasionally sweep public opinion.

To live in a political realm with neither authority nor the concomitant awareness that the source of authority transcends power and those who are in power, means to be confronted anew, without the protection of tradition and self-evident standards of behavior, by the elementary problems of human living-together. Historically, we may say that the loss of authority is merely the final, though decisive, phase of a development which for centuries undermined primarily religion and tradition. Of tradition, religion, and authority, the Roman-inherited trinity, authority has proved to be the most stable element. With the loss of authority, however, the

[42] Professor Norman Jacobson mentioned to me certain remarks of John Adams which would justify these assumptions.
[43] *Prince,* ch. 6.

general doubt of the modern age also invaded the political realm, where things not only assume a more radical expression, but become endowed with a reality peculiar to the political realm alone. What perhaps hitherto had been only of spiritual significance for the few, now has become a concern to one and all. Only now, as it were after the fact, the loss of tradition and religion have become political events of the first order.

When I said in the beginning that I did not wish to discuss "authority in general," but only the very specific concept of authority which has been dominant in our history, I wished to hint at some distinctions which we are liable to neglect when we speak too sweepingly of the crisis of our time and which I may perhaps more easily explain in terms of the related concepts of tradition and religion. Thus, the undeniable loss of tradition in the modern world does not at all entail a loss of the past, for tradition and past are not the same, as the believers in tradition on one side and the believers in progress on the other would have us believe. Therefore it makes little difference that the former deplore this state of affairs while the latter extend their congratulations. With the loss of tradition we have lost the thread which safely guided us through the vast realms of the past, but this thread was also the chain fettering each successive generation to a predetermined aspect of the past. It could be that only now the past will open up to us with unexpected freshness and tell us things no one has yet had ears to hear. Yet it cannot be denied that without a securely anchored tradition — and the loss of this security occurred several hundred years ago — the whole dimension of the past has also been endangered. We are in danger of forgetting, and such an oblivion — quite apart from the contents themselves that could be lost — would mean that, humanly speaking, we were to deprive ourselves of one dimension, the dimension of depth in human existence. For memory and depth are the same, or rather, depth cannot be reached by man except through remembrance.

It is similar with the loss of religion. Ever since the radical criticism of religious beliefs in the seventeenth and eighteenth centuries, it has remained characteristic of the modern age to doubt religious truth, and this is true for believers and nonbelievers alike. Since Pascal and, even more pointedly, since Kierkegaard, doubt has been carried into belief and the modern believer must constantly guard his beliefs against doubts; not the Christian faith as such, but Christianity (and Judaism of course) in the modern age are ridden by paradoxes and absurdity. And whatever else may be able to survive absurdity — philosophy perhaps can — religion certainly cannot. Yet this loss of belief in the dogmas of institutional religion need not necessarily imply a loss or even a crisis of faith, for religion and faith, or belief and faith, are by no means the same. Only belief, but not faith, has an inherent affinity with and is constantly exposed to doubt. But who can deny that faith, too, for so many centuries securely protected by religion and its dogmas, has been gravely endangered through what is actually only a crisis of institutional religion?

Some similar qualifications seem to me to be necessary regarding the modern loss of authority. Authority, resting on a foundation in the past as its unshaken cornerstone, gave the world the permanence and durability which human beings need precisely because they are mortals — the most unstable and futile beings we know of. Its loss is tantamount to the loss of the groundwork of the world, which indeed since then has begun to shift, to change and transform itself with ever-increasing rapidity from one shape into another, as though we were living and struggling with a Protean universe where everything at any moment can become almost anything else. But the loss of worldly permanence and reliability — which politically is identical with the loss of authority — does not entail, at least not necessarily, the loss of the human capacity for building, preserving, and caring for a world that can survive us and remain a place fit to live in for those who come after us.

7. Knowledge, Tradition, and Authority: A Note on the American Experience

NORMAN JACOBSON

From one vantage point the history of political theory in the West is the history of conflicting claims to the exercise of political authority. A particular theory might seek either to support or to demolish a single claim, or it might seek to reconcile or adjudicate those in conflict with one another. The assertion that some person or class of persons possesses special competence in the discovery and application of the good in civil society begins with Socrates and reaches an early crescendo in the attacks of Plato upon his sophist and democratic opponents. It is safe to say that we have not heard the last of such assertions. The fact that they are often unsupported claims, more in the nature of ultimatums than of reasoned cases, or that they are misleading or merely clever makes little difference. All of them are grounded, whether explicitly or implicitly, in the notion that political authority stems from special competence in politics and government. Special competence in these matters is thought to be based upon special skills and special knowledge, analogous to skills and knowledge appropriate to the exercise of authority in fields other than politics and government. And, characteristically, the kind of knowledge and the skills believed competent to the exercise of political authority derive from the particular view of the nature and ends of the state. Thus the knowledge and skills appropriate to the exercise of authority might be philosophical, or they might be theological or historical or scientific or even astrological, varying as the image of the state varies.

The image of the state has varied not only from age to age in western development but from tradition to tradition and from school to school within a given age and even within a given society. For it is an image constructed by the political theorist. To one theorist the state is a school, to another it is a church; the state is a hospital, the state is a family, the state is a commercial enterprise, the state is a prison, the state is an army, on and on almost without end. Hence special competence in the exercise of authority is the competence of the teacher or the priest, of the physician, the businessman, the jailer, or the general, depending upon the kind of knowledge and skills demanded by the particular image of the state. But the image of the state, with its appropriate picture of authority, is not merely formal. Its power to touch men resides in its ability to appeal to everyday experience and common sense. It must be plausible. Every powerful theory of political authority has found some analogy in a significant aspect of human existence. Who would diminish the importance of the scholar in erecting and supervising an educational system? Does the patient prescribe for himself or does he bow before the superior knowledge of medical science possessed by the physician? Conscious of his sinfulness and preoccupation with the goods of this earth, does mortal man dare oppose his own views of God and salvation to those of his priests? But it is not merely in the person of authority that the image of political authority finds an analogy. Ordinary language is enormously helpful in this respect, and the recent diffusion of technical literacy with its quite obvious tendency to encourage respect for the written word, for printed "authority," has only strengthened the role of language in sustaining authority. From a common recognition of the difficulty of knowing with anything approaching certitude what is best for one, as well as from a common experience with "authority," personal and impersonal, in different life situations, the analogy implicit in any compelling image of political authority derives strong support.

For it to be complete the image of political authority requires one further ingredient: a "founder" distant enough and powerful enough to sustain a particular kind of political authority by providing a link between the purposes of the state and the special competence to rule. The founder is the divine embodiment of those qualities thought proper to the exercise of political authority in achieving the highest ends of the state. Men create gods not in their own image but in the image of what they wish to become. The Divine Legislator has had a long history in the western world. It makes little difference that men could invest him with such diverse qualities and powers. Happily his flaws are few. This is because so little is ever known of him. Omniscience and glory are assured as the flesh-and-blood figure, indeed if he actually existed at all, recedes in time. Distance, it is true, has the capacity to diminish the stature of most things. It also possesses the power to magnify our great men, perhaps because the dimensions of ordinary beings are commonly known while there is little experience of the great. That which is shrouded in mystery and touched with a sense of the divine looms, like the Godhead, ever greater with distance.[1]

The most detailed, ingenious, and enduring image of political authority is to be found in the Platonic dialogues. In presenting his case for authority Plato set the style for generations of political theorists. His case was expressed in a series of analogies that are the most compelling in the history of thought. Political authority and the qualities proper to the exercise of political authority are vested in the philosopher-king just as specific authority is vested in their own fields of competence, in the blameless physician, the master pilot, the brilliant mathematician, the gifted musician, the inspired artisan. In his fascinating essay on "Plato's Political Analogies,"[2] Renford Bambrough contends that the reason Plato relied so heavily upon the analogy between the statesman and these masters of the arts and sciences is that the latter are obviously

[1] Were it possible to designate political authority (in our usage) in the pre-Roman classical world, there is no question that it would rest squarely upon the image of the Divine Legislator. The constitution of Sparta was not merely wise, it possessed the virtue of having been thought the product of a single magnificent mind. Thus could Descartes credit Lycurgus with the grandest contribution to the science of government. Yet it is impossible to suppose that Descartes' tribute was a tribute to Lycurgus the man. The image was instead that of Lycurgus the founder, the divine legislator, the authority.

[2] In *Philosophy, Politics and Society,* ed. Peter Laslett (1956).

"experts who can find and give . . . answers as men speaking with authority." Let us consider for a moment one of the most famous of the Platonic analogies, the parable of the ship in the *Republic*. It is in this parable that Plato's case for the special knowledge and skills demanded by political authority is perhaps most succinctly set forth.

Plato would have us imagine the following situation aboard a ship or a fleet of ships. The captain, though more impressive physically than any of the crew, is nevertheless as poor a navigator as they. The crew members are engaged in an endless and destructive dispute for control of the helm. They are convinced that steering a ship requires no special skill and that a system of apprenticeship is unnecessary because there is nothing to teach. In their scramble for possession of the helm each crew member attempts to persuade the captain, by any means, that he would make a more satisfactory helmsman than the rest. After a tumultuous period the crew finally succeeds in subduing the captain and in commandeering the vessel. Only those who abetted them in their schemes are designated as skilled navigators. The others are quieted or tossed overboard. What the crew refuses to understand or will not admit is that "the genuine navigator can only make himself fit to command a ship by studying the seasons of the year, sky, stars, and winds, and all that belongs to his craft; and they have no idea that, along with the science of navigation, it is possible for him to gain, by instruction or practice, the skill to keep control of the helm whether some of them like it or not. If a ship were managed in that way, would not those on board be likely to call the expert in navigation a mere star-gazer, who spent his time in idle talk and was useless to them?" Plato then has Socrates draw the obvious analogy: "I think you understand what I mean and do not need to have my parable interpreted in order to see how it illustrates the attitude of existing states towards the true philosopher." [3]

Bambrough points out, correctly I believe, that the parable presupposes a distinction between knowledge and skill, "between

---

[3] *Republic*, Book VI, 488a–489a, Cornford translation. Jowett's translation makes even more explicit the relation in Plato's theory between special knowledge and skills and political authority. Socrates impresses upon Adeimantus that the crew (the people) will never recognize "the possibility of this union of *authority* with the steerer's art . . ." VI, 488. Italics mine.

knowing *that* and knowing *how*." It is clear that Plato was intent upon demonstrating that the qualifications of the true statesman "consist of both science and skill, of theoretical knowledge and the ability to apply it in practice." Bambrough's specific arguments that Plato's analogy, though plausible, is seriously misleading need not concern us here. The point is that beyond any doubt Plato was convinced that the people are inherently mutinous. They simply will not recognize true authority, for they lack the capacity to understand that authority demands special knowledge and special skills. What Plato in turn refuses to recognize is that the people, having had ample experience of such voyages, might choose to behave the way they do from a fear of falling prey to anyone who can convince them, even briefly, of his competence as a pilot. If the crew wants the discrimination to distinguish the master pilot from the pretender, how can it afford to accept *any* pilot unconditionally? Seen in this light, the task might be one of guarding against the inconvenience of frequent mutinies on the one hand and the abuses of the pretender on the other. It must be conceded that in the process the contributions of the superior pilot, if one should ever come along, are likely to be diminished through the restrictions placed upon his authority by the crew. Even so, the judgment is a prudent one. At least this was the conclusion of the crew that participated in the founding of Plymouth in America. The founding had great theoretical significance, especially in terms of the image of political authority which accompanied it. That the theory had been literally conditioned by a voyage across the seas is extremely interesting.

In 1620 a disgruntled band of settlers arrived at Plymouth. They had been bound for Virginia but had lost their way. Under the threat of mass desertion the leaders were compelled to accede, in writing, to the demands of the rest of the party. A document was drawn up in the form of a compact among all the members. Certainly this did not mark a new departure. The same party had covenanted as a church body before leaving the Old World. It is tempting to believe, however, that the experience of incompetent leadership suffered during the long voyage had influenced the mutinous crew to demand a restatement, this time in political terms, of the basis for authority. They simply refused to land on strange soil without first having taken the precaution of establishing a constitution of government. The party "solemnly and mutually" bound themselves "together into a civil body politic" for their "better ordering and preservation"; and they agreed to "enact, constitute, and frame" laws for the common welfare to which they promised "all due submission and obedience." It should be remarked that submission and obedience were to be granted only to the *laws duly enacted, constituted,* and *framed.* No person or class of persons was empowered by the instrument to assume authority in the new community. And there was no mention of any special knowledge or skills appropriate to the exercise of political authority. The Mayflower Compact became the model for all future agreements of government in America. It is the only form of social contract of which Americans were to have any experience at all.

Later, after the community had been liberated from the rule of the British, this theory of political authority was reaffirmed in both the Declaration of Independence and the Constitution. At the "second founding" the people displayed no more readiness to prostrate themselves before a personal authority than they had in 1620. The second, figurative, voyage had only served to reinforce the instincts and sentiments manifest so strongly during the first. The people had been the beneficiaries of over a century of political *experience,* the greatest single antidote to Platonic theories of authority. Thus they reaffirmed the position assumed earlier. Governments are established by the consent of the governed. They function only with their continuing consent. For the purpose of government all men are considered equal. The right to revolt is a right lodged in the community, to be invoked when the rulers behave in a tyrannical manner, that is, when they are no longer willing to acknowledge the superior, indeed ultimate authority of the laws. It should be noted that this theory does not recognize as crucial the question of the special skills or knowledge of those exercising authority. The test established in the Declaration and reiterated in the Constitution is simply *how* the rulers behave, and not the justice of their original claims to dominion. Do they acknowledge the legitimate authority? Then they are qualified to exercise legitimate authority.

This line of reasoning had its basis in liberal theory as it had developed since the seventeenth century. Before Hobbes and Locke political obligation had almost always involved obligation to some tangible authority — to some person or class of persons. With the rise of a body of theory stressing self-interest, equality, and the rule of law the concept of political obligation underwent drastic change. It was divested of much of its traditional meaning. Fealty to the person of the monarch or to a class of nobles was gradually replaced in the minds of men by loyalty to particular governmental arrangements. Not until allegiance became more depersonalized could liberalism, by its very logic a political theory jealous of individual rights and distrustful of rule by fiat, become a viable ideology. So long as there was in America no king or established aristocracy as a party to the original contract "popular sovereignty" alone was created by the instrument, and individual obligation was thought to extend no further. This is most strikingly reflected in the history of the transformation of the traditional contract theory from a defense of established authority to a vindication of individual right or interest. In Europe this development was sometimes obscured by the existence of lords and nobles, of great churchmen, and of grand monarchs. In America the absence of feudal institutions from the very beginning served to confirm the theory and to strengthen it.

At the same time the absence of feudal arrangements and feudal loyalties contributed to the difficulty of locating and sanctifying personal authority in America. Any system that originates and flourishes in a rational context, exalting individual reason and self-interest and dubious of exclusive claims to the exercise of authority, is seriously handicapped in the search for tradition as a bulwark for authority. The Plymouth founding had been the accomplishment of ordinary Englishmen who were careful to make a record of it. The second founding not only was a clear extension of the logic of 1620, but in addition deprived Americans of the luxury of appealing, along with their fellow Englishmen, to an origin sacred for its distance and obscurity. As a matter of fact, the necessities of their position compelled the American patriots to attack the notion that obscure origins possessed any binding force whatever for rational men in the playing out of their political destinies.

In his service for the cause of independence Tom Paine had argued not merely against continued loyalty to a haughty and oppressive monarch. He challenged the very idea of monarchy itself. The institution had originated either in usurpation or in election or lot. If its origin lay in usurpation it could make no claims on the loyalties of free men; if in election or lot the claims of monarchy as an institution were forfeit at the moment when the practice of hereditary succession was established. While irreverent in the extreme, Paine's expression of antimonarchical sentiments had at least the virtue of directness. "A French bastard," he wrote in *Common Sense,* "landing with an armed Banditti and establishing himself king of England against the consent of the natives, is in plain terms a very paltry rascally origin. It certainly hath no divinity in it." As for Englishmen, "let them promiscuously worship the Ass and the Lion, and welcome. I shall neither copy their humility nor disturb their devotion." The "plain truth" was that the "antiquity of English monarchy will not bear looking into." [4]

Now it is true that for a time during the Revolution the patriots rested their case to some extent upon the defense of the traditional English constitution against what they chose to believe were the despotic acts of a contemptuous monarch. Moreover, in the Philadelphia Convention and afterwards, many of them accepted the view that the new Constitution was much more a summary of the best in the Anglo-American tradition than a novel experiment in free government. Like Columbus they attempted to convince themselves that the new world they had brought into being was actually an old one. There is no question that the familiar is always more comfortable than the novel. Yet the logic of their true position is indisputable; they had founded a new nation. And owing to the nature of the system they established and the values they decided were to be privileged in the Constitution, the founders virtually guaranteed against the founding's ever really becoming obscured in antiquity or clothed in tradition. If it could be said that an "American tradition" had existed at all at the time of the framing of the Constitution, its life was so brief that an impressive defense of it was almost impossible. Anyone bold enough to attempt such an act would have been faced with a staggering problem, the kind of problem which

[4] *The Life and Works of Thomas Paine,* ed. W. M. Van der Weyde, Thomas Paine Historical Association (1925), vol. II, pp. 117, 118.

would have taxed even the ingenuity of a Burke compelled to defend the continuity of the English tradition scarcely a century after the Norman Conquest.[5]

The problem was further complicated by the fact that the founders not only were well known to the people, but were from the beginning participants in the great game of interest politics. The people had had as much experience of these leaders as the passengers and crew aboard the *Mayflower* had had of their captains. The unrestrained attack upon the institution of monarchy during the course of the Revolution was not soon forgotten. Despite John Adams' fear that an end to thrones and crowns would mean an end to all dominion and justice, no mystique was to surround an American head of state. It might be true that, as Adams put it, the common people of foreign nations as well as American soldiers and sailors would despise plain George Washington, but plain George Washington he remained. And by his second term even Washington was subjected to public abuse by his political opponents. The presidential succession that endured down to Jackson did not succeed in obscuring the fact that the founders themselves were engaged in the most active kind of politics. With the triumph of Jackson even the limited advantage of the succession in shielding an American president from open vilification, as well as the movement toward a definition of the qualities appropriate to the exercise of political authority, was lost.

How is it that the system has managed to thrive so well without the divinity which has usually hedged the figure of the founder, without a theory of personal fealty, without a mystique surrounding the exercise of power, without an image of the special skills and special knowledge competent to rule — without, in a word, traditional political authority? If there is any miracle at all here, it is the miracle of interest politics. Machiavelli had been the first great political theorist to discuss political authority in nontraditional, utilitarian terms. He had exalted the politics of contingency in theory; the American republic provided the first impressive empirical test. There are, to be sure, certain specifiable skills and kinds of knowledge appropriate to the exercise of political authority in a free

---

[5] For a more detailed discussion of this point see the author's "Political Realism in the Age of Reason: The anti-Rationalist Heritage in America," *The Review of Politics*, 15: 446–449. (October 1953).

republic. Given the existence of pluralistic contingency, however, the competence required is for the most part dictated by particular social, economic, and political situations. Even the traditional virtues must be justified at the same bar of public opinion. Such an approach is in a sense "procedural." The special knowledge and skills proper to the exercise of political authority may be spelled out only in the most vague and general terms, for it is the "objective situation" which is decisive in the demands made upon political talent. Contingency must always be taken into account. *There is no unique American image of political authority that is truly substantive.* The competence to rule must be representative in character. In a political system based upon contingency, where the politics of interest takes precedence over the politics of reason or the politics of love, authority simply cannot be said to reside ultimately with any person or class of persons trained to the responsibility in any specific manner. Even were it impeccable in its logic, which by the way there is ample reason to doubt, the Platonic parable would thus be irrelevant and inapplicable. No parable seeking to construct a substantive image of authority is possible in such an environment. If it is to be located anywhere, political authority in America may be found only in the impersonal document establishing the rules and limits of political conflict, the Constitution itself.

Despite oft-repeated claims — their own included — to the contrary, the founders *did* establish a novel system in America. Had they failed to do so it is barely conceivable that there could have remained a trace of respect for political authority. After all, it was they who had helped undermine the traditional claims to the exercise of authority. The old symbolism was now either dead or dying. The new possessed tremendous vitality, tremendous appeal. In the absence of a durable, concrete image of the qualities most desirable for the exercise of political authority, competence was what the public said it was. And the public spoke often enough to keep even the general image a highly volatile one. The unique qualities of each powerful political leader in relation to the needs of the age could be made to serve as a substitute for a specific image of political authority within the broader context of the authority and symbolism of the Constitution. To some extent the effect has been cumulative. Yet there is a huge gulf between the special knowledge and skills of, say, a James Madison or a John Adams and those of a Harry Truman or a Dwight Eisenhower. Nor is that all. Because there is almost as much known about Madison and Adams as there is about Truman and Eisenhower (some would contend that actually we know more about the first two), distance has failed to secure their qualities against reinterpretation or their reputations against reassessment. In a liberal political community the competences of its great men, even of its founders, are never definitively settled. They are always fit subjects for dispute. Hence the specific image of political authority, if it is sensible to discuss it at all, will always be in flux.

The fact that loyalty in America is thought to extend primarily to the instrument which brought the system into existence makes the search for an American conservative tradition extremely arduous and probably unrewarding. If it is hardly possible to conceive of conservatism without a constant specific image of political authority, where in the American experience may such an image be found? In the "rules of the game," or in as prosaic a concept as the "decision-making process"? Toward the end of his long life, as outstanding a conservative-by-instinct as John Adams made a rather ludicrous figure in an attempt to invoke a traditional American image of political authority. At the Massachusetts Constitutional Convention of 1820, Adams, then in his eighty-sixth year, joined with Daniel Webster in a spirited defense of the property qualifications for electors and office-holders. "The great object," Adams declared, "is to render property secure." The French Revolution had recently furnished a convincing demonstration of the "utility and excellence of universal suffrage." But Adams went beyond empirics to the ultimate irrefutable argument. "Our ancestors have made a pecuniary qualification necessary for office, and necessary for electors; and all the wise men of the world have agreed in the same thing." [6] Adams was referring to the provisions of the first Massachusetts constitution of 1780. It is rather difficult to believe that Adams had forgotten that he himself had drafted that constitution, or that he had introduced there a property qualification substantially higher than the one which had existed under the old provincial charter. "Our ancestors," indeed! Webster was on much firmer ground when he based his defense on

---

[6] *Journal of Debates and Proceedings of the Constitutional Convention of Massachusetts, 1820–21* (Boston: *The Daily Advertiser*, 1853), pp. 277–279.

the Harringtonian doctrine that the "true principle of a free and popular government would seem to be, so to construct it as to give to all, or at least to a very great majority, an interest in its preservation; *to found it, as other things are founded, on men's interest.*" [7] The interests of men, and not the wisdom of "our ancestors," are the final arbiter in the American system.

The appeal from the elder to the younger Adams is after all an appeal from experience to relative inexperience with the practices and problems of American political life. Yet puny and misdirected as it is, this kind of appeal must perforce continue as part of the American case for conservatism. It will most likely prove ineffectual, but what alternative, regardless of the environment, is open to the true conservative? The freshness of the American experience, its sheer novelty, thus serves to illuminate the single most obvious shortcoming in the conservative image of authority. Francis Bacon saw this very clearly. In the field of science men had been retarded "as by a kind of enchantment" owing to an inordinate "reverence for antiquity, by the authority of men accounted great in philosophy. . . ." The view of antiquity which most men accept is misleading and hurtful:

For the old age of the world is to be accounted the true antiquity; and this is the attribute of our own times, not of that earlier age of the world in which the ancients lived; and which, though in respect of us it was the elder, yet in respect of the world it was the younger. And truly as we look for greater knowledge of human things and a riper judgment in the old man than in the young . . . so in like manner from our age, if it but knew its own strength and chose to essay and exert it, much more might fairly be expected than from the ancient times. . . .

And with regard to authority, it shows a feeble mind to grant so much to authors and yet deny time his rights, who is the author of authors, nay, author of all authority. *For rightly is truth called the daughter of time, not of authority.*[8]

Bacon's argument could scarcely have been so persuasive in an age of quiescence. Had it not been articulated at a time when there loomed a new philosophic and scientific system, a new intellectual

[7] *Journal of Debates,* p. 311. Italics added.
[8] *NOVUM ORGANUM,* lxxxiv, in *The Works of Francis Bacon,* J. Spedding, R. L. Ellis, and D. D. Heath (1875), vol. IV, pp. 81–82. Italics mine.

world, the case against traditional authority would have lacked the compelling quality it seemed to possess. Nor would Bacon have bothered to make the case at all. Where there is no unique experience, no new world, and equally important, no feeling of great optimism, antiquity is either casually accepted or implicitly defended. Traditional authority persists unchallenged. The American experience called into being a new political system which demanded, if not novel theories, at least novel attitudes. The appeal to authority vested in antiquity could no longer be expected to exert its traditional influence. But there is more to it than that. The political world discovered in the seventeenth century was unique in that it was by nature inhospitable to the construction of any specific image whatever of political authority. Deference to traditional sources of authority could no longer be regarded as automatic, and there existed no ready substitutes at hand. To use Bacon's figure, in the American adventure experience as a product of time and not the prescriptions established by authority has been the genuine parent of political truth.

8. Authority and Its Critics

GEORGE E. GORDON CATLIN

I

"In any given society," writes Proudhon in *Qu'est-ce que la Propriété?*, "the authority of man over man varies in inverse proportion to the intellectual development of the society." The implication is that, were men perfectly intelligent, authority would disappear. Only freedom and self-control would reign or, if "reign" be thought here inappropriate, there would be an anarchy of preestablished harmony, founded on free moral choice. Maybe intelligence would guide all to choose the same thing. God would become (as some democratic divines have suggested) a cooperative republic. Authority and freedom are here regarded as not only contraries but contradictories.

Proudhon's view, while characteristically "modern," is yet in certain significant respects not new. Although Leo XIII may say, in *Libertas praestantissimum* (1888), that "the highest duty is to respect authority," and in *Immortale Dei* (1885), that "to despise legitimate authority, no matter in whom it is invested, is unlawful; it is a rebellion against God's will," yet there is a respectable array of patristic writers and canonists to declare that *dominatio est contra naturam.* Since no opposition is to be supposed between the canonists and Leo's encyclicals, we have to note a distinction between "authority" and "domination," touched on by Santayana, which raises the question whether such truth as there may be in Proudhon's statement may apply, not to all kinds of authority including those that reason supports as legitimate, but only to one species, itself dubious, to wit, dominative power and force. On the other hand, there are those who would seem not only to make social approval a constituent of that power which is authority, but also to deny to power, exclusively identified here (wrongly) with authority, any connection with force. Thus so good a political critic as John Plamenatz, in his *German Marxism and Russian Communism*, flatly says: "It is a mistake to suppose that power is prior to right and obligation . . . All exercise of power is subject to rules." [1] This is either ambiguous, identifying the genus "power" with the species "authority" and legal rules with scientific laws, or it is misleading. We shall return to it.

Philologically, the word "authority" has the implication of "to grow," as "propaganda" has that of "begetting." It has the implication of the accumulation of people under one aegis, of cumulative momentum. The word "power" carries the meaning of potency and potentiality; and "domination" has the meaning of lording and mastery. If, however, we are to discuss the subject of authority with profit and avoid logomachy, it is necessary to consider and state the context of our usage and the plane of discourse.

For example, we may discuss the matter on the level of psychology, as do Adler and Freud and numerous more recent writers from Dodge and Kahn to Erich Fromm.[2] We may make a study of the drive to domination such as Adorno and his colleagues did in their extensive work *The Authoritarian Personality*, which is primarily concerned with German National Socialist and Fascist phenomena. This book makes an identification of authoritarianism and totalitarianism, against which others protest as biased and theoretically unsound.[3] Again, I would sharply distinguish, beyond the difference between the psychological and the political planes, between discussion of authority on the level of political science, where it is a term with an assigned and precise meaning within the general schematism, and debate on the plane of political philosophy, with its con-

[1] (1954), p. 136.
[2] See R. Dodge and E. Kahn, *The Craving for Superiority* (1931); D. W. Harding, *The Impulse to Dominate* (1941); Ranyard West, *Conscience and Society* (1942); H. D. Lasswell, *World Politics and Personal Insecurity* (1935); Erich Fromm, *The Sane Society* (1955).
[3] T. W. Adorno *et al., The Authoritarian Personality* (1950); see also Erich Fromm, *Escape from Freedom* (1941).

cern with evaluations, popular and critical. The two latter levels
will be our subject here, although the dictum of Bryce, following
Sidgwick, holds perennially true, that the foundation of the study
of politics will be found in psychology, so that it is indispensable to
bear in mind the results of research on the first level.[4]

2

In political science, the first requirement for profitable discussion
is the choice of neutral, or of what Bentham calls "descriptive,"
terms, without "evocative," moralistic, or evaluative "loads" or overtones. We must have what Professor David Truman, in *The Governmental Process* (1951), calls "the neutral precision requisite to
careful discussion." For the purposes of political science, authority is
neither good in itself nor bad. It carries no poison necessarily, whatever may be the warnings of psychologists and others (since Arch-
bishop Fénelon), but also no necessary implication of goodness and
awe, unless brought in, as in papal encyclicals, by the words "legitimate" and "rational." If the purposes of which it is efficient cause are
stated to be "good," then *ex hypothesi* the authority is here "good."
But the scientific issue is that of its efficiency and *virtù* in Machiavelli's sense. Hobbes can adopt another usage only because he has
first made his authorities, if sovereign, then by definition the judges
of good and bad. Likewise, in the complementary field of discussion of freedom, we must agree with Professor K. J. Scott, of Wel-
lington, New Zealand, in his article "Liberty, License and Not Being
Free,"[5] that the term "freedom" is neutral — "freedom is a non-
moral thing." We must also be allowed to include "license," although
according to my definition of "liberty" as "freedom under law," we
can always argue that what the law allows is at least not contrary to
the substantial public interest and that, although there may be a lawful freedom and what Kant calls "a wild, lawless freedom," the im-

---

[4] Apart from the classical work of Freud and Adler, and the illuminating studies
of Erich Fromm, R. E. Money-Kyrle's brief *Psychoanalysis and Politics* (1951)
merits notice. A companion study to this one on authority will be found in the
present writer's contribution "On Freedom" in the *Festschrift* for R. E. Cushman of
the same title (Cornell University Press, 1958), ed. Clinton Rossiter and Milton
Konvitz.

[5] In *Political Studies* (June 1956).

pulse towards freedom is among the deepest instincts of man and *pro tanto* is good.

What, then, in the functioning of politics, does the neutral term "authority" describe? It is my argument here that it is, not just by chance but necessarily, one of the key terms in political science, a term of a relation from which, indeed, the entire science follows in its abstract scheme, just as classical economics follows from the linked relation of demand and supply, and of competition in demand for the supply, and in supply for the consumer demand. The theme, as I have stated and developed it in the *Principles of Politics* is:

Control is the first object, for which the liberty-demanding will will require power, in order to execute a wish . . . Authority is power exercised in accordance with a convention, whether between two people, one of whom is under conventional obligation to the other, or over a group of people by those whose function is to enforce the convention of the group.[6]

Under some circumstances such a convention can be called, as with T. H. Green, a "constitutional morality." In *A Grammar of Politics* Harold Laski appropriately writes, "Will that is made by activity, as distinct from consent [or assent] that is inferred from reception, is the foundation upon which authority is based."[7]

It is not irrelevant to recite the psychological derivation of authority. The primitive and "innocent" condition is that of wish. Here, no hard choices have to be made and, in the Eden of imagination, every man is king. The God which is the principle of reality has as yet uttered no veto. There is no disobedience or temptation to it. Adam is lord of all creatures in "oceanic omnipotence," or rather, in a condition of "oceanic" being which is innocent of limits. Reality's power and limit he has not yet challenged. It is a mistake of old-fashioned liberalism to ignore how much of political action takes place through close connection with this world of imagination, in identification with Hollywood-style princes and with fantasies of national omnipotence; it is a world of various opiates (including Marxist predestination to victory), with attendant sedative or intoxicant dreams. The more developed condition is that where, by the

[6] (1930), pp. 160, 164.
[7] (1925), p. 244.

guidance of reason and through what Lippmann calls "maturely facing facts," the will to achieve an object (and, incidentally, the formal will to have one's way) is determined upon. Where there are no obstacles brought to consciousness — the "real" obstacles, maybe, having already been circumvented by a reason that avoids them: whatever the lame man may dream, his common sense prevents him from placing his hopes in the Olympic race — a rational trust is established, a sense of competence. Kropotkin indeed optimistically placed here, in a kind of "kingdom of Grace," the bases for a spontaneous cooperative society.

Where there are obstacles to freedom in the achievement of the willed object, the mind, losing its natural innocence, becomes preoccupied with the *power* to overcome them. Will is not power but can require it. As against K. J. Scott, we can say that increase of power increases potential freedom. First there is the innocent, oceanic sense of the limitless; then the sense of limit to wish; then the desire for freedom; and then the consideration of power to overcome obstacles and to realize freedom, whether by trustful competence or by struggle for domination, and thereby also realize the freedom of wish and will. From obstacles and frustrations, not least if dictated by objective reality, arise, as Dollard and his associates insist in their *Frustration and Aggression,* the tendencies to aggression and those moods of discontent with civilization elaborated by Freud. This can become obstinate attachment to the pride of self-will and the bias of "original sin." But, no less naturally (for it is not artificial), when the freedom-striving will finds that others have had like obstacles and like objects, a rational bond of choice, later re-enforcing habit, is forged with them. The joint support and power meet with the approval of each. They are prepared to pay all the costs — restrictions — of its support and to perform duties. They recognize this power as, for themselves, an authority, under which they enjoy both liberties and approved rights, even though it remains an irrational and brute force of power for those who constitute the obstacle and repudiate the objective. Others will assent to the power as authority for general purposes, finding (as Bryce says) one of the grounds of obedience in indolence,[8] even if they have no wish re-

---

[8] James Viscount Bryce, "Obedience," *Studies in History and Jurisprudence* (1901), p. 467.

lated to the particular purpose. In brief, authority with the political goals of security and the like, which it has to offer, guaranteeing the successful execution of any will, springs directly and logically from what Pavlov calls precisely the "instinctive" drive for freedom. And the freedom which, in turn, authority chooses to recognize is negatively called liberty — here is that which the law permits — and is positively called specific rights.

3

In *The Future of Public Administration* Professor John Gaus says: "Authority follows the successful exercise of function." In one sense this is true; in another, false. There is not first "function" and then "authority." There is an exercise of power functionally for the achievement of a willed objective. When several persons concur about the desirability of that goal and join their power to achieve it, then within the ambit of that group and for its members that power is not mere force but is, *pro tanto,* an approved power or authority. Authority is approved power; whether it is successful or not is strictly and *de jure* irrelevant. But power that repeatedly moves from potential into actual achievement is reinforced cumulatively; and approved power, which is authority, is also reinforced cumulatively and "greater power follows." Successful authority is more authority. Here indeed we may adapt Spinoza and say "the more power, the more rights." This additional authority, insofar as it builds upon a presumption of successful exercise of power upon the next occasion, we may call prestige or "face" (*persona*).

Some people are spoken of as having authority either as a matter of status, by reason automatically of the position which they hold, or as a matter of qualities of individual personality, going beyond what status will confer, or both. Following on certain psychological investigations, but almost certainly with overstress, David Truman asserts that "leadership is an inter-actional function of the personality and of the social situation." [9] We may agree, in less academic language, that men are more readily hypnotized by those to whom, even if quacks, they have allocated greater prestige in hypnosis. And the

---

[9] *The Governmental Process* (1951), p. 191, quoting from C. A. Gibb, "The Principles and Traits of Leadership," *Journal of Abnormal and Social Psychology*, vol. 42, no. 3.

same observation may apply to the *mana* or authority of leadership, as with a Hitler (who modeled himself on Rienzi). A society may be so structured, on the contrary, as to be obdurately unreceptive to the Hitler type of leadership, and more inclined to follow some gray, neutral personality who relies almost entirely upon the principle of keeping to the rules as laid down in committee. However, in *The Web of Government,* Robert MacIver, whom Truman quotes, states the matter far more cautiously. He writes:

The power a man has is the power he disposes; it is not intrinsically his own. He cannot command [effectively?] unless another obeys. He cannot control unless the social organization invests him with the apparatus of control.[10]

Here Laski's distinction between will and assent, as the basis of authority, is corrective. Quite clearly power through leadership is not a private quality, like curly-headedness or muscular strength. There must be the mood to accept and the apparatus of enforcement. This type of power is by its nature in part social, even in the case of a semi-tyranny (although here the element of sheer power of force enters in). This Hume pointed out in a famous essay, commenting on Henry VIII. Authority flowing from leadership goes beyond any individual strength or the wit to combine, such as reason dictates. It is addressed to the performance of a function, at least possible, and it is socially and physically conditioned by the nature of the obstacles to be overcome. In a situation of human obstruction, it can be put to the social test of effective ability to command cooperative obedience or passive acquiescence. Yet its bearer may also have, as other men have not, the wit and gift to know what the situation requires for leadership. Not everyone is a Tudor, even if on a throne. It was not only "the situation" which destroyed the Stuarts.

Political problems indeed vary as to the kind of leadership required. There are great war ministers, and again, there are men with a gift for knowing what the situation requires in peace, and with the prestige to be able to do it. The issue may "require" leadership, but no man, speaking as one having authority, may arise to meet it. On the other hand, the editors of *Life* Magazine (November 19, 1956) commenting on the American Presidential election, wrote in

[10] Robert MacIver, *The Web of Government* (1947), pp. 107–108.

the opposite sense to Professor Truman's, but perhaps with no less humor and judgment:

> There is another lesson from the returns which may be even more useful in the long run. Ike is not the only strong and attractive personality who won this year. In scores of local contests, after all the other explanations are in, personality was a decisive factor . . . Give the voter a choice between a dim and a forceful candidate — especially when there are no great party issues — and the voter will pick the latter . . . [Personality] is a mysterious but permanent key to success in American politics.

Situations may indeed arise where the voter, far from emphatically identifying himself with such a "father figure," better gratifies his own vanity by reacting against an authoritarian personality and subscribes to the program of somebody he feels to be more democratic and folksy, indeed just like himself. Hence this may run the gamut from a Churchill to a Kefauver. Occasionally the voter may react in favor of Crippsian Puritanism and against any extrovert personality whatsoever.

Whether by false deduction from the view that "the power a man has is the power he disposes," and with which others will cooperate, or from some other cause, John Plamenatz — like Isaiah Berlin an able commentator on Marx, who also has made a useful pioneer contribution in the application of logical analysis to politics — writes, in a passage to which reference has already been made:

> It is a mistake to suppose that power is prior to right and obligation. No man has power unless his right to command is acknowledged by some at least of those who obey him; it is only because they obey him that he has power. All exercise of power is subject to rules; it is in principle regular and cannot last long or be effective if it is often arbitrary . . . It is of the essence of power that it supports rights and enforces obligations; and it is inevitable that it should appear as much oppressive as protective to those with the fewest rights.[11]

There seems to be here an odd ambiguity, unless words are being used in a highly idiosyncratic fashion, through a confusion between power and authority. By Plamenatz's argument as it stands in the text, the Russians have power in Hungary only insofar as they

---

[11] *German Communism and Russian Marxism*, p. 136 and footnote.

receive obedience and as their right to command is acknowledged
by a significant portion of the Magyar people. The historic tragedy
lies in the opposite *realpolitik;* and, although this power may indeed,
like a fire, "not last long" (which is a different argument), it may
last too long for some people to remain alive. As Lord Keynes
pointed out, this is the disadvantage of statements about "the long
run." The argument is a strange piece of academic abstraction —
and misleading abstraction. It is, further, true that power (as we
have said) supports rights; but it can also support wrongs. Authority
is indeed oppressive to those who present obstacles and who are in
the market for other kinds of liberty than those preferred by its
supporters. But, although the man with few rights — for example,
the feudal vassal who is not *baro* or *liber homo* — is clearly not doing
well in the political market, and *pro tanto* at some stage may come
to have the sense of being defrauded or underprivileged, it is improbable that this humble man will present the outstanding recalci-
trant obstacles to authority or primarily feel the weight of its hand
against outlaws. A sound analysis of authority will lead us to expect
what historically we find. And certainly there is nothing to lament
in the desire of the common man for the maximum freedom or in
his resentment against such particular authorities (as distinct from
authority) as are for him functionless and unprofitable or cater to
another class or race.

"The Power of man," says Hobbes, "is his present means to obtain
some future apparent good." If we accept that these "present means"
need not be exercised but may remain potential, we have no reason
for quarreling with this definition. "Desire of Ease disposeth men,"
Hobbes continues, "to obey a common Power . . . the right of doing
any action is called Authority. So that, by Authority, is always understood a Right of doing any act." This is sound doctrine; that is, the
concept of recognized right enters into authority, such as may come
from the habit of recognition or the original consent of a group, or
the emergent approval of many of its members or a rational ground
for such approval. But this concept does not essentially enter into
power, for force apart from right is nevertheless truly power (which
is neutral and must not be moralized); and the force of one exercised
habitually over another is dominion, whoever consents or consents
not and whether or not it be rationally *secundum naturam.* The

argument of Hume that even tyranny requires the support of opinion, although not utterly untrue since all social power requires *some* support, yet ignores the graded nature of organized society and the extent to which, not active consent, but passive assent (even with the intent to disobey at better convenience) may be commanded by fear of violent death or other cowardice. The obedience may be from terror of illicit power and without obligation in conscience — or rather, may coexist with a plot to disobey — but the power to compel may nevertheless persist; and it is an optimism contrary to history to presume otherwise. What is indeed true in science is that such a violent or dominative power structure is, as it were from its own chemistry, unstable, fissionable, and explosive. In other terms, it involves too costly and burdensome a power monopoly.

4

Dr. Hannah Arendt, in her admirable *Origins of Totalitarianism* (1951) and in her article, "Authority in the Twentieth Century," [12] very rightly refers to "the distinction between legitimate and illegitimate power on which all authoritarian government hinges." Illegitimate power can end in tyranny, even if it has emerged (as Aristotle warns us) from popular forms of government — not the same forms, however, as what the Anglo-Saxon world means by "democracy" and Aristotle by *politeia*. It can end in totalitarian domination. Of legitimate authority, the caliphate was an instance. Here the notion of the caliph under the Koran gave legitimacy and authority, but the caliphate always involved also the characteristic of military power. The Catholic Church (as Dr. Arendt implies) offers a singularly pure instance of authority with power and legitimacy, but divorced from military force. It is a body politic, as a *societas perfecta* of social controls, but, except for the minor (if diplomatically important) exception of the Vatican State, it is without direct secular power. This authority, functioning apart from the secular arm of society, does not possess the *vis coactiva*, the hallmark not of the law, as Holland too broadly says,[13] but yet of the secular state — the hallmark of the secondary social organization, as Augustine remarked (and Toynbee recently followed him by remarking), which func-

---

[12] In *The Review of Politics*, vol. 18, no. 4 (October 1956).
[13] T. G. Holland, *Jurisprudence* (1916 ed.), p. 23.

tions *ratione peccati* but also by reason of natural ignorance, and with the imperfection of force as part of its essence.

Following Fénelon, Lord Acton observed to Bishop Creighton that "power tends to corrupt," which may be psychologically correct, as a man may say that lust for speed corrupts. But it should not be construed as the opposite of Plamenatz's position, implying that all power has an inherent quality antipathetic to right; or as denying that the authority which is purged of force is nevertheless power, even if cooperative and not dominative. In this last case of "pure authority," indeed, it is true that power is contingent upon voluntary obedience to suggestion. But it also can *control;* and perhaps more steadily and lastingly than violence. There can, then, be authority without force, coercive power, violence. Patently, however, there can also be force without authority. Power, as neutral guarantee of control, includes both concepts. As Dr. Hannah Arendt writes,

> The same [functional] argument is frequently used with respect to authority: if violence fulfills the same function as authority, namely makes people obey, then violence is authority . . . All those who call dictatorships "authoritarian," or mistake totalitarianism for an authoritative structure, implicitly have equated violence with authority.[14]

The question of legitimacy arises. Conversely, authority possesses power but is not barely to be equated with power, and it is fallacious to make the identification (perhaps especially when discussing the dialectical material power-philosophy of Marxism, however complicated by immaterial ideals of non-dominative "administration").

In another passage on the same page already quoted, Plamenatz continues:

> There has been for centuries a strong popular inclination towards anarchy; it has been more than balanced by an even stronger need for security, but has been nevertheless a considerable influence on many societies. Men need the protection of power, and all resent the burden it imposes; and the poorer they are, the less they need the protection and the more they feel the burdens.

The political synthesis of freedom and authority is here incomplete, and hence so is the explanation (although the helpful language of exchange on the market is used). The passage quoted does not

---

[14] "Authority in the Twentieth Century."

clarify *why* the poor have the alleged paradoxical interest in the anarchy of nonprotection. On the contrary, as recent trends have shown, the democratic electorate and especially the modern proletarians, like the ancient, have a strong interest in the security of employment which can be given by authority, even at the cost of other liberties. Earlier there was the interest of "the ruled" in security of the person, guaranteed through the courts. The objection then is not to authority and its power, but to a particular authority, for example, when, as for Adam Smith, the state is primarily a night-watchman protecting the possessors of private property against burglary, and offers less in the way of substantial rights to other citizens. The unorganized poor, especially in a society of warrior-power (notably equestrian warrior-power) or of finance-power, are weak bargainers in the market. They need protection but they do not get the goods; and they resent an authority which, while imposing the costs of restrictions and inviting support, provides goods desired by rival bargainers. Substantially the poor man has less freedom and less advantage in anarchy than the more powerful warrior-nobleman, and obtains less from near-anarchy or "anomie" than the rich, protected by minimal law, whose interest often is in *laissez-faire.* But the strength of these interest groups changes. Organized trade unions, as providers, replace the clumsier goods in sumptuary provisions made by local magistrates. The forces of power alter with the shift of politically effective support in the swing and chaffer of the market. In the modern, "other-directed" democracy of America, according to David Riesman's view in *The Lonely Crowd,* authority is shaped by the fact that the consumer controls the market, to use Riesman's own terminology.

Professor Guglielmo Ferrero, in his distinguished book *The Principles of Power* (1942), discusses further this issue of the legitimacy of power, once found dynastically under the influence of Talleyrand as the key to settlement at the Congress of Vienna. Now Ferrero finds it in the popular mandate, which is where Jefferson had placed it, in his letter of 1821 to Spencer: "All authority belongs to the people." Other authority is that of pretenders to recognition. What *ought* to be the whole people's guide or principle in using it is another matter, whether majority principle, individual rights, the law of nature and nations, compromise, revelation, or what. And the term "the people" can vary in meaning from the majority in Sybaris or Sodom to the consensus of humanity.

Whatever the judgment of "the people," or of its majority or stronger element, *ought* to be, at least we can say that legitimacy is, in part, a matter of actual recognition of a particular authority in its particular set-up or against the background of an overriding "constitutional morality." This itself is a matter of custom and actual recognition. Authority, as used in political science, is of its essence social and objective. Legitimacy is a name for wide, enduring recognition, flowing from the constitutional morality and modifying it, as a basis for law, stable order, and "habitual obedience." Today such wide recognition is normally tested by free elections, with alternatives; and its enduring quality by the repetition of the elections, whatever the momentary will, or madness, of the people to be bound to a dictator. (In my own view, the only complete democracy is, as once was accepted as axiomatic, a pure democracy of perpetual plebiscites or polls, to which rulers must listen. The technical difficulties visualized by Aristotle have vanished.) What we are saying in brief is that today "the mandate of heaven" is regarded as moving in accord with the *vox populi* and mass recognition — unlike the illegitimate situation in South Africa — and, when this recognition is enduring, as moving prudently. The task of a minority (apart from such commerce as it may conduct on its own) ought to be, maybe as educators or as an aristocracy or "clerisy," to persuade and invite, not to monopolize; and the opposite oligarchic structure will be technically unstable at this stage of popular consciousness. Just insofar as "the poor" are the majority, authority to be legitimate must primarily cater to these common men, "who have a claim to especial consideration" (*Rerum novarum,* 1891); but this ought not to nullify the individual rights (even despite Ferrero) of the minority — otherwise an unsatisfied market — or indeed the rights of the poor or destitute themselves, when they are only a minority.

5

The issue of wide recognition, and of persuasion and education of the majority and the minority, raises the question of what recognition is prudent and of what ought to enter into a far-sighted prudence. The question is no longer one of political science, but of political philosophy, in which it is improbable that we shall be able to prove any conclusions. To what pattern *ought* constitutional morality, as the over-all social form, and derivative authorities, as providers of rights, to conform in our judgment in order to secure recognition and clients? This is an issue not only of behavior and actuality but, as it touches width of recognition, an issue of education. It is an issue of the *kind* of goods which the truly prudent man will demand in society, allowing practically for what any actual authority is able to provide under the conditions. It is also, however, an issue of priorities in the support of authorities. What authority do we support most? This will determine our system or pattern. A picture is involved of our "good society." Mazzini, while himself offering an ideal fusion (which is unrealistic) of freedom and authority, quotes a passage from Louis Blanc which leaves authority out of the "good society," as contradictory to freedom. Blanc describes authority as "a principle that entrusts the life of nations to blindly accepted beliefs, to a superstitious respect for tradition, to inequality and that employs force as a means of government." This statement rightly seizes upon the abuse of functionless authority or monopoly of power, but verges upon the kind of argument which Bentham described as "bawling upon paper."

T. H. Green in his *Lectures on the Principles of Political Obligation,* though discarding the doctrine of social contract, argues that men have an obligation to obey political authority due directly to the social nature of man. No detour via contract is logically required; and the Robinson-Crusoe individualism of the contractualists is false. However, the revolutionary or radical reformer, the Marxist, the pacificist may all with passion uphold the doctrine of the social nature of man; but it does not follow that they will be impelled to obey some particular state authority. The ideal and the actual may be in conflict. Indeed the Marxist may urge that the proper course is to "smash" the actual organization, in the name of insurgent society. The question then is not that of social obligation in general but of obligation to a specific society in particular, the obligation of an individual and the obligation of a minority social group. We may urge that on a calculation established authority has a balance of advantage. But we may ask, with Marx, whether change, spurred by a different education, might not procure an even wider margin of advantage,

Many writers, especially, among the more recent, Dr. Erich Fromm in his *Man for Himself* (1948), have stressed a contrast between authority, and the authoritarian-educated personality, and "autonomy" or "self-realization," in the tradition of Green, Mill, von Humboldt, and Goethe. However, Dr. Fromm, in critical passages, himself adopts the position that every man shares both authoritarian or "externally dictated" and autonomous elements in the direction of his behavior. David Riesman makes a very modest plea, as a matter of degree, for "a more autonomous type." All too seldom asked here is what is the nature of the *nomos* for the autonomous personality, and what "self" ("real" or "actual") is "realized" or "improved." The Freudian answer is clear: the *nomos* is implanted or "in-built," as a super-ego, from an outside tradition. This, however, would certainly not be acceptable to Dr. Fromm, who would probably find the answer, with Archibald MacLeish, in man's own conscience — however we choose to define this — or in reason, which can expose the bad, narrow, or complacent conscience. Even if we (rightly) repudiate the position of the Kierkegaardian and fundamentalist writers, who deny the competence here of calculating reason and accept as authoritative a tradition, rejoicing in its paradoxes, it is intolerable to hold that reason is merely private. Hence we come back to the notion — as a canon of autonomy and self-realization, and in spite of certain existentialists who deplore "the tyranny of reason" — of an external and objective authority, although, as St. Thomas indicates, only such a one as our common natural reason, verifying natural law, can endorse.

The concept of "self-direction" (to such limited extent as this approximation to reason in direction ever can or ought to be the atomic "self") is highly aristocratic, as Milton shows clearly enough. Fromm denies that what a man feels to be his actual interest is an educated view of "his *true* self-interest." For many people, who are unprepared to go to the labor of adequately instructing their judgment or cultivating their reason, authority must necessarily, from lack of leisure, be in large measure what Riesman and Fromm describe as "other-direction." Insofar as this springs from strong community sentiment among ordinary folk or a neighborly pragmatic advice that confronts pretentiousness, itself "springing from the grass-roots," there is no need to deplore it. But, against rootless

mob sentiment and fear of "not getting on," the corrective is to replace such mass "other-direction," in Ortega's and Riesman's meaning, with a cultivated and rich "tradition-direction," "musical," in
the Greek sense, a Grand Tradition of history and civility, as I have
urged in my *History of the Political Philosophers,* as the authority
on values.

Dr. Hannah Arendt, in her paper in this volume, has argued that
authority — not simply as political means to individual or group
ends, even if it springs naturally from human life and its social im-
pulses, but as the deliberate confirmation of what is generally received as the pattern of the good society, an object of reverence and
duty, an *ought* which obligates and not merely a calculated means —
must spring from the *founding act.* Even if this act is not that of
some Platonic or Rousseauistic law-giver with a heroic aura, at least
it must be regarded as something beyond dispute in the history of the
particular society. To put it briefly, there has to be a founding myth
from which develop the national (or religious) pattern of the desirable, the tradition in education, the "public philosophy," the concept
of the *summum bonum.* As usual in ethics, we here enter into the
realm of speculation and the final aesthetic judgment, although history and anthropology can of course make their contribution. We
have, for example, what Ernst Cassirer calls "the myth of the state,"
by which he does not mean an illusion. Dr. Arendt herself chooses
to make the myth of Romulus and Remus and the founding of
Rome her outstanding illustration — although the dubious morality
of Romulus as a fratricide, emphasized by Augustine and by Pope
Gregory VII in his famous letter to Bishop Hermann of Metz,
somewhat weakens this particular illustration. The binding of the
Jewish people under the Covenant of the Law, as given by Moses
from Sinai, seems to offer a more telling instance, as do the divine
laws of Manu and the Koran.

Cassirer[15] shows indeed that these myths of authority are by no
means always healthy, whether they are strict state myths as in
Fascism or folk myths and "national patterns." The secular religions
— in many characteristics far more "religious" than the philoso-
phized and sublimated ancestor worship of Confucianism, for instance — such as the *mystiques* of the materialist dialectic and of

[15] Ernst Cassirer, *The Myth of the State* (1946).

race, are among the least healthy. We may indeed emphasize with
Cassirer that "since the times of Plato all great thinkers have made
the greatest efforts to find a rational theory of politics," and with
Cassirer aspire to escape from the "astrology" of politics into what
he terms a science positive and exact. (Personally I have more respect for Comte than, for example, Sir Isaiah Berlin showed in his
First Comte Memorial Lecture.) We may yet think that the reduction of political philosophy to a kind of "science of culture," such as
is the aspiration of the scientific humanists, is alike improbable and
even undesirable. The most we can say is that there is possibly a
natural basis for our degree of uniformity of aesthetic judgments.
But men will continue to develop their social myths, pictures, and
patterns, with their complementary rituals of behavior; and judgments on them cannot be equated with the methods of experimental
science. The final ends transcend calculations of means.

The social myths about the good society take the form of dramas,
and not least, of religious dramas. We do not, therefore, have to
say that intellectual comparison and analysis have here no place,
and to declare a bankruptcy or skepticism in political philosophy.
The five-and-forty tribal ways are not all equal; nor need we accept
historical relativism as the final word.[16] It is true that, beyond
calculations of advantage from authority or exaltations of individual responsibility in assessment of its correspondence with our
private moral ideals, there lie a conscious loyalty to our own
particular societies as such, and even a strong subconscious community feeling which does not reason about authority but accepts
it (just as many ages have accepted particular economic systems
as providential). We may learn from, but need not slavishly follow,
C. J. Jung about the basic nature of this feeling. What we may say
is that some social dramas of authority and tradition directions
are chiefly matters of ceremony and pomp; others reach deeper into
the collective memory of a people. And moreover, as among

[16] Plamenatz, pp. 30, 314, not only states, as he says in accord with Marx, that
"the proper study of man is not man but institutions" but that, while reciprocally
shaped by morals, these morals are "the moral codes prevailing in [men's various]
communities." He then comes near to the marsh of historical relativism himself,
thanks to an initial antipsychological error, incompatible with natural law and
concurrent with Marx's antihumanist theme (not sustained without contradiction),
that men and their wills are but jetsam on the stream of matter in dialectic flow.

peoples, some make little contribution to high civilization; others have had the genius to produce a drama (usually, as Toynbee says, a religious drama) which penetrates more subtly than others to the depths of the human spirit and interprets it. That interpretation shapes for us our picture of what the good society may be. It is an interpretation of an authority that tends to silence dispute, for as was said of a certain famous painting, "it is not it that is there to be judged."

Although I hesitate to attach so much importance as does Dr. Arendt to the historical founding act, as by Moses or in the Marxist religion of Lenin, I concur with her presentation of the relation of authority on ends with the myth as concrete focus or *désir collectif personifié* and, in its completest form, as historical incarnation. The comparison between one vision and another will, first, be of a simple aesthetic character concerning how far it satisfies. Here the uncorrupted and unsophisticated judgment may be best. How far does the social picture involve revolting inhumanities, of which no talk of destiny can obscure the ugliness? Nevertheless, there is an educated and desirable sophistication in judgment, the judgment of musicians of music, of which Plato spoke. The profoundest dramas of humanity must satisfy its taste. Nor can I accept the criticism made on Wittgenstein, that the aesthetic judgment is merely speculative or contemplative, whereas the ethical judgment is practical and one of action. The theoretic judgment in aesthetics is still empathic, and moves to action and to the assessment of it.

What, however, it may be objected, have the plays of Shakespeare about the dignity and tragedy of kings or the Eleusinian mysteries to do with authority? The answer is that Shakespeare's plays, although concerned with the human condition and seeming to bear a message of tolerance, do not, unlike the work of Goethe and Dante, come to a focus in their picture of man and his society. The greatest social myths must subsume the nature of power as well as of pity. Dante does this when he gives the answer that power is not neutral, but good, when it is the divine power which is also love, placed above hell, a love which by its order rules the stars. The founding act here is placed in the macrocosmos, as the act of creation of the cosmos itself, which the human microcosm can reflect. Authority archetypally lies in natural law, supremely willed. All authority lies on high (and not below, save as it touches the choice of mundane means), because it is placed in reason, which is no more democratic than is mathematics. And its service is freedom, because the illuminated will must seek to accord itself to that reality, which prevails over obstacles, if not by "dialectic," then by logic of the *logos*. This picture, which Dante learned from St. Thomas, the ethical judgment of some may repudiate in favor of some more pragmatic structure which sees the authentic ends of the good society solely in promoting the means of education for information, health, wealth, and more technical power. But no reputable philosopher can ignore it.

9. Authority, Progress, and Colonialism

WOLFGANG H. KRAUS

It has been well observed, most recently by B. de Jouvenel,[1] that the conception of the absolute monarchy most dramatically set forth and embodied by Louis XIV was revolutionary in its repudiation of the old limitation of reason and natural laws which had long constituted an essential element in the pattern of legitimate public authority. Yet, for a while, until the age of the eighteenth-century revolutions, European society would continue to accept legitimate authority as an agency strongly personal in character, pretty securely rooted in the complex web of hereditary and traditional status, privilege, and obligation which maintained the social order in the face of increasingly severe strains. The new absolutism was a major challenge, deepening the latent crisis of confidence which belongs to the climate of opinion of the Enlightenment.

Two developments roughly coincide in time with the forging of the new absolutism, one in the realm of government practice, · the other in that of ideas; both of them illuminate, directly and indirectly, the growing quandary of legitimate traditional authority. One involves the increasing institutionalization of personal monarchial authority. The other relates to certain aspects of the evolving doctrine of progress.

The institutionalization of the monarchy had, of course, been

[1] *De la Souveraineté* (1955), pp. 239ff.

under way for centuries. The requirements of a broadening range of public activity, both at home and abroad, the setting up of military establishments, and the like, had all made the contemporaries increasingly conscious of a problem which Spinoza, for instance, formulates in these terms:

They are very much mistaken who suppose that one man *can* by himself hold the supreme right of a commonwealth. For the only limit of right is power. But the power of one man is very inadequate to support so great a load. And hence it arises, that the man, whom the multitude has chosen king, looks out for himself, [a] general, or councillors, or friends, to whom he entrusts his own and the common welfare; so that the dominion, which is thought to be a perfect monarchy, is *in actual working an aristocracy, not indeed an open but a hidden one, and therefore worst of all . . .*[2]

What makes this comment relevant here is Spinoza's emphasis upon some sort of informal delegation and division of labor in the managing of matters of state, and the contention that this normally leads to a dispersal of power and the diminution of true authority in favor of an aristocratic cabal — an authority which, as he stresses elsewhere, in the case of monarchial rule should be within the grasp of one who "should be something above average humanity, or should strive to get himself accepted as such."[3]

The risk of sharing the substance of power with councilors and thus impairing the majesty of unified authority had preoccupied James I, troubled Louis XIV, and it would still preoccupy Frederick II of Prussia in the eighteenth century. It is this atmosphere which develops to the highest degree a concern for mysteries of state, for secrecy which would long endure. It springs not only from a justifiable fear of external rivals, but also from the deep need of this type of authority to maintain that exclusiveness and social distance which would keep the common man in awe; even so the suspicion and ridicule of the intellectuals were mounting, never to be stifled again:

[2] *Tractatus Politicus,* ch. VI, secs. 5–8, in *Writings on Political Philosophy by Benedict de Spinoza,* ed. A. G. A. Balz (1937), pp. 115f. Emphasis added.
[3] *Tractatus Theologico-Politicus,* ch. V, in Balz, pp. 25f.

it is far better for the right counsels of a dominion to be known to its enemies, than for the evil secrets of tyrants to be concealed from the citizens. They who can treat secretly of the affairs of a dominion have it absolutely under their authority, and, as they plot against the enemy in time of war, so do they against the citizens in time of peace. Now that this secrecy is often serviceable to a dominion, no one can deny; but that without it the said dominion cannot subsist, no one will ever prove.[4]

The Sun King, in what Schevill has called his "Gallicly flavored version of the papal baroque," [5] zealously seeks to uphold the principle of personal rule. Thus he formulates methods by which, he believes, the emergence of a first minister or the banding together of any powerful group of principal councilors can be avoided: the King "must know his business thoroughly," so that he does not come to "depend" on those who serve him. He should divide his trust among several persons, and this will bring on rivalry among them: "the jealousy of one serves often as a restraint to the ambition of the others . . ." [6]

Coupling the panoply and circumstance of baroque majesty with the carefully calculated manipulation of its minions was meant to safeguard the personal and dynastic charisma. In a developing scheme of a governmental division of labor it might also be seen, by hindsight, to convert the Most Christian King of France into a general manager of the system. The King's last-ditch efforts to extricate himself from the toils of the government machine and to restore the image of personal mastery over it were bound to become a target of the opposition. "The King," writes the Huguenot leader P. Jurieu, "has taken the place of the state. It is the service and the interest of the King, it is the preservation of the provinces and property of the King. Finally, the King is everything, the State is no longer anything." [7] While Louis XIV could not possibly conceive of a lack of royal capacity to achieve this goal, Frederick II of Prussia would later urge his successor that while the ruler

---

[4] Spinoza, *Tractatus Politicus,* ch. VII, sec. 29, p. 144.

[5] Cf. also C. J. Friedrich, *The Age of the Baroque* (1952), ch. VII.

[6] Supplement of the Memoirs of 1666, quoted by Henri Sée, *Les idées politiques en France au XVIIme siècle* (1923), p. 133.

[7] Pierre Jurieu in his *Soupirs de la France esclave,* 1689, quoted from G. H. Dodge, *The Political Theory of the Huguenots of the Dispersion* (1947), p. 150.

really should retain the conduct of business in his own hands, he might, if he felt he lacked the ability altogether, have to designate a first minister to take on this essential unifying function.[8]

The main responses to this development are too well known to require much elaboration. Two important phases will illustrate our point. The doctrine of the separation of powers repudiates the new exaltation of unlimited authority; it is also its obverse, in both the aspects here suggested. In one aspect, it elevates the judicious dispersal of the powers hitherto assembled and usable at the arbitrary whim of these rulers into a principle, so as to limit (or weaken) an authority which has gone out of bounds. In its other aspect, it counters the latent notion that the complex new machinery of government with its somewhat haphazard division of labor requires a firmly controlling hand, a masterful royal manager, with the idea of a simple and apparently practical division into three main functions and the suggestion (aided by the traditional precept of socially mixed government) that a sweetly rational equipoise would normally prevail as regulator among the functional groups of government.

While this response emphasizes the need for curbing and reducing legitimate authority, it also denies, at least by implication, the inherent charismatic superiority of anointed rulers. The first response goes much farther and is not often clearly articulated until Rousseau's doctrine of the general will calls for a new legitimate authority and denies the validity of the old.

Yet three-quarters of a century before, in justifying the Glorious Revolution, Pierre Jurieu made claims for the legitimacy of an absolute popular will, as unlimited by any higher reason as was Louis XIV's very own. Defending the British Convention Parliament, Jurieu declared that there were some forms and procedures which, in order to be legitimate,

[8] Frederick's cruder father, Frederick William I, bluntly stated to the Saxon King's accredited envoy that rather than use as ministers people of rank and merit who often "refuse to carry out orders blindly," he would in future turn to "ordinary persons, yapping little dogs, less intent on their honor, whom you can push around without getting them angry." See H. Hausherr, *Verwaltungseinheit und Ressorttrennung* (1953), p. 11.

need not be established by laws and by the terms of the law; absolute necessity alone renders them rightful . . . it is not a question even of knowing if the nation was right at bottom in all this. For even if it were wrong it is necessary that there be a certain authority in communities, which is not obliged to be right in order to make its acts valid. But this authority is only in the nations [peoples].[9]

While this declaration greatly exceeds Rousseau's position (which is tempered by his faith in the rational infallibility of the general will), it constitutes a clear equivalent of Louis XIV's contemporary royal positivism. Thus are laid the intellectual foundations for the making of a future system of institutionalized authority, based on a new legitimacy.

The idea of progress begins to contribute most effectively to the ferment spreading since the latter part of the seventeenth century. The heated French controversy between the "Ancients" and the "Moderns" over the crucial issue whether the authority of classical literary standards should remain binding in perpetuity, helps to center attention on much more far-reaching questions. The dominance of theological authority over knowledge had of course been challenged ever since late scholasticism. Renaissance humanism had put the authority of the ancients on a pedestal, recognizing the *auctoritas majorum* in the arts and letters very broadly, including such practical knowledge as the law. The scientific revolution of the sixteenth and the seventeenth centuries and its application to technological change forced re-examination. Pascal, in his *Fragment of a Treatise on Vacuum*[10] distinguishes between types of knowledge capable of being informed by authority and those that clearly are not. He then proceeds to point out that the ancients were elevated to the rank of authority because posterity treated them with greater deference than they had treated their own ancestors. And not only does "each individual man progress from day to day in the sciences, but mankind as a whole constantly progresses in proportion as the universe grows older . . . So that the whole suc-

[9] Jurieu's Eighteenth Pastoral Letter, quoted (in translation) from G. H. Dodge, *Political Theory of the Huguenots of the Dispersion*, pp. 66f.

[10] See F. J. Teggart and G. H. Hildebrand, eds., *The Idea of Progress: A Collection of Readings* (1949), pp. 164ff.

cession of men, throughout the course of so many centuries, should be envisaged as the life of a single man who persists forever and learns continually." B. de Fontenelle[11] adds the proposition that there was no reason for believing that the talents of the ancients could not at least be equaled in succeeding generations. At the conclusion of the debate such diverse strands as the principle of an order of nature of which man is a part, the faith in the continuous emergence of creative individuals in society, and the suggestive analogy of the life of the individual and the race as a whole had been fused into a fervent belief in the possibility of unlimited advance.

These aspirations, assembled into a program, are most movingly set forth by Condorcet under the shadow of the revolutionary terror. Knowledge itself, liberated from the control of both the ancients and the theologians, is to become the fundamental activating principle by which a mediocre present lays the foundations of a golden future, with or without the blessings of public authority. This principle of progressive knowledge is, in fact, incompatible with the contemporary principle of exclusive authority, with its insistence upon submission and conformity. What Condorcet calls that desired equality in instruction and diffusion of knowledge

excludes all dependence, whether forced or voluntary . . . , the entire mass of a people can be instructed in all that they have need of knowing . . . for the administration of their affairs, and for the free development of their industry and their faculties . . . that they may not depend blindly on those to whom they are obliged to confide the care of their affairs or the exercise of their rights; that they may be in a position to choose them and to watch over them.[12]

Thus, while repudiating the rude external sovereign authority of the old regime which had long lost its vaunted and jealously guarded capacity for leadership, the theory of progress, intimately associated with that of constitutional liberalism, projects an image of a new and once more rationally bound authority. To the conservatives of the reaction, it spells the end of all authority. Small wonder

[11] In his *Digressions sur les Anciens et les Modernes;* see Teggart and Hildebrand, p. 187.

[12] From his *Historical Sketch of the Progress of the Human Mind,* in Teggart and Hildebrand, pp. 321ff.

that now those like de Maistre give voice to the indictment that authority had been subverted by a conspiracy of the intellectuals, the heretical prophets of progress. Yet, as the concept and practice of the old regime's authority crumble under the impact of Enlightenment and Revolution, they are, in a sense, put together again to function within the rapidly expanding system of colonial rule over nonwestern peoples. There was, of course, no lack of precedent. The opening up of the Americas by the Spaniards since the sixteenth century had given rise to an exercise of authority over indigenous peoples of a different culture almost unrestrained and unrelieved for long periods, despite the efforts of some notable men to re-examine the assumptions and purposes of a rule in such alien conditions. Now, during the course of the eighteenth century and after, large communities of Asian and then African peoples were to come under colonial dominion, in an age when, by a curious historical coincidence, the image and role of authority were undergoing a rapid transformation in all the colonizing "mother countries."

Under what conditions did this new complex of authority come into being? Colonization involved the contact, sometimes casual and peaceful, often aggressive and violent, between peoples of different cultures, with the colonizers blandly assuming the superiority of theirs. To give force to his contention that the East India Company merely administered a trust, Edmund Burke sought to dispel this view with respect to India. He likened India to the German Empire and described its people as "forages civilized and cultivated — activated by all the arts of polished life, whilst we were yet in the woods." [13] It was an assumption of superiority generally backed by superior force and technology and frequently found acceptable for extended periods by the peoples under control.[14]

[13] In discussing Fox's East India Bill: see R. Hoffman and P. Levack, *Burke's Politics* (1949), p. 260.

[14] This assumption of superiority is still natural to a modern humanitarian religious mind like Albert Schweitzer, who is quoted as saying: "Am I to treat the black man as my equal or as my inferior? I must show him that I can respect the dignity of human personality in everyone . . . The Negro is a child, and with children nothing can be done without the use of authority . . . With regard to the Negroes, then, I have coined the formula: I am your brother, it is true, but your elder brother" (as reported in *Dissent,* vol. 3, no. 3, Summer 1956, p. 247).

Furthermore, colonialism involved establishment of agencies of government on the spot, usually at vast distances from the government of the home country. Thus, the local rulers became to the people whose lives they directed the sole symbol of authority. They appeared as representatives often not only of faraway overlords from whom they held office, but at times also of the old rulers of the country whom they had displaced or superseded (and who were sometimes permitted to carry on a shadowy semblance of their old majesty). Thus there developed the characteristic and ubiquitous phenomenon of the colonial governor who,

> to the inhabitant of such a colony appears as an alien autocrat backed by the prestige and physical might of the dominant powers. This does not imply that he will be an unpopular figure. When a community's history has been one of tribal wars, of oppression by stronger enemies and of technological backwardness, a powerful protector is generally welcome. The greater and more openly apparent his power, the higher the regards he elicits from oppressed masses.[15]

The institution recalls the setting and the growth of authority in the West in earlier stages.

Hand in hand with this goes the special and privileged position, not only of the lower agents of public authority, but of the western settlers, normally very small minorities both in Asian and in African colonial development. The circumstances of their coming, the differences of culture and of color, make them as a group, both officials and nonofficials, the extensions of emanations of an often distant authority. Obviously, this occurs in different degree and in different form under various colonial regimes and is always affected by the level of culture in the host society. Yet, by and large, even the nonofficial residents can be said to form the outer fringe of an alien authority which, in all its elements, typically contrives to maintain a considerable social distance between itself and its subjects. The representative quality of officialdom comes out vividly in Lord Lugard's description of a British district officer in Africa:

> The British officer comes of a class which has made and maintained the British Empire . . . His assets are usually a public school and probably

---

[15] T. R. Adams, *Modern Colonialism* (1955), pp. 29f.

a university education, neither of which have hitherto furnished him with an appreciable amount of positive knowledge adapted for his work. But they have produced an English gentleman with an almost passionate conception of fair play, of protection of the weak, of "playing the game": they have taught him personal initiative and resource, and how to command and obey . . .[16]

The description suggests a catalogue of valuable qualities required of a bearer of authority. Whether it makes that authority acceptable and legitimate would depend on the values and responses peculiar to the indigenous community. The foreigner's lack of easy communication and instinctive communion with those under his guidance would, in John Stuart Mill's opinion, tempt him to despise the natives and prompt the natives to disbelieve that "anything the strangers do can be intended for their good." [17] Surely until most recent times, precisely this unavoidable yet characteristic lack of adequate communication and understanding has been a distinctive component of the colonial condition, especially conspicuous in the relation between the indigenous community and the people of the ruling power and its home authority.

If due allowance is made for his assumptions, some of which are no longer ours, Mill's remarks of a hundred years ago still go to the heart of the matter:

To govern a country under responsibility to the people of that country, and to govern a country under responsibility to the people of another, are two very different things. What makes the excellence of the first is that freedom is preferable to despotism: but the last *is* despotism. The only choice the case admits is a choice of despotisms: and it is not certain that the despotism of twenty millions is necessarily better than that of a few, or of one. But it is quite certain that the despotism of those who neither hear nor see, nor know anything about their subjects, has many chances of being worse than that of those who do . . .[18]

All told, the difficulty of communication points up the dilemma of an authority derived from and part of the fabric of responsible

---

[16] Lord Lugard, *The Dual Mandate in Africa,* pp. 131f., quoted from D. C. Sommervell and H. Harvey, *British Empire and Commonwealth* (1954), p. 303.

[17] *Representative Government,* ch. XVIII; see *Utilitarianism, Liberty, Representative Government* (Everyman ed.), p. 384.

[18] *Representative Government,* p. 383.

government at home, maintaining something much less than responsible government in the colony. The dilemma results in an exercise of authority which, whatever its intention, must in due course appear to have elements of arbitrariness, caprice, irrationality, and even malevolence in the eyes of its subjects. At length there emerges an image of authority in the colonial world as an increasingly vast institutionalized apparatus, extending from the "mother country" into the ranks of officialdom and "colons" in the colony, led by mighty dignitaries whose will is law, and separated by the uniform of color and the troubles of understanding from the mass of its subjects. Here, in a new guise, is a reincarnation of the authority which had become obsolescent in the West.

The system is confronted with a new element in evolving colonialism. Early colonial rule had, quite characteristically, limited its activities to those without which the possession would not yield returns or might rapidly deteriorate: maintaining peace and order and collecting revenue. But times, needs, and colonial theories underwent change. The task of developing colonial societies and their resources made it imperative to advance education, disseminate knowledge and thus, sometimes deliberately (as in India) and sometimes inadvertently, to spur the growth of modern, assimilated indigenous elites. From these groups would come the people who were capable and willing to assume whatever share of the "white man's burden" they might be permitted to bear.

This released energies not unlike those which had brought on the transformation of authority in its western setting. The story is familiar. The modern indigenous elites of the nineteenth and twentieth centuries were absorbing the seminal ideas of the eighteenth and nineteenth centuries. The doctrines of progress, liberal constitutionalism, democracy and nationalism, and eventually of socialism and communism were taking root, through the medium of literature and "useful knowledge." Henceforth questions, many of them already voiced by oppositional opinion in the "mother countries," are raised, first hesitantly and apologetically, by the elite who are turning from "native friends of authority" into popular leaders. Can a paternal authority exercised at a distance through alien officials be informed by the people's needs? Are not the demands of interest groups in the "mother country" and of settlers in the colony receiving more consideration than the welfare of the people? Can or will an alien authority ever take measures which will promote colonial welfare but hurt domestic interests? How can lasting progress be achieved except through the active and unfettered participation of the dependent people in their own public affairs?

In the long drawn-out process of denying the validity or timeliness of such questions and deriding the qualifications of the questioners, the authority of colonial regimes was worn threadbare.

It is only a quarter of a century ago that Mr. Churchill called it alarming and also nauseating to see Mr. Gandhi, a seditious Middle Temple lawyer, now posing as a fakir of a type well known in the East, striding half-naked up the steps of the Viceregal palace, while he is still organizing and conducting a defiant campaign of civil disobedience, to parlay on equal terms with the representative of the King-Emperor . . . It can only encourage all the forces . . . hostile to British authority . . . The Indian National Congress . . . represent neither the numbers, the strength, nor the virtue of the Indian people. They merely represent those Indians who have acquired a veneer of Western civilization, and have read all those books about democracy which Europe is now beginning increasingly to discard.[19]

In the place of the old colonial authority — and usually employing elements of its machinery — a new authority, that of indigenous revolutionary Asian and African elites, is coming to life. These groups are turning into true founders or rebuilders of their communities. Coming into their own, they have learned to give at least symbolic or formal deference to the *mores* and *auctoritas* of their tradition; but not so much that it would prevent them from freely borrowing from the no longer so alien West whatever is vital to their task of founding and developing. Yet, here too, they must be circumspect lest it appear that they are indiscriminate imitators of alien authority and its values. When, a number of years ago, a West African political organization demanded the election of representatives to serve in legislative councils, it wished to have this point clearly understood: in demanding the franchise, it stated, the people of West Africa are "not asking to be allowed

[19] Speech of February 29, 1931, in Eric Williams, *Documents Illustrating the Development of Civilization* (Howard University, Washington), vol. III (1948), p. 461.

to copy a foreign institution," rather, they wish to preserve and apply principles of elective representation traditionally used in the family and tribal order of West Africa.[20]

This generation of founding fathers, the Gandhis, the Nehrus, the Nkrumas, Jinnahs, Kotelawalas, and Bandaranaikes,[21] are citizens of two civilizations which they seek to weld into something new. They have long understood that the prolonged association of western and nonwestern peoples has induced far-reaching social, economic, and cultural changes whose extent and direction only a handful of leaders can assess. The generation of founders, having broken away from the moorings and traditions of imperial authority, has, in substance or at times in form, turned to the people for democratic legitimacy and proposes to infuse engrafted institutions with the spirit of their national future.

[20] "Memorandum from National Congress of West Africa to the Secretary of State for the Colonies" (1920), in Williams, *Documents Illustrating the Development of Civilization*, III, 483.

[21] The name of Solomon West Ridgeway Dias Bandaranaike, Prime Minister of Ceylon since 1956, is symbolic of the process: his first name is his father's; West Ridgeway was a British Governor of Ceylon much admired by Sir Solomon; Dias recalls the earlier Portuguese period of Ceylon. The whole name spells out a successful political leader who, raised as a Christian, chose to turn to Buddhism, his people's dominant religion.

PART THREE

Authority in Socio-political Perspective

10. Authority: The Efficient Imperative

BERTRAND DE JOUVENEL

The polyvalence of individual words is a boon to the literary writer, but not to the scientific. Our claim to be political "scientists" is currently denied by other scientists, and not without reason. We lack the first requisite of a science — a vocabulary of uniquely defined terms. The difficulty of endowing our political words with unambiguous meanings is of course great, because we share our vocabulary with political operators, who have a vested interest in ambiguity. Nobody can gain by twisting the meaning of the word "cycloid": it is not so in the case of the word "democracy." As the audience of political operators is very much larger than that of political scientists, the words we wish to use neatly come back to us glittering with many facets. Against this we have two means of defense: one is to mint completely new coins but these will also circulate on the hustings, and be debased; the other is to bind ourselves to use words only in acceptations agreed among ourselves. The scope of the present paper is quite modest: it is merely to propose a definition of the term "authority."

THE EFFICIENT IMPERATIVE

Let us start with a social phenomenon open to our observation at all times and everywhere. An agent A formulates an imperative statement; thereupon the action indicated in the statement is performed by an agent B or a set of Bs. Compliance of the Bs establishes for the observer an empirical relation, namely, that for the complying Bs, A's statement has proved an *efficient imperative*. If we find this process regularly repeated between the same agents, we shall feel inclined to say that A has a certain power to move the Bs, or again that he enjoys a certain authority over them: at this stage we need not pick our terms.

This power or authority has three dimensions: it is *extensive* if the complying Bs are many; it is *comprehensive* if the variety of actions to which A can move the Bs is considerable; finally it is *intensive* if the bidding of A can be pushed far without loss of compliance. It seems important to introduce this notion of intensity at an early stage. No power relationship is of unlimited intensity; there is always a point at which compliance breaks down, and it is at different stages for the different Bs.

Bidding and complying fall within the general pattern of human relationships, that is, suggestion and response. But bidding and complying differ from bargaining. In bargaining, A offers to perform a certain action *a*. This is a proposition which is either taken up or left alone or over which haggling may occur. However B responds, his response is prepared by a process of weighing in his mind whether the benefit to him of *a*, the action promised by A, is greater than the inconvenience to him of performing the action *b*. Therefore in the bargaining relationship, the response of B is mediated through a rational process.

This process is completely different in kind from the immediate response to A's imperative. All too many political authors, and indeed some of the greatest, have sought to make the relation of bidding and complying a special case of the bargaining relationship. Since in the case of the efficient imperative, no *quid pro quo* is mentioned, these authors have pulled in an imaginary *quid:* the "social contract" writers, for instance, will have it that B weighs against the inconvenience of complying the advantage to him of the social bond or his once-for-all "contracting-in." This is purely imaginary. Others will have it that B weighs against the inconvenience of the performance demanded of him the retaliation which A can mete out to him in case of refusal. The cases in which this fear, *metus,* intervenes cover but a very small area of the manifestations of the efficient imperative. We shall deal with

them. The point to be made now is that bidding and compliance
are a phenomenon *sui generis*.

Political authors have concerned themselves almost exclusively
with the relations between the sovereign and the subjects in an
established commonwealth. Then of course A is in a position to
reward compliance and to punish noncompliance. Even though
no inducement or threat is contained in A's imperative statement,
all Bs know that A has means of rewarding or punishing, and
there is no doubt that this "aura" of possibilities inherent in the
sovereign contributes to his being obeyed. It is, however, a major
error to regard the phenomenon of compliance as basically rooted
in the feeling of fear. This would fail to explain a great many
phenomena of compliance and, further, would fail to explain whence
the means to threaten originated at the outset of political relations.

Let us now consider the great many cases in which we find compliance while A, the formulator of the imperative, has no means to
reward or punish. He may, however, bear some outward signs
which impress the Bs. For instance, A sits in a certain place, or
bears certain stripes, or wears a certain hat, and the Bs are used
to executing imperatives formulated by people thus sitting or thus
adorned. Insofar as we shall find that B's compliance is due to
association with these trappings, we shall say that the authority
exercised by A is *derived authority*.

Finally we divest A of these trappings. Not only has he no means
of bribing or threatening, but further, his prestige is not built up
by any accessories. If then he obtains B's compliance, we find a
pure relation of authority. Such a relation exists by our definition
whenever B does A's bidding without A's enjoyment of any en-
dowment whereby he may bribe or threaten B or any superadded
prestige.

Is it important to focus attention upon such a relation? I believe
that nothing is more important to our science, that here we come
to the fundamental element upon which the whole complex fabric
of society is reared.

THE GENEALOGY OF ESTABLISHED AUTHORITY

Political science has all too long dwelt upon a massive and ancient construction, the State. Why do subjects do the bidding of men whom as individuals they quite often admire or respect? Because civil obedience is second nature? Granted. How did it so become? Because initially subjects feared the punishment meted out by their ruler? Question: whence did the ruler secure the means of punishing insubordination? The Austinian genealogy of civil obedience resting upon acquired respect sired by initial fear of punishment will not do. The formation of the power to punish remains unexplained. Hobbes, who fostered this view, perceived that the first stage in the process was lacking, and filled in the void by the supposition of an initial agreement to endow the ruler with the means to punish. But such an agreement is a fiction. The reasoning which might lead men to make such a covenant postulates a vision of their long-range interest, which is not a universal feature even of our most advanced commonwealths, as Hume pointed out.

An enormous amount of intellectual effort, and of the highest quality, has been wasted on imagining the prehistory of the State while it is easy to watch the emergence of power relationships in our day and age. The birth of any association displays the building power of pure authority as we defined it.

It is a legal fiction that an association arises out of an encounter of wills. The founding members are assumed to have had the same notion at the same time and to have thus met upon common ground and coalesced naturally. But things do not happen that way. There must be an individual who takes the initiative, who calls others together, and prevails upon them (or some of them) to join with him. Thus, at the inception of a body politic of any kind, there is a relationship of pure authority.

The duration, growth, and success of the body generates in its members a loyalty toward *it,* and whenever the inceptor drops out, the historical loyalty lends prestige to the inheritor of his position who thus enjoys derived authority. Finally the means which are placed at the disposal of the body's ruler allow him to reward or punish the performance of members. Logically, this comes last and not first.

A CONFLICT OF AUTHORITIES

If we picture things this way, we must immediately recognize that conflict is a necessary feature of human society and that it is in essence a conflict of authorities. It is a vital necessity of civilization that bodies politic should endure. If companies of men had always fallen apart at the death of their convener, mankind would never have risen above predatory roaming. Securing a long lease of life to corporate entities has been one of the major achievements of our species and has been a fundamental condition of our other achievements.

But the relative endurance of bodies breeds problems. Consider the organized bodies in existence at a given moment with their appointed leaders. These leaders enjoy what we may call composite authority, an authority into which enters their own raw capacity of obtaining compliance, the prestige they derive from their status in the organization, and the powers with which their control of the organization provides them. At the same time, there are, footloose as it were within society, a number of people who have the naked capacity of mustering assent, of causing others to follow their suggestions. These people have an inherent tendency to pull down existing fabrics in order to build up new aggregates.

Is this a restatement of Pareto's well-known theme, "the circulation of elites"? No: Pareto's argument is that unless social ladders are provided whereby the gifted may rise to the top, they will wreck the existing structures. If this were the only problem, then the solution would be simple at least in principle; it would be enough to provide free competition for the leading positions. But it is not the case that the "new men" only want to run the existing bodies, nor are they necessarily the best qualified to do so. They may call upon men to do other things than those which are being done, and their appeal may cut right across the existing bodies. There is very little reason to believe that either Lenin or Hitler would have been quite happy and competent as the president of a big corporation in his particular country.

Such notorious examples are cited only for the sake of clarity, but the very same problem arises in the workroom of a plant, where men are subject to the formal authority of a supervisor but

come under the informal spell of one of their number, who may
not necessarily wish to take the place and perform the functions of
the supervisor. Formal and informal authority are potentially at
war at all levels of society, a fact amply recognized by American
sociology. I wonder if political science does not blur it by reason
of its vocabulary.

AUTHORITY AND THE INDIVIDUAL: A FALSE PROBLEM

During the last few years we have had an enormous volume
of discussion on the theme "Authority and the Individual," sometimes stated as "Authority and Freedom." I submit that the problem
is wrongly stated. I have yet to meet the individual who moves
freely on a field where the only prohibited areas and mandatory
paths are those traced by the state — the individual who, but for
these public restrictions, runs his life entirely by a continual process
of bilateral bargaining with his fellows. The individual whom I
can see is institution-ridden and institution-supported. The whole
social field is built over with structures of various natures, offering goods, services, positions, and posting up the conditions on
which they will deliver these goods or confer these positions; and
with no one of these structures can the individual haggle: it is not
for him to discuss the conditions of his joining either the staff of
General Motors or the Union of Automobile Workers. This is a
universe of posted prices, in the most general meaning of the
word "price." And it is highly doubtful whether any other kind
of social universe can exist.

Understanding of this is widespread, as such terms as "adjust-
ing," "fitting-in" testify. The individual per se moves within this
organized world, reaching the goal he has chosen insofar as he has
taken the paths provided and satisfied the conditions. The individual
cannot fight an organization unless he happens to be at the head
of another organization (say Walter Reuther), or unless he initiates
a move among his fellows (say John Hampden).

It is therefore clear that social conflict is in essence a conflict of
authorities. We may find an established authority clashing with
another established authority: the classic example is the fight between emperor and pope in the Middle Ages. Or we may find
an unrecognized authority raising a powerful wind against an

established authority: the classic example is provided by Luther. Far be it from me to argue that everything which occurs is the work of strong personalities, though I think it is much greater than we like to admit. It is irrelevant to my purpose to discuss whether the genesis of a drive is due in greater measure to the dispositions of the Bs, the *causa materialis,* or to the call of A, the *causa efficiens.* It might be quite interesting to show by the confrontation of different instances, that the relative importance of the *causa materialis* and of the *causa efficiens* varies considerably from case to case, and one might be tempted to comparisons with chemical reactions, some of which set in only under the influence of a very specific catalytic agent while others develop under the impact of almost any shock. Such fancies may be suggestive and may be also misleading.

All that matters for my purpose is to stress the role of the efficient imperative. For purposes of illustration it has been necessary to cite instances of imperatives which have had gigantic results, which have gone down in history. This choice of illustrations should not obscure the fact that the efficient imperative is manifested every day in the most minute phenomena of social life.

CONSERVATISM AND LIBERALISM

This view leads us to a classification of human societies. Commanding suggestions may arise anywhere in a society, and we can regard them under two aspects: their origin and their character.

The extreme conservative feels that commanding suggestions should arise only from properly appointed sources, and that the character of each should be ever the same. Without question this provides maximum regularity. It should be stressed that nothing is further from totalitarianism: first, the appointed sources in such a system will be very diverse, and each will have its proper scope; second, the intensity of command will be experienced as very slight since the performances demanded are customary. Once more, to avoid any ambiguity, extreme conservatism is characterized by a dual constancy of imperative statements; constancy of sources and constancy of contents. In other words again, the members of such a society are told what to do (and what to avoid) by voices ever originating from the same places and saying the same things. It is obvious that under such circumstances, these voices, unaffected by the passage of time, must come to be regarded as starting timeless obligations. In other words, the voice of authorities is the very voice of social conscience. (For me social conscience is a shape which custom gives to the sense of obligation, innate in man.)

The extreme conservative arrangement has been described in positive terms. But it is just as valid, and more convenient, to describe it in negative terms: stating that commanding suggestions should not arise from unacknowledged sources or be of a novel character. Let the first exclusion be rule one and the other, rule two. When the proposition is so stated, it appears that an extreme conservative arrangement is practically impossible. For it must happen at some moment that a person invested with authority makes a commanding suggestion which is not hallowed by custom: he is thus breaking rule two. Rule two remains broken unless this innovating leader finds himself contradicted by someone who moves his fellows to disobey the imperative issuing from a seat of authority; and this contradictor may himself not be seated in a place of authority: therefore he is breaking rule one. This situation is by no means imaginary: the Bible offers instances of the bold king commanding something out of the ordinary, and of a prophet arising to condemn him. Therefore a system of extreme conservatism, such as we defined it, is not self-conservative. It is a pure concept of the mind.

The extreme liberal view is the exact converse of the extreme conservative view. Anyone may formulate an imperative statement, whatever his place is in society, and this statement may have any content. Such is the theoretical basis of our society. Without any title or office, I have the right to formulate a commanding suggestion and this suggestion may be anything. Further, with very few exceptions (and this is a legal point of considerable interest), I shall never be guilty by virtue of my commanding suggestion, while those who shall do my bidding may be guilty for having performed at my suggestion actions which are formally illegal.[1]

[1] In French law, it is a general rule that suggestions are per se innocent. This rule has been impaired only by special statutes adopted at the time of anarchist bomb-throwing at the turn of the last century, which are practically never invoked. On the

This throws considerable light upon what we so clumsily call "a free society." [2] It is in fact a society where members are equally entitled to utter commanding suggestions, and where they are free to utter any such suggestions. The inherent possibilities of such a system are softened by the unequal readiness of individuals to adopt suggestions by reason of the latter's origin or nature. A commanding suggestion originated by a recognized authority has an advantage over the suggestion originated by a mere individual, and a suggestion which by its nature runs counter to custom or belief has a slender chance of acceptance. Nonetheless, every man is allowed to issue the imperative. Every man is entitled to be the generator of other men's actions.

THE SELECTIONS OF IMPERATIVES

From the foregoing statement it follows that a liberal society is one in which the selection of imperatives is achieved by those to whom the imperative statements are addressed. Every one of us is a potential A, capable of uttering commanding suggestions. And every one of us is a B, who chooses between a number of such suggestions. These suggestions may be materially incompatible, or worse, they may be morally conflicting.

It is therefore of immense importance to study the conditions of response to imperative statements. When and why does a call to action "ring a bell" and give rise to the action demanded? In other terms what makes the imperative an efficient one for me, an individual? Let us think of the suggestions actually compelling as a message duly received. What are the factors which ensure its reception?

This is presumably a problem for politically minded psycholo-

---

other hand, if criminal actions can be unquestionably traced back to one who has counseled this particular action to that particular person, then and then only is the adviser accounted an accomplice. The foregoing statement is all too simple, and a competent jurist may criticize it. The point is raised only to stress that it would be of the utmost interest to have a study of comparative law on guilt by suggestion, a study which does not, to my limited knowledge, exist.

[2] The term "a free society" is blatantly improper. Literally it can mean only a society independent from any authority lying outside itself, that is, as Hobbes put it, "not the liberty of particular men, but the liberty of the Commonwealth" (*Leviathan*, Part II, ch. XXI). The term is, however, taken above in its common meaning, i.e., a society where particular men enjoy individual freedom.

gists. But here is another which is truly a problem for political philosophers: is there, within the process of reception, a "natural selection" such that those messages which are most conducive to the preservation and development of human cooperation are more readily and widely received than others?

The mere statement of the question opens up, or so I believe, enormous vistas. Just to trace one of the perspectives, let us think of those enjoying vested authority as being in a position to broadcast their message far more widely than those who stand in the crowd at the foot of an established structure. Is this inequality a means for biasing men in favor of the most innocuous messages on the assumption that the men who have risen to the top of the pile have been tested on the way for common sense and prudence? A comparison immediately springs to mind. In our society anyone may speak freely, but not everyone is invited to broadcast, and while the sayings of broadcasters are indeed diverse, they are less so than the sayings of individuals. We find here an undevised but nonetheless operative selection of utterances a priori, which tends to bias the *ex post facto* choice of opinions of hearers.

One may attack this state of affairs on the grounds that all views do not get an equal chance. It is permissible, however, to think that any society needs a narrowing down of the range of opinions propounded and imperatives suggested. Not that these should be ever the same through time but that they must not be too far dispersed at any given moment. This is achieved in a liberal society, not by the suppression of extreme opinions or out-of-the-way imperatives but by weighting the near-to-median opinions or imperatives, which alone can be propounded from dominant and privileged positions.

The emphasis has been put here upon the elementary phenomenon of prompting, which I take as the common "root" of all manifestations of authority. Elsewhere[3] I have sought to work up from this first step towards elaborate relations; to show how this phenomenon permits the erecting of human aggregates and constructions, ensures their conservation, and thereby constitutes "fields" wherein the members of the "set" are susceptible to mutual prompt-

---

[3] *Of Sovereignty: An Inquiry into the Political Good.* To be published by the University of Chicago Press.

ings. Also I have stressed that it is the essential function of established authorities to preserve the "field," standing surety to individuals for the continuation of the cooperative condition established. In other words, I have attempted to study the "domestication" of this natural phenomenon, the efficient imperative, for the purpose of ever more confident and fruitful intercourse between men. But in this paper, no more could be attempted than to delineate a "root" which intervenes in every social complex. I shall account myself lucky if this is accepted as a useful tool of analysis, and used more efficiently by other hands.

11. The Perception of Authority and Political Change[1]

DAVID EASTON

The study of political change may be approached from a number of directions. We can search out the impact on political systems of variations in the economy, social structure, culture, or use of force by other political systems. We can examine changes that occur in patterns of voting, attitudes towards authority, political movements, and circulation of political elites. But each of these approaches by itself is fragmentary in the sense that it contributes to our understanding of only one or two factors in the processes of change. What is clearly lacking is first, some way for drawing together many of these items conducive to change so that the various complex processes involved in the basic changes of a political system can be at least partly synthesized and viewed as they influence a single process. Second, there is clearly a need to select for special study a process that not only reflects the effect of the various important factors influencing change, but that is also empirically manageable. That is, it must be of a kind that lends itself to a rigorously formulated program of research. In this paper,

[1] Research for this paper has been supported in part under contract N6onr-25133 (NR-047-004) of the Office of Naval Research and in part by the Social Science Research Committee of the University of Chicago. Sections 3 and 4 of this paper have borrowed freely from preliminary discussions with Professors Robert Hess, Committee on Human Development, and Peter Rossi, Department of Sociology, both at the University of Chicago, in connection with a joint research project we have under way concerning the development of political opinions and attitudes among adolescents.

with these criteria in mind, I shall focus on a specific aspect of the relation between political authorities and the rest of the members of a political system as a useful way for describing the processes that produce, if not a direct transformation in a political system, at least a state of readiness among the members to accept, promote, or countenance change.

I. AUTHORITY AND CHANGE

A fundamental transformation in a political system will be said to occur when support has shifted from one set of authorities to a different set, in which the organization, solidary symbols (that is, symbols validating and defining limits of power), and central characteristics with regard to the way in which power is used have all undergone change. Once support begins to shift away from these aspects of authority which I shall call collectively the structure of authority, the system will be said to be in process of change.

Although a shift in the support of authority as a criterion of change could be justified purely on grounds of its convenience for present purposes, it has in fact more than transitory significance. The reason for this is that the existence of authority is fundamental to the working of a political system. To appreciate the part that authority plays in a political system, let us examine briefly the function of a political system itself for the maintenance of a society.

If we view a political system from the standpoint of its consequences for the society of which it is part, we can see that one of its major functions is to help integrate the behavior of the members of the society. Integration can occur in two fundamentally different ways: through autonomous or private interaction on the part of the members of society, and through deliberate intervention on behalf of society. In every society there is scarcity of some of the major values or things desired. If the society is to maintain itself, it must be able to assure a minimal degree of order in the conflicts resulting from the pursuit of these scarce values. In part the values of the society are allocated through the development of customary norms and patterns of behavior that succeed in regulating the degree of conflict, preventing it from passing beyond a destructive point. The mechanisms here are all autonomous in the sense that each individual or group in the society works out his adjustment with others without the intervention of any special group or institution that presumes to speak for the society as a whole.

There is, however, a large segment of conflicts over values that are not resolved in this way. Where members of the society are unwilling or unable to negotiate their own differences, or where various groups seek special objectives with which others might not find themselves in accord, every society has developed characteristic institutions to mobilize the resources of the society for the purpose of regulating the differences. The fact that these means are regularly found in all societies has led scholars to identify and label them political institutions. The whole set of such institutions in a society may in turn be described as a political system.[2]

The significance for society of a political system and its component institutions is that through them it is possible to contribute to the maintenance of order. Where values in dispute cannot be privately negotiated, it is through the political system that decisions allocating them are made, put into effect, and normally obeyed or accepted by most members. These political processes must result in the making and implementation of authoritative decisions, if that minimal order requisite for the mere survival of society is to occur. Without attempting the necessarily involved proof here, I shall simply postulate that if it were not for the existence of a political system authoritatively allocating values, minimal integration could not be achieved.[3]

If for a moment we set aside the relation between society and its political system and direct our attention to the political system itself, we can appreciate the fundamental role that authority must play. Without it the system could not fulfill its social function, and the society could not endure. If in turn this necessary structure of authority is to prevail in a political system, it must obtain support from the members of that system. Basic changes in the structure, as defined above, will alter the whole character of the political system. It is for this reason that decisive cessation in the input of support for

[2] For an elaboration of the implications of this concept see my volume, *The Political System* (1953), and "An Approach to the Analysis of Political Systems," *World Politics* (1957).

[3] For the further development of this theme, see my paper, "A Theoretical Approach to Authority," Technical Report No. 17, prepared under contract N6onr–25133 (NR–047–004) for the Office of Naval Research (1955).

a given structure of authority will be construed here as a sign that the members of a political system are ready to entertain a crucial alteration in their system.

2. IMAGES OF AUTHORITY

To discover the extent to which the members of a political system stand ready to give or withdraw support for the structure of authority, I suggest that it is useful to focus on the perceptions or images of authority in the minds of the members themselves. My hypothesis is that the way the members view their authorities, their structure, influence, mode of exercising power, and other characteristics, will significantly reflect the degree to which these members are ready to give or withdraw support.

If we look for a moment at a kind of research prevalent in the study of political change, we can appreciate why it is useful to single out perception for special study. This research adopts as its point of departure the description of the way in which transformations occur in the bases of legitimacy of the authority structure in political systems. In this regard the threefold typology presented by Max Weber has captured the imagination of some research workers. A number of studies of underdeveloped areas have sought to apply this classification and to test its utility by analyzing the shifts in the bases of legitimacy for traditional to legal-rational systems through the vehicle of charismatic leaders.

Such an approach to the study of authority particularly interests us here, since it explicitly seeks to understand the process through which a political system changes its characteristic structure of authority. Change is viewed largely in terms of a shift in the support of symbols validating different structures of authority, coincident with a corresponding transformation of these structures themselves.

Aside from the merits of this classification of legitimacy, which is not beyond challenge, the Weberian typology, as it has been utilized, has certain shortcomings for purposes of understanding the dynamics of political change. First, it views change largely from the point of view of the holders of authority, such as the administrative staff and political chief, and the symbols attached to their roles. The subjects of authority play a very shadowy part in the processes of change, reflecting Weber's typical overemphasis on the influence of great men in history.

Second, it approaches the problem from a formal level. This may seem a rather strange accusation, since Weber operates within the framework of the concrete actor and his actions. Nevertheless as it turns out in this instance, the Weberian classificatory scheme offers only a gross description of principles of legitimacy and the various types of authority structures to which they correspond. At one level, change is described as the net result of the operation of economic and other social factors that makes it possible for any one of the given types of authority structures and validating symbols to break down. At another level, change is explained as the appearance of a charismatic leader whose authority at some stage becomes routinized into one of the other two types, traditional or legal-rational.

Of course, as an ideal type the Weberian description was calculated not to describe any given process of change but only to draw attention to the major components at work. Yet recent research has assumed that this typology does in fact broadly describe the major elements at work in political transformations, at least in underdeveloped areas. However, even if the Weberian description of the process of change should prove to be valid, it would still have to be supplemented with an explanation of the dynamics underlying the gross description.

To see what I mean, let us assume first, with Weber, that all the factors constituting the social environment of a political system[4] contribute in one way or another to the rise of a new basis for legitimacy and a new structure of authority. Let us agree further that the pattern of change typically involves the appearance of a charismatic chief whose charisma later becomes routinized. Presumably changes in culture, economy, personality types, and the like would be transmitted to the political system and account for the loss of power and validity of the existing authorities. However, in terms of this Weberian analysis, correct as it may formally be, we are still left with the problem of how in fact we are to trace through and sum up the impact of these changes in the environment upon the patterns of authority in a political system.

[4] For the concept "social environment of a political system" see "An Approach to the Analysis of Political Systems," cited above, footnote 2.

A useful device for drawing all these strands of influence together would be establishment of the effect of these changes upon the way in which the members of a system perceive their authorities and related solidary symbols. By concentrating on perceptions of authority, we could develop an index of the predisposition for support to shift towards or away from a given set of authorities.

To establish such an index we would need to begin with the members' perceptions of their authorities and relate the resultant images to their conceptions of who the authorities ought to be, the characteristics they ought to have, and the symbols in terms of which their power ought to be limited. If there is a gap between what is perceived as existing, on the one hand, and as desirable, on the other, the hypothesis is that the measure of this gap provides an index of the state of readiness in which the individual finds himself with regard to shifting his support. Up to a certain point, a discrepancy between perceptions and expectations may be tolerated or tolerable; but if the gap stretches beyond a certain magnitude, presumably a state of readiness arises.[5]

It is of course one matter to be ready to transfer support from one to another structure of authority and quite another matter to act so as to implement this state of mind. Just what is involved in the relation between the state of readiness and implementation I shall examine at a later stage. The important point here is that an inquiry of the present sort could lead not to an index of the probability of change but only to an index of the psychological state indicating a predisposition to change.

For the purposes of economy and uniformity of expression, I shall designate as the "perceived image" the way in which the members

[5] From time to time, the presence and implications of this gap are intuitively recognized in the literature of politics. For example, "What is central to the situation (in the conflict between generations in the USSR) is the inherent cleavage within a society where the young are brought up to revere certain broadly humanistic tenets which Soviet Communism shares with Western liberalism — only to make the shattering discovery on leaving school, that no more than lip service is paid to these fine ideals of social justice and fellowship in the actual society in which they are expected to take their place. One would not wish to claim that this problem is altogether peculiar to the USSR but owing to the totalitarian character of the regime, and *the immense gap between promise and performance,* it is perhaps more sharply accentuated in the Soviet Union than in any other country at the present time" (*Soviet Survey,* 12 (1957), 3; italics mine).

of a political system do in fact view the authorities and related properties. For lack of a more appropriate term I shall use the phrase "expected image" to refer to the way in which the members think the authorities ought to be organized, to act, and to be limited in the exercise of power.

3. POLITICAL AUTHORITIES AS A CONCEPT

If we are to explore the problems raised by an attempt to build up information about these perceived and expected images of authorities, we must first have some idea about what we, as professional students of politics, have in mind when we speak of the political authorities. This will give us some clue to the kind of objects of perception to which we shall have to refer when we deal with the problems of eliciting from the members of a political system the nature of their image of authority. Professional students of politics could be looking at the same phenomena as other members of a political system, or more likely, at something quite different.

To settle at the outset just what the concept "political authorities" signifies, let us examine the idea of authority itself. We may understand authority in one of two senses: either as a property of an individual or group or as the property of a relation between two or more individuals or groups. The difference may seem at first glance rather slight but in fact it turns out to have a wealth of significance for research.

In the way that the concept is used today, it sometimes seems as though authority is a quality attaching to or inherent in an individual, possessed much as he possesses hair of a certain color, or a particular stature or weight. The possession of this quality does not depend upon the kind of relationship in which the individual stands to others but solely upon other signs that indicate whether or not he has it. Colloquially we are accustomed to saying that a policeman has the authority to prevent crimes, so long as he is a policeman. Once we are aware of the fact that he does hold this position, we may automatically ascribe the authoritative characteristic to him.

To a certain point, this view of the nature of authority may be used without leading us into great difficulty. But its utility dwindles if we should discover that for a variety of reasons it happens that the policeman is not obeyed with regard to certain matters; and let us assume that he is not able to enforce his presumed authority. In practice this happens when violators of the law have special connections that enable them to flout the orders of the policeman on the beat. Now there arises the difficulty of determining how we are to interpret that percentage of cases in which the policeman issues orders having no visible consequences in the way of compliance by members of the system. If authority is a characteristic independent of the kind of relationship existing between its holder and others, clearly we must say that even in those cases the policeman continues to possess authority. Although qualities like his strength or the color of his hair may change, they do not change merely because some other person refuses to recognize their existence. To insist upon ascribing authority to him, however, even when he is not obeyed, becomes meaningless if not nonsensical, if we assume that to have authority is to have the capacity to obtain compliance to orders. We are driven therefore to look for other possible meanings to the proposition, which seems intuitively correct, that the policeman nevertheless has authority even at the very moment of being flouted.

There is a possible sense in which this is correct. What we may mean is that the law prescribes that he shall have the power to require others to do certain things, even though in fact for one reason or another, these persons may refuse to obey and may get away with it. In this case, all we are saying is that the law declares that a certain kind of relationship shall exist between a policeman and others. If the relationship does not in fact prevail, this does not change the prescription of what ought to exist. In characterizing the role as authoritative, we are not in reality *describing* one of its properties but we are rather attributing to it a quality that we think it *should* have. Authority here becomes a term of evaluation masquerading as a descriptive concept. Because the law says that the policeman should be obeyed, even when he is not, we continue to insist that he has authority because we believe that he ought to have it.

We need to be able to overcome this curiously ambiguous meaning, and to avoid having to shift from a descriptive to an evaluative frame of reference for the same word within the same context. For this purpose it is useful to conceive of authority, not as a characteristic that attaches to a member of the political system regardless of its consequences, but as a type of power relationship between two or more members or groups. The presence of authority in each case will depend upon the exact nature of the relationship.

To understand clearly just what this use of the concept implies, it will be necessary to indicate the class of similar relations of which it is a part and the distinctions among them.[6] Authority is a type of relationship that we can call *influence*. A person stands in the relationship of influence with respect to another when his behavior modifies the acts of that other in some way. It may lead the other person to change his action or in some cases to maintain his current way of acting if, but for the exercise of influence, he would have altered his behavior.

We can divide influence into two types depending upon the presence or absence of intention on the part of the person who exercises the influence. Those cases in which A influences B but does not intend to do so, we can call *mere influence;* those cases in which A does in fact intend to do so and is effective, we can call *power*.

For example, let us suppose A is a political leader who has become aware of a move to increase tariffs on a product in general demand in his district and at the moment intends only to sound out his constituents on the matter. If upon learning of the proposed increase, his constituents send a stream of protests to the appropriate members of the government, A will clearly have influenced their behavior, even though he might be very much surprised by the results of the information he had imparted. He had intended only to elicit information but instead accidentally stirred up a hornet's nest. This situation is one of mere influence. It differs markedly from one in which A might apprise his constituents of the proposed increase in the hope that he could lead them to protest the action. The consequences would be intended, and thereby A would have a measure of control over the behavior of his constituents. This type of control is so vital to the operation of a political system and is in fact so often equated with the whole of politics that it is useful to distinguish this case from the former by calling it an exercise of power.

As in other cases of definition, we could argue whether this is

[6] For a similar and suggestive classification of types of power see H. Goldhamer and E. A. Shils, "Types of Power and Status," *American Journal of Sociology,* 45:171–182 (1939). For conceptualization of power in relational terms, see C. J. Friedrich, *Constitutional Government and Democracy* (1951), ch. 1.

what one really and truly means by the concept "power," and whether intention must always be present. There would be little prospect of ever terminating the discussion of a question posed in this way. The most I am saying is that the presence of an intention to modify the behavior of others constitutes such an important element in an influence relationship and is so different in its consequences from other relationships that it is useful to signalize its presence by referring to it as power.

We can distinguish two basically different types of power relationships, and authority falls into one of these. The property differentiating these two types is that of the presence or absence of awareness, on the part of the subject, of an attempt to exercise power, that is, of an intention to modify his behavior. When B is *not* aware of A's intention to influence him but A does in fact manage to get B to follow his wishes, we can say that we have an instance of *manipulation*. For example, without informing B of his desires, A may so work on B through the use of propaganda and other instruments that B does what A desires even though B is entirely innocent of the fact that he is serving A's ends.

In the second general class of power relationships, A's intention *is* known to B. Here we have three subtypes: force, persuasion, and authority. In the case of *force,* A physically seizes B and compels him to do what A wishes. The police may seize a political dissenter and jail him, thereby removing him from the realm of active political participation, to the extent that the imprisonment is effective.

In the case of *persuasion,* A may seek to get B to change his behavior by presenting him with arguments intended to show him why this change is desirable. If B reviews these communications, evaluates them in the light of his own criteria of what he considers best under the circumstances, and then accepts them as the basis of his actions, we can say that B has been persuaded to execute A's intentions.

On the other hand, if A sends a message to B and B adopts this message as the basis of his own behavior without evaluating it in terms of his own standards of what is desirable under the circumstances, we can say that A has exercised *authority* over B.[7] B here

---

[7] Authority was interpreted in this way quite some time ago by L. Stein, in "The Sociology of Authority," *American Sociological Society,* 18:116–120 (1923), at p. 117,

has accepted a message from A as authoritative for or binding upon him and without further contemplation of its merits acts to carry out A's intention as incorporated in the communication. There may be a number of determinable grounds leading B to accept the message as binding. He may like A; he may feel that he ought to act in accordance with A's commands because it is right to do so; he may fear possible sanctions that A can impose; or he may feel that it is in his own material interests to accept A's directives in this situation. But regardless of these and other varied grounds upon which one person might be induced to obey another, the fact that in practice he does obey the other is sufficient evidence for describing the power relationship as one of authority.

This interpretation of authority conflicts with the way it is often used even by those who would agree that authority is a quality not of a person but of a relationship between people. In this use authority is indeed an aspect of power but refers to legitimate as against coercive power. Authority stands in contrast to coercion. In a political system in which the governing group, say, bases its activity on the principle of hereditary divine right of kings, and in which the members of the system consider this principle to be adequate grounds for obeying their rulers, the power is said to be legitimate or in accord with the generally accepted moral standards for ruling. In this event, the holders of political power can also be described as the political authorities. If, however, in the given system, the bulk of the members reject hereditary royal divinity as an acceptable basis for complying with the decisions of the rulers, and large elements of force must be used to bring about obedience, then the holders of political power are coercers. They rule through coercion and cannot be said to hold political authority in the system.

As I am using the terms here, the above situation would be interpreted differently. Both in the case where the legitimacy of the rulers is accepted and where the rulers are obeyed only because they possess a predominance of effective, violent sanctions, the rulers can be described as the authorities. The difference does not arise from

where authority was defined as "the 'untested acceptance of another's judgment.' To submit to authority implies the surrender of one's own judgment in favor of another." In recent years, others have adopted a similar definition. See for example, C. I. Barnard, *The Functions of the Executive* (1938), and H. Simon, *Administrative Behavior* (1947).

the presence or absence of authority, that is, the capacity to obtain compliance in either case, but rather from the varying motivations for obeying. In the one case, authority rests on the fact that most members of the system accept rulers based upon divine right as legitimate and accordingly feel they ought to be obeyed. In the other case, even though the members of the system would if they could change their rulers, nevertheless out of fear of the consequences for themselves or because they simply have no acceptable alternative, they do in fact obey. The grounds of obedience here we can designate as fear or necessity. In the one case we have legitimate authority; in the other nonlegitimate or coercive authority.

As was true for the identification of power, there would be little point in debating whether the one or the other interpretation of authority conveys its presumed real meaning. All we can do is to indicate which description of the concrete phenomena is more useful. For purposes of signalizing the differences between systems with regard to the amount of violence involved in the relationships between the rulers and subjects, the authority-coercion dichotomy undoubtedly has some value. Beyond that, however, use of this type of classification runs into certain obvious difficulties. Authority clearly refers in this definition to a relationship of obedience. By contrasting it with coercion, although it points up the important differences in grounds of obeying, it obscures the fact that in both the authoritative and coercive relationships, the subjects of the acts of the rulers do in fact obey. It draws attention almost exclusively to the one factor: the degree of legitimacy or illegitimacy attached to the decisions and positions of the rulers.

An adequate analytical scheme for understanding the way in which political systems operate demands, however, that our concepts incorporate the widest range of relevant political phenomena. If we view authority as one among four kinds of power relationships, we are able to embrace a wider range of behaviors known to be relevant to the operation of political systems. This more comprehensive classification points not only to the differences between but also to the similarities of systems we have spoken about, those based on principles of legitimacy and those based on fear of violent sanctions. In both cases obedience is forthcoming.

This fact poses two questions: what are the means used to achieve this obedience, and on what grounds do those who obey act in conformity with the decisions of the rulers? It points up what seems to be obscured in the authority-coercion dichotomy, namely, that in both types of political systems communications or commands are issued by the rulers and are accepted as the premises of action by the bulk of the members of the system. In this sense the relationships between ruler and ruled are identical regardless of the presence or absence of legitimacy and coercion. To call attention to this similarity it is useful to designate the relationship as one of authority and to accept the fact that in both types of systems authoritative or binding decisions are made. It leaves open for further inquiry the task of establishing why people obey. In doing so, it draws attention not only to legitimacy as a possible ground, but also to the threat of violence, coincidence of material interests, identification of the subjects with the ruler as in the case of a charismatic ruler, and the like. This classification, therefore, draws together in a more economical way a broader range of related political facts vital for understanding how a political system functions.

But we are confronted with a certain inconsistency in the application of this concept. Among those writers who implicitly adopt the authority-coercion dichotomy, the day-to-day makers and executors of binding decisions are frequently designated as the political authorities, even in the case of coercive systems. This usage indicates that the notion of authority is being applied in the neutral sense I have suggested. Anyone who is regularly obeyed is an authority.

It would be misleading, however, to imply that the political authorities are always able to execute their intentions solely through their use of the authoritative elements in the power relationship of which they are part. To put the matter in another way, those who occupy authority roles in a political system may be able to execute their decisions through means other than authority itself. This raises the problem as to the extent to which we are achieving adequate clarity and consistency in continuing to apply this label to this set of roles.

The fact is that political authorities typically utilize means other than authority to perform their tasks, and for this reason it is in a sense misleading to characterize them as the authorities. To the extent that my classification of power is exhaustive, they have three other typical relationships through which they can implement their decisions. They may utilize pure force, as when they physically seize members of the system and compel them to act or usually not to act in a given way. The political police are the main instrument for the accomplishment of this end in totalitarian systems we know today. I distinguish here between force and the threat of force. In the latter case we have an example of the exercise of authority. There is a significant difference between actually eliminating a person from the political system by jailing him and merely threatening him with incarceration. When only threats are made, the individual may be inclined to obey, thereby participating in an authority relationship, whereas in the case of pure force the individual continues to refuse to obey but is nevertheless compelled to conform to the decision of the authorities.

The authorities may also use manipulation to achieve their goals. Since the point is quite clear, we may pass over it rapidly, indicating only that this type of power finds its place in democratic as well as autocratic systems.

It is persuasion, however, that is by far the most prevalent type of power in all systems operating under the conditions of modern mass-industrialized societies. The diffusion of democratic doctrines and attitudes has led to a pronounced resistance to commands, even when by circumlocution they are phrased as requests. There is a widespread preference for acting not because someone tells us to act in a given way, but because we have had the opportunity to weigh the pros and cons and to arrive at an independent judgment concerning the desirability of the proposed activity. This is particularly, although not exclusively, true of modern democracies. Here the presumed authoritative element in a law is reinforced, if not at times largely displaced, by appeals to the members of the system to conform to legislation because it seeks to meet long-range or broadly conceived needs and interests. In recent decades the burgeoning of "fireside chats," the increase in activities of public-relations experts in governmental agencies, and the popular diffusion of the reasons and need for particular kinds of legislation, represent attempts to obtain conformity to decisions, not only because as the "law of the land" they are supposed to be binding, but also because they are reasonable in terms of the interests of the various persons and groups involved.

In one sense, then, the designation of those who make the important decisions in a political system as the political authorities is a misnomer. It stresses the authoritative aspects of their power relationships and tends to gloss over the other types of power relationships typically brought into play, at least in modern times. Its usage reflects earlier historical periods when authority played a greater part in the organization and processes of political life.

In the literature, the special roles embraced by the idea of political authorities are variously called the government, rulers, governors, elite, decision-makers, or policy-makers. The indecision in terminology is a symptom not only of dissatisfaction with any one term but also of indeterminacy concerning identification of the specific members of the system in this way. Yet the phrase, political authorities, continues to have considerable utility. The terms ruler and governor are no adequate substitute, since they too have a number of unfavorable subsidiary connotations. Even the relatively neutral contemporary hyphenations, decision- or policy-makers, do not fill the need. The actual *makers* of policies or political decisions do not exhaust the members of a system normally included in the idea of the authorities. But the term as used refers also to those who *execute* policy.

Furthermore, the advantage of the term political authorities is that it continues to stress the element of authority which is necessary in the relationships between the makers and executors of policy and the rest of the members of a political system. It is empirically observable that no political system has endured without the existence of the power of authority in the hands of a determinable subset of members. This is true of all but the smallest, least organized primitive societies, and there is some reason to believe that even in these cases, authority roles appear to be absent only because anthropologists have not been sufficiently sensitive to the political aspects of these societies.[8]

It is also true on logically deducible grounds. We could show that it would be impossible for a political system to maintain itself if the initiation, formulation, and execution of political decisions had to rely on any combination of force, manipulation, or persuasion, ex-

[8] See, in this respect, the interesting preface by A. R. Radcliffe-Brown to M. Fortes and E. E. Evans-Pritchard, eds., *African Political Systems* (1940), pp. xi–xxiii.

cluding authority entirely. The outlay of energy involved in having to force, manipulate, or persuade members into conformity with a decision would exceed the resources of any but the smallest face-to-face political system.[9] It is for these reasons valuable and logical to continue to label as the "political authorities" those who in fact formulate and execute decisions accepted as binding by the members of the political system.

In brief, then, for purposes of political analysis, the authorities are those members whose communications are in fact obeyed, disregarding for the moment the reasons for compliance. Although there is no need to probe the matter further here, it is obvious that not every last member of the system needs to obey. In general terms, we can say that the bulk of the members spread over most of the territory over which the authorities presume their decisions and acts to apply need to comply most of the time.

4. PERCEIVED IMAGES

If we are to understand the part that images of authority play in political change, it is not enough merely to describe the referents of the concept of political authority and then pass on to a discussion of the popular images of the characteristics of this authority. The image of political authority raised by my description is one present in the mind of the social scientist; it need not, and normally will not, coincide with the picture in the mind of the participants of the authority relationship, assuming they are not themselves trained in social science. That is, the presence of a gap between perceived and expected images that generates a readiness to transfer support does not require that the members of a political system see as the authorities those who are so defined for research purposes by the social scientist. To expect this would be to commit the fallacy of misplaced images, since we cannot assume that the average person views the world through the conceptual lenses of the social scientist. The task for the social scientist, then, is to put himself behind the lenses of those persons whose perceptions he is exploring. He must seek to discover just whom the members of the political system see as the

[9] This theme is elaborated in "A Theoretical Approach to Authority," cited above, footnote 3.

persons who are responsible for making and who do make and implement the authoritative decisions for a society.

To take a concrete illustration, students of politics have described the patterns of behavior that developed as some of the members of the German political system transferred their support from the Weimar authorities and symbols to those of the Nazi regime. We can describe what occurred as the displacement of one set of authorities and solidary symbols by another. But this tells us little about how the shift occurred. Presumably some members of the system at one stage sensed, however inarticulately, that their image of the authorities did not coincide with their view of who the authorities ought to be; as the discrepancy between perceived and expected images widened, there was a greater propensity to accept a new structure of authority and associated symbols. This is not to say that the Nazis rose to power solely because of the existence of such a gap in images. All that I am suggesting is that the inner dynamics of the process of change would not have led in this direction unless the members of the system who initially did in fact support the Nazi regime were placed in a state of readiness to shift their support. Others of course never did support the Nazi authorities, except to the extent to which they were coerced into doing so.

The point here is that even though we may describe the consequence of the behavior of those who did seek the change as that of lending support to the Nazi authorities, we really do not know whom these members saw in their own interpretation as the outgoing and incoming authorities. The images they had of the Weimar and of the Nazi authorities could have and probably in most cases did diverge appreciably from the *ex post facto* conclusions of political research. Until we clearly established whom they saw as the authorities under both regimes, we would lack an important link in understanding the relationship between the authorities and their subjects. We would not know toward whom the members of the German political system were orienting their behavior when they transferred their support, and to that extent we would be neglecting an important element involved in the shift.

On purely a priori grounds — and this has been suggested by preliminary investigation — we could expect that the members of a political system would be able to include within their perceptions a number of alternative elements in varying proportions. Conceivably when we seek to discover whom it is they see as responsible for making the decisions and taking the action necessary to meet the problems with which the country is confronted, we might find that at least in a democratic system, the members think primarily of the people at large, "people" in this sense meaning the voters. The voters would be perceived presumably because they select the representatives whose task it then is to make day-to-day decisions within the framework of the whole electoral process. The element of the people as the ultimate political authority in a system might loom so large in some images as to reduce to relatively minor significance the other aspects included within the image.

The mental picture of others, however, might come to a sharp focus not on the voters but on the formal authorities. In this event, the details of this image would be of considerable interest. For instance, to what extent does this image correspond with what the professional student of politics conceives to be the existing components of the structure of political authority? If we adopt the description offered by social scientists as the closest approximation to the correct identification of those who make and execute authoritative decisions for a society, we will find that popular images vary from those that show the individual to be extremely well-informed and correct in his perceptions, to those that display considerable ignorance and confusion.

A final element in the picture might be that of the authorities as the "real powers behind the scenes": as various social groups and individuals who hold no formal place in the political structure making and influencing decisions and actions. These groups might be perceived as the real authorities, with the formal government considered, if not an epiphenomenon, at least of secondary consequence. Such a perception might include a wide range of objects from prominent personalities, interest groups, and lobbyists, to such specific categories as the wealthy members of the system, labor, and the military establishment.

I am not suggesting that the images reported would necessarily include only one or the other of these various categories of elements. Rather, we could expect that aspects of each category would appear in the picture of authorities held by any one member. We might, however, find that some elements loomed larger in the image than others, thus reducing the other elements to comparatively insignificant proportions. In any event we would elicit in this way images of the structure of authority in the minds of the respondents. We would have some concrete basis upon which to determine the kind of objects toward which the individual orients his behavior when, for example, he obeys the laws sanctioned by the political authorities. This image would represent the concrete reality to which the perceiver, depending upon the degree of his political awareness and participation, would be subconsciously or quite deliberately comparing his expected images of authority.

The readiness of the members of a political system to maintain or shift their support for political authorities is a function not only of who they think the authorities are, but also of their perceptions of the way in which the authorities act. Different images of the characteristics of the political authorities would result in different types of responses to the demands imposed upon the members of a system by these authorities, if only because we interpret the meaning of the acts of others in the light of what we think of them.

It would be useful to uncover the many different perceptions of various characteristics such as the following: to what extent are the authorities seen as competent, honest, trustworthy, prestigeful, dedicated, representative, responsive to demands, morally responsible, powerful, punitive, or disciplinary, as against inept, corrupt, unreliable, degrading, self-seeking, unrepresentative, impermeable to demands, irresponsible, weak, protective, or nurturing?

Whether we selected for examination these or other qualities would depend upon an evaluation of the kind of expectations members of the system have of the way in which their authorities ought to behave. It would then be possible to develop a measure of disparity concerning those aspects of the images that are conceived as important by the members themselves.

We would also need information concerning the distance in perceptions between the kind of limits within which political authorities do in fact act as compared to those that are expected of them. This would bring out the symbols of legitimacy and solidarity most closely associated with political authority.

Political and legal philosophy has exerted considerable effort to inquire into the kind of limits that *ought* to be imposed upon political authorities. From the perspective of our present concerns, moral inquiry of this kind can be interpreted as the expectations held by political philosophers and constitutional lawyers concerning the limits of authority or zones of obedience. There is little reason to assume that the images held by the political philosophers and lawyers would coincide with those held by other members of a political system, although insofar as there is homogeneity in political culture, there should be some minimal convergence of expectations.

Furthermore, a large amount of research has been devoted to identifying the actual limits of authority. The minute examination of the Constitution and related legislation in the United States, for example, reveals the kind of limits that have in practice been accepted by the authorities. The study of the decisions of the Supreme Court in interpreting the meaning of the Constitution has contributed to our knowledge of the kinds of limits that at least this segment of the authorities has sought to put into effect.

However, in spite of this tremendous body of available data about the desired boundaries of political authority or those adopted in practice, we have little if any reliable knowledge about the kinds of limits that the members of any political system see as in fact restricting and legitimating the behavior of their authorities. Yet this would seem to be an inescapable starting point if we sought to predict the kind of response that any expansion or for that matter retraction in the powers and scope of intervention permitted to political authorities might elicit from the members of a political system.

The identification of the nature of the perceived images is only the first step. We can anticipate that these images will not be homogeneous for the members of a political system. We would need to discover why various types of images do emerge in different parts of the population.

To this end, the impact of a variety of factors upon a person's image would need to be tested, such as the individual's age, sex, personal experience in and awareness of politics, and his socio-economic, religious, and ethnic background. To illustrate what I mean, let us take socio-economic status. It is well-known that one's position in this respect provides differential access (and response) to education and to the mass media and thereby at least to information about those who are most influential in making and effectuating political policies. In addition, social and economic position helps to shape one's way of life and thereby to create wide gulfs in types of political experience; this would be reflected in the way in which various elements combine in a concrete mental image.

We would also want to inquire into the effect upon this image of the fact that for the overwhelmingly large proportion of the members of a political system, those political authorities about whom we have some views are not familiar to us as the result of personal contact. Almost exclusively we come to know them either through formal education and mass media of communication or through personal information from others who themselves have obtained their opinion from these media. This aspect of the process of political perception tends to be neglected if only because it seems so apparent.

For most of the people, there is little opportunity to establish direct personal contact with those whom a social scientist might designate as the authorities and associated influential groups. We are prone to forget that for the vast majority of the members of the American system, for example, contacts with the authorities are normally confined to licensing agencies, police, firemen, tax officials, agricultural agents, educational officials, postal employees, and the like. We might perhaps go so far as to include local party officials, such as precinct captains, who are sometimes confused in the public mind with appointed officials, although not without justification when the party officials also hold public office.

These various types of public authorities are relay points between the vast network of elected and appointed officials and effective interest groups associated with them, on the one side, and the members of the system who are affected by their behavior, on the other. There are of course other relay points connecting the higher reaches of the authorities with the members of the system, as for example, where persons in their private capacity act as informal administrators of the law, even though we do not usually view them in this light. I have in mind here the employer, from corporation to housewife, who collects income or social-security taxes for the national authorities, and the storekeeper who collects sales taxes from the public. But it is doubtful whether this category would ever appear as part of the authorities on the political map of the average member of the system.

In brief, the bulk of the members of a political system such as ours, to the extent that they interact personally with the political authorities, experience that relation at the tail end of an involved process of making and implementing binding decisions. We would therefore be justified in expecting that whatever image of authorities the member of such a system has might arise in part as a by-product of the kind of relation in which the individual finds himself with the specific members of the political authorities at his end of the network. In fact, however, preliminary inquiry suggests that these last find little place in his mental picture. Instead there appear on his visual horizon primarily those groups or members of the authorities who are socially and usually spatially most remote and with whom he has little or no personal contact or access and, what is equally important, little or no chance in his lifetime of having anything but contact at a distance.

To the extent that this is true, the members of a bureaucratized democracy such as ours, in contrast to smaller traditional societies, have become habituated to conceiving of themselves as subject to the acts and decisions of other members or institutions that are personally remote and inaccessible. This state of affairs is not only the product of a mass bureaucratized political system but also of the effort to maintain practices consonant with the norm calling for a government of laws, not of men. One of the effects of this impersonality and remoteness of political authorities is that the members of a political system must rely heavily on indirect channels of communication to transmit material out of which cognition arises. In mass societies the lines of communication become attenuated and complicated, introducing distortion and partial, if not at times complete, blockage of information. As a result the members of such a system are normally exposed to inadequate stimuli for purposes of forming an accurate image of who the political authorities are and how they act.

5. EXPECTED IMAGES

For the purpose of estimating and understanding the reasons for the distance between perceived and expected images of political authority, I have indicated so far that it would be necessary, first, to establish the empirical referents of the concept political authority as it could be used in research; second, to discover the kind of picture of political authorities in terms of which various sets of members of a political system orient themselves as they respond to acts by and communications from authority; and third, to account for the differences in images by relating them to various socio-economic characteristics and contact points with authorities. The next step involves the acquisition of data about the kind of organization of authority the members of a system would prefer and the characteristics they would like the authorities to possess. This would constitute the expected image.

The discovery of this image is equivalent to an inquiry into one aspect of the members' belief systems. The technical problems here are considerable but the objectives can be indicated very briefly. We would need to find answers to this major question: What kind of persons would the members of a political system like to see as the political authorities? This question involves several subsidiary items. First, who would the members of a system like to see play some significant part in making and executing authoritative decisions? In some systems, as in the United States where the political culture is homogeneous, clustering around the axis of democratic theory, we might be able to anticipate with some degree of accuracy the various types of responses. But in other political systems, such as the French or Indonesian, the range of response might show considerably greater variations. It is these differences that both reflect and contribute to the lack of political homogeneity at the level of behavior.

Second, what sort of relationships would the members of the system prefer to see among all those who participate in making and executing authoritative decisions? This would get at their preferences with regard to the organization of authority. Even if it should turn out that in many political systems, members were fundamentally satisfied with the given structure and therefore were not inclined to offer alternatives as more desirable, this would be very significant from the point of view of their state of mind with regard to their readiness to support political change.

Third, we would require data about the kind of qualities the members would prefer the political authorities to manifest and the limits within which they would wish the authorities to confine the exercise of their powers. Here we would be tapping their implicit political philosophy, that is, their conception of what the solidary symbols ought to be.

In this way we could elicit and identify the basic expected norms held by the members of a system. We would then be in a position to establish the distances between them and the actual perceptions.

6. LIMITATIONS OF THE INDEX

As I indicated at the outset, it is important to bear in mind exactly the kind of knowledge we obtain through discovering the distance between perceived and expected images. One way of doing this is to specify what such an index does not tell us.

In the first place, even if we had such an index of discrepancy, it would not tell us how far apart the two images have to be before sufficient discontent will be generated to stimulate hostile action against the existing authorities. Theoretically it would be extremely difficult to undertake to specify in advance any meaningful measure of the degree of tolerance of discrepancy that a member of a system could entertain.[10]

However, if we look at the components of the image of authority, we may be able to shed a little further light on this problem. For example, we can anticipate that this tolerance will vary for different characteristics perceived in and expected of political authorities. As an illustration, even though subjects may wish authorities to conform to the general norms of honesty, they may be quite ready to tolerate a thoroughly dishonest regime if what the subjects see as their vital material interests are being adequately satisfied. On the other hand, if the prevailing cultural notions with regard to fairness and justice were flagrantly violated, the degree of tolerance might be significantly less.

To approach this problem at a general level, we would have to determine what aspects of the political culture are considered the most salient in the behavior of the members of a given political system. We might then be able to test to discover whether the degree of tolerance of discrepancy between perceived and expected characteristics of authorities varied inversely with those qualities which the

[10] Recent research in psychology with regard to the tolerance of ambiguity might be suggestive in this respect.

culture emphasized as vital. In this event, if with respect to fairness and honesty, for example, the distance between perception and expectation were equal, we would anticipate that the unfairness of the authorities would be likely to induce greater discontent than their dishonesty, assuming the culture ranked fairness above honesty.

In the second place, although the existence of a discrepancy between images together with even a high level of consciousness on the part of the members of a system of its presence may stimulate a desire for a new structure of authority, the desire may still be insufficient to invite the kind of action necessary to effect the desired changes. There is a profound difference between a felt need and its implementation. Historically it has often happened that the members of a system have even gone so far as to deplore vigorously the failure on the part of the prevailing authorities to measure up to expectations, and yet the counterbalancing conception that the means for transforming the structure of authority were not at hand has inhibited the required action. The actual attempt to alter the basic structure of authority and its associated solidary symbols depends not only upon the readiness of the members of the system to act but also upon their conception of the availability of the appropriate means. For this reason the existence of even a great distance between perceived and expected images, although a prerequisite of change, may be only a necessary rather than a sufficient condition. At most it prepares the ground for possible negative action against the prevailing structure of authority by reducing the degree of support available to it. Our understanding of the nature of and reasons for the existence of this distance can therefore inform us only of the degree of readiness on the part of the members of a system to transfer their support.

In the third place, the state of mind of those subject to authority is relevant only when they are called upon to participate in introducing or maintaining a given structure of authority. But we know that there are numerous occasions when the structure is fundamentally altered with most of the subjects of authority having very little to do with the matter. For example, the structure of authority may be changed because new aspirants for power have the means to bring this about, even though the members of the political system would have preferred to maintain the old structure.

In this case the distance between perceived and expected images of authority is irrelevant.

It will, however, have some significance for the permanence of the change. If there is a considerable distance between images of the new authorities, we can expect that the degree of legitimacy attributed to the new authorities would be at a minimal point. Stabilization of the change would, therefore, depend in part upon the success that attended any attempts on the part of the new authorities to close the gap between perceived and expected image.

This brings us to a final point. Although the discrepancy in images may be an index of readiness to shift support, and even though the means for doing so may be available, these conditions in themselves would not permit us to predict the necessary alteration in the structure of political authority. It is of the very nature of political processes that the presence of such a gap in images would trigger attempts on the part of the prevailing authorities to close the gap. Political perceptions and preferences with regard to authority need not be fixed for life. There is always the opportunity through manipulation of symbols, new policies, more adequate dissemination of information, and the like, to bring perception into closer harmony with expectations or even to modify expectations themselves. In this way the predisposition of the members of the system to transfer support might be reduced.

It is clear, therefore, that before this predisposition will lead to the act of withdrawing support, the discrepancy must reach an unspecified magnitude, and the magnitude may vary depending upon the characteristics in question; even if the members are ready for action, they may not have the means; and before action is or can be undertaken, the existing authorities may succeed in narrowing the distance between images, thereby reducing the degree of readiness to shift support. Recognition of these limitations only serves to stress the modest claims that can be made on behalf of the hypothesis that there is a significant relation between the index of discrepancy of images and readiness to alter the input of support for authority.

However, this discussion also serves to emphasize that to the extent that political authority depends for its persistence, not on force exclusively or largely, but on acceptance by the bulk of the members of the system, knowledge of the distance between images will provide us with a direct clue to the stability of the structure of authority. It indicates the potential for change waiting to be released by the appropriate events.

Furthermore, the discrepancy index is a single index for a vast variety of factors contributing to change in a political system. Innovations in technology, economy, culture, social structure, and the like all contribute to important modifications in the operations of political systems. They leave their mark on these systems in two characteristic ways. First, they change the distribution of power and thereby make it possible for new structures of authority to emerge, regardless of the initial support available from the members of the system. Second, they normally influence perceptions and expectations of authority. As I suggested at the outset, by concentrating on the impact of these factors on perception and its relationship to readiness to support authority, we have a method for synthesizing and isolating the potential effects of these multiple factors upon changes within a political system.

12. Authority, Legitimation, and Political Action

TALCOTT PARSONS

The general field usually referred to by the term "authority" is an important meeting-ground between several of the sciences of human behavior, notably political science, sociology, and psychology. Like so many other terms in general usage it has been employed in a variety of different senses, not only by proponents of different disciplines, but within the same one. In such a situation it is often useful to attempt to analyze the different parts of the complex of social relations with reference to which the term is used by different writers. I shall concentrate my attention on the aspects which lie on the borderline between sociology and political science.

The main problems with which this paper will be concerned involve the interrelations between three important functional aspects or imperatives of social systems. The first aspect is the way in which values and other facets of a common culture are shared by the members, internalized in their personalities, and institutionalized in the social structure. The second concerns the ways in which values are involved with the more differentiated social structure through particular institutions which regulate the main different relationship complexes of the society. The third concerns the ways in which the system is organized for the formulation and implementation of effective collective action toward collective or "public" goals: what is usually thought of as the political aspects of the organization of the society. These three, the value aspect, the institutional aspect, and the political aspect stand in complex, but, I think, relatively definite relations to each other.

This classification of problems derives from a general classification of the structural components of social systems. The first, least differentiated level, which can be taken as an analytical point of reference for structural analysis as a whole, is the system of values, which, relative to the other elements, must be formulated on a high level of generality. Values are modes of normative orientation of action in a social system, which define the main direction of action without reference to specific goals or more detailed situations or structures. The second level is that of institutions. Institutions are still normative patterns, but on a less general level; they are differentiated according to the situational exigencies and structural subdivisions of the system. Property and authority, as I propose to use the terms, are institutional patterns or complexes.[1] Institutions are still generalized and "regulate" action at more differentiated and particularized levels. The third level, then, is what I call that of collectivities. A collectivity is a concrete system of interacting human individuals, of persons in roles. The term "group" is applicable to at least some collectivities, but not to institutions. One is a member of a collectivity, but not of an institution in my sense — thus to be a "member of property" is clearly nonsensical, but to be a member of a university faculty is not. Roles, finally, are the complexes of organized participation of individuals or categories of individuals in the functioning of collectivities.

VALUES AND THE LEGITIMATION OF ACTION

That a system of value-orientations held in common by the members of a social system can serve as the main point of reference for analyzing structure and process in the social system itself may be regarded as a major tenet of modern sociological theory.[2] Values

---

[1] In common usage, even in the social sciences, the word "institution" is often used to designate what I shall here call a collectivity. Whatever words are employed it seems to me essential to make the distinction and keep it clear.

[2] The tradition of sociological theory to which I have reference derives particularly from the work of Max Weber and Emile Durkheim, particularly, in the present context, Weber. See especially his *Theory of Social and Economic Organization* (translation of Part I of *Wirtschaft und Gesellschaft*, 1925). My own general sociological

in this sense are the commitments of individual persons to pursue and support certain *directions* or types of action for the collectivity as a system and hence derivatively for their own roles in the collectivity. For sociological purposes, values are deliberately defined at a level of generality higher than that of goals — they are *directions* of action rather than specific objectives, the latter depending on the particular character of the situation in which the system is placed as well as on its values and its structure as a system. Still, values (and goals) may be formulated at many different levels of generality. What level is appropriate will depend on what social system is taken as the point of reference for the analysis in question. For purposes of this paper it will be the total society, so the level of generality will be very high.

To illustrate, for contemporary American society, I assume a value system which may be called "instrumental activism." It involves an attitude of active mastery toward the empirical situation external to the society, a situation which includes both physical and psychological nature and other societies. This attitude favors increasing the level of adaptive flexibility primarily through increase of knowledge and economic production.[3] It avoids commitment to a specific societal goal but is characterized by pluralism on the goal level and a commitment to indefinite generalized "progress." It is also committed to universalization of the prerequisites of valued achievement, hence to relative equality of opportunity and its realization above all through civil rights, education, and health. Finally, instrumental activism involves a broadly pragmatic attitude toward organization and authority, accepting them when

---

point of view is most fully stated in *The Social System* (1951). For the concept sketched here of the economy as parallel with that of the polity, see Parsons and Smelser, *Economy and Society* (1956). A recent brief essay into a related field of political sociology is "Voting and the Equilibrium of the American Political System," in *Continuities of Social Research,* ed. Burdick and Brodbeck, III, "The Studies of Voting Behavior" (1957). From the side of political science three sources which deal with the same broad problem area from somewhat differing points of view, are C. J. Friedrich, *Constitutional Government and Politics* (1st and 2nd eds.); H. D. Lasswell and Abraham Kaplan, *Power and Society* (1950); and David Easton, *The Political System* (1953).

[3] This statement does not imply that the American social structure *as a whole* tends to be predominantly flexible — for example, the Constitution has been relatively unchanging. Economic production and knowledge do, however, serve as special instruments of flexible adaptation to changing exigencies.

needed for specific approved goals but repudiating any suggestion of generalized hierarchical superiority.[4]

No value system is ever perfectly internalized and institutionalized, but its status is uneven in different personalities and subcollectivities of the society. The value does not "actualize" itself automatically, but maintenance of relative control in its terms is dependent upon a whole series of mechanisms of institutionalization, socialization, and social control.[5]

I have suggested above that values are in the first instance commitments of the individual personality — they are in some sense ways for him to live with his fellows in society. As such they must be "grounded" in three main directions: first, in his *existential beliefs* about the world; second, in his own *motivational needs* as a

[4] It should be clear that a societal value system ordinarily has not been deliberately or consciously "instituted."

[5] It should be clear that using values as the initial point of reference for the structural analysis of social systems does not imply that they are the sole or even the most important *determinants* of particular structures and processes in such systems. I do not think it is useful to postulate a deep dichotomy between theories which give importance to beliefs and values on the one hand, and those that stress allegedly "realistic" interests, e.g., economic, on the other. Beliefs and values are actualized, partially and imperfectly, in realistic situations of social interaction, and the outcomes are *always* codetermined by the values and the realistic exigencies; conversely what on concrete levels are called "interests" are by no means independent of the values which have been institutionalized in the relevant groups. Thus churches have "interests" just as definitely as do business firms or trade unions, though of course the content is different. Marxian theory does not escape this difficulty of circularity, since Marx explicitly includes what I have called institutions, e.g., the law of property, in the "relations of production."

Another problem of interpretation which may be raised in this type of theory concerns the stability of values relative to change. In recent discussion "value" has come to be an overpopular term and there has been a tendency to use it simply as a label for any fairly general type of behavior — thus if people tend to seek security more than in the recent past, the values are said to have changed in the direction of greater security-seeking. This is similar to the uses of the term "instinct" a generation ago. I do not wish to quarrel over definitions, but here I use the term "value" in a technical sense for the *most general directional commitment of persons to action in a social system*. Its content and level of generality are technically defined relative to the system of reference. In these terms change of the values of a social system has a special technical meaning. Adaptive or equilibrating processes in general do *not* involve change of values, nor does the process of structural differentiation, for example, most broad social change in the United States in the last century. If the value system in our technical sense changes, it means a profound change in the *type* of system. Analysis of such changes involves special problems of technical theory and is not to be equated with "social change" in the most generalized sense.

personality; and third, in his relations to others in the society. On the level of belief the "justification" of values leads beyond empirical knowledge and has roots in the realms of religion and philosophy. The existential propositions that men invoke to answer what Max Weber called the "problems of meaning," the more or less ultimate answers to questions of *why* they should live the way they do and influence others to do so, may thus be called the field of the *justification* of values.

There is also, however, the dimension of "meaning" of values which concerns their integration in the individual personality and their relation to the balance of gratification and deprivation, of personal fulfillment or frustration involved in living up to professed values or failing to do so. This relation may be called the *internalization* of values or value-commitments.

Finally, the third "grounding" of a personal value system is in the social context, the network of rights and obligations in which an individual's value-commitment involves him in his social situation, and which the sharing or nonsharing of his values with others implies. This context, so far as it involves values which can be said to be *common* to the members of a social system, I would like to call the *legitimation* of social action.

Legitimation in this sense is the *appraisal of action in terms of shared or common values in the context of the involvement of the action in the social system*. It is a value-reference at what is clearly a very high level of generality, and as such is applicable to any mode or type of action in the social system. It also operates through many different kinds of mechanisms and modes of symbolization.

As I see it, legitimation is the primary link between values as an internalized component of the personality of the individual, and the institutionalized patterns which define the structure of social relations. As an operative process in social systems, legitimation in this sense is not a simple entity the content and strength of which depends only on the nature of the values themselves; it is rather a function of several variables. These variables are, first, the value-content itself; second, the nature and solidity of the cognitive justification involved; third, the mode and order of internalization of the values in personalities, that is, of their motivation; and fourth, the nature of the situation in which the actor who accepts some kind of commitment to the values is placed in the social system in which he undertakes to implement them.

It may be well to illustrate these points. The justification factor of legitimation may thus in some cases be most prominent where commitment to the relevant values is directly linked with highly explicit transcendental religious beliefs, for example, on the part of the early Puritans. To a psychologically sophisticated observer, however, in such cases often the very emotional vehemence of the adherents of such beliefs (as communism, for example, at present) suggests an insecurity of motivational grounding — the adherents "protest too much." Again it is one thing to be committed to implementation of a value when the situation presents a fairly favorable opportunity of success and another when it is realistically hopeless that anything but martyrdom could ensue from a serious attempt. From the present point of view "counting the cost" is definitely an aspect of legitimation, though how heavily the cost will be weighed will depend on the particular value-content. Legitimation thus is the set of criteria by reference to which "adherence" to a pattern of values is translated *by the individual* into implementing action — that is to say, it is the *action* rather than the values themselves which is legitimated. It is important to understand that action can, however, be legitimated on a variety of different levels of generality — all the way from highly specific acts to the most general directions of action over a lifetime, and involvement in a total society.

The *functions* of legitimation are here defined with reference to the pattern of values itself. The process of legitimation is the bridge by which values are joined to the differentiated subsystems of action and the situations in which action takes place, looked at from the point of view of the degree to which, and the mechanisms by which, the values can be understood to play a part in the empirical regulation of action. What this degree is in a concrete case is always an empirical question and must never be assumed on a priori grounds.

LEGITIMATION AND INSTITUTIONALIZATION

The primary reference point for the linkage of values through legitimation with the structure of the social system is *insti-*

tutionalization. This I conceive to be a category for the analysis of social systems as such, whereas both values and legitimation are more general than that and apply to *any* systems of action, including cultures, personalities, and, in certain ways, organisms.

Institutions are generalized patterns of norms which define *categories* of prescribed, permitted, and prohibited behavior in social relationships for people in interaction with each other as members of their society and its various subsystems and groups. They are always *conditional* patterns in some sense. *If* you occupy a certain status in a social group or relationship, and *if* certain types of situation arise, you are expected to behave in certain ways with respect to the prescribed, permitted, or prohibited. Institutions as such incorporate what I have called "value-content," that is, *legitimate directionality* of behavior. But they also do more than this. They *relativize* rights and obligations to status in the social system, and to the structure of the situation in which persons of a given status are placed, and they define and legitimate *sanctions,* that is, types of consequences of the action of an individual, "intentionally" (which need not mean consciously or deliberately) imposed by the actions of others in reaction to the person's own. Sanctions, of course, being conditional, may be anticipated and hence, within limits, may control behavior through motivating the avoidance of negative and the securing of positive sanctions.

Values define, as I have suggested, a broad direction of action. They do not, however, tell the individual what to do in a given situation; they are too general. When values are institutionalized, statuses and situations are differentiated, and differentiated and graduated sanctions, positive and negative, are attached to them. Conformity with different institutional expectations, and different degrees of conformity and infraction of the same ones, are ascribed to different categories of statuses and roles in the social system.

Values as such are undifferentiated with respect to the internal structure of the social system. A person's values are the same, that is, they are definable and describable, independent of who he is in social-status terms, what situations he faces, and what the probable consequences of different alternatives of his action are for him.

Institutions, on the other hand, are differentiated in the first instance with reference to function in the social system. They define the situation for, and regulate, collective life and, relative to the same shared value system, permit, prohibit, and prescribe different types of action for different parts of a functionally differentiated system. Thus we may speak of complexes of institutional patterns as regulating all the major functional contexts and group structures of a social system — economic, political, integrative, educational, cultural, and the like.

Authority I conceive to be[6] a category of institutionalization, not one of legitimation as defined above, nor of what, on a somewhat more concrete level, I shall call "authorization." As such it is cognate with such categories as contract and property. Perhaps a brief delineation of these concepts will be helpful in approaching that of the institution of authority. In a society with a widely ramified division of labor there is an immense network of continually shifting contractual arrangements. The terms of these arrangements are settled *ad hoc* in each particular case by agreement of the parties. But in the concrete structure of the social relation involved in a contractual relation there is more than the *ad hoc* agreement of the parties; there is a set of socially defined expectations and norms as to what *kinds* of agreements may or may not be made, what means may be employed in securing the other party's consent, how the interests of third parties may affect the agreement, what will happen if, for various reasons, one of the parties fails to fulfill his obligations, and the like. Norms and expectations on this more general level underlie any particular contract, a situation which Durkheim called the *institution* of contract.[7]

Contract, like other institutions in a differentiated society, is in general partly defined and enforced by legal process. Thus some types of agreements are clearly approved by law and interpretable and enforceable at law; others, while not prohibited are declared *ultra vires* so that legal sanctions may not be invoked; still others, like those involving slavery, are explicitly prohibited. The essential

---

[6] That is, I find it convenient to define it this way. There is, of course, an arbitrary element in this and I do not claim it is *the* right way.

[7] Emile Durkheim, *De la Division du travail social* (1893), Book I, ch. VII.

point for present purposes is the existence of a system of relatively general norms which regulate the entrance into and the consequences of contractual agreements, but which do not prescribe either that any given persons should enter into any given agreements under given circumstances, or, within the institutional limits, what the content of such agreements should be.

The institution of property is a cognate set of norms regulating the relations of persons, individual and corporate, to economically valuable objects of possession. They involve the definition of types of rights of use, control, and acquisition or disposal with reference to such nonsocial objects. Though in the first instance a set of rights and obligations with reference to nonsocial objects, property always involves and helps to define social relationships in that the right of any actor in relation to an object entails at the very least the obligations of others to respect that right, and, conversely, the basis of the obligations of property is the impingement of the owner's rights on the right of others. It is the social-relation aspect which is at the focus of the *institution* of property.

Similarly, I think of authority as an institutionalized complex of norms which do not involve the prescription, permission, or prohibition of *particular* acts, but which on a general level define the conditions under which, in the given social structure and given statuses and situations within it, acts of others within the same collectivity *may* be prescribed, permitted, or prohibited. In order to say more it is necessary to discuss what I referred to above as the political aspect of a social system.

It seems to me that what are very generally called the political processes of social systems need to be dealt with in relation to the two different levels of the structure of social systems already mentioned — levels which unfortunately are often not discriminated in the literature of either political science or sociology. One is the level of institutions in the sense I have just been discussing, the other is that of *government* as involving a specific complex of *collectivities,* of organizations in which specific decisions are made and specific administrative tasks carried out. The distinction is one which runs throughout the analysis of the structure and functioning of social systems. Thus property and contract concern the institutional level of the structure of economic function in societies, while the structure of business firms, and of markets which articulate them with each other and the like, concerns the collectivity level. Property and contract are not types of firms, and similarly authority in my usage is not a branch or agency of the government.

If I may continue with the parallel between economic and political categories, what economists call the *economy* is a functional subsystem of the society — not as such a "structure" which primarily articulates the institutional and collectivity levels of the organization of social action in this field.[8] An economy is the set of processes by which, within a framework of institutional norms, the mobilization of the factors of production — for example, through employment and investment — and commitment to the production of goods and services are carried out. Collectivities are the active instrumentalities of these processes — and so, of course, are individuals *in their roles* in collectivities.[9]

Cognate with the economy in this sense, I conceive that we can speak of a functional subsystem of the society in the political area, conveniently referred to as the "polity." The goal or function of the economy is *production,* in the economic, not the physical sense, and the product is income or wealth. The goal or function of the polity I conceive to be the mobilization of societal resources and their commitment for the attainment of *collective* goals, for the formation and implementation of "public policy." The "product" of the polity as a system is *power,* which I would like to define as the *generalized capacity of a social system to get things done in the interest of collective goals.* Again, collectivities are the active instrumentalities of these processes, operating within an institutional

---

[8] Cf. T. Parsons and Smelser, *Economy and Society,* for a full discussion of the nature of an economy in these terms.

[9] The purely "individual" producer, e.g., the independent artisan, may from this point of view be treated as the limiting case of a one-man firm. For relatively refined purposes it is also important to distinguish the *plant* as the collective organization engaged in physical production from the *firm* as the superordinate organization concerned with the mobilization and commitment of the factors of production and the disposal of the product through the market mechanism.

framework. Primarily, but by no means exclusively, in the political case it is the network of collectivities we call government which constitutes such instrumentalities. Through such collectivities resources are mobilized and through the decision-making process, committed to goals, and then the "product" is distributed to the ultimate beneficiaries.

A brief word should be said about the concept of power as used here. It seems to me that it is one of the two principal alternatives which are current in the literature of political theory, the other being what may be called the "zero-sum" concept.[10] This is the conception that power is the capacity of one unit in a system to gain its ends *over the opposition* of other units — hence, if the power of two units is equal, there is a stalemate between them. The concept I am using here does not make opposition a criterion as such, though since I am talking about capacity to attain goals, it *includes* the overcoming of opposition. I thus consider the zero-sum concept to be a special case of the more general concept employed here.

Power and wealth have in common that they are both generalized categories of "means," that is, of capacities to get desired things done. They differ in that though production as such is a collective value, the product (wealth or income) has no specific reference to *collective goals;* it is a means to *any* goals valued in the society. Power, on the other hand, has specific reference to the goals of the collectivity, and hence implies, for its generation, *integration* of the collectivity with reference to such goals, in a sense which production of wealth does not.

Our immediate concern, then, is with the institutional framework within which power is produced and allocated in a social system, which sets the main norms that must be observed in the process. Coming a little closer to the problem we may note that, though in one connection institutions constitute the "spelling out" of values for the more differentiated contexts of social action, in another connection institutions constitute the primary focus of the integration of a social system. It is only by virtue of institutionalized norms that internal conflict can be held within tolerable limits

---

[10] Used, for example, by Max Weber and H. D. Lasswell.

and that different units of the social structure can be channeled
into mutually supportive relations with each other.

Ever since Hobbes, if not much longer, it has been acutely
realized that power was a central focus of the integration problem
in societies. If a social system is to be stable, the circumstances
under which power can be generated, and thus "acquired" and
allocated, cannot be left unregulated by institutional mechanisms,
or on occasion by overt goal-directed collective action.

POLITICAL INSTITUTIONS: THE PLACE OF AUTHORITY

Authority I conceive to be part of a wider complex of institutionalization in social systems with reference to power and to
political function. The broadest category of political institutions,
from which more specific ones may be derived, may be called
"differential responsibility." By this I mean that it is a general
feature of the institutionalized structure of a social system that
responsibility for the effective performance of all functions in the
system is not diffusely spread among all statuses in it. In one sense
the division of labor results in differential responsibility in that
de facto different groups assume different specialized functions.
But what I have in mind now goes beyond this in one respect: that
there comes to be differential responsibility for effective performance
of functions which are held to be, for the system in question, "affected with a public interest," that is, for collective goals.

Differential responsibility in this sense is an aspect of what
sociologists call social stratification. The reference, however, is not to
stratification in general but is political, namely to the achievement
of collective goals where positive action binding the collectivity
and its members is necessary. It is theoretically possible, and in
limiting cases in small groups approximated, for all members
effectively to bear equal responsibility in such matters, but in
general, and the more so the larger the system, there are fundamental factors making for inequality. Though these are in general
familiar, the importance of clarity of decision, range of planning
in terms of time and subject-matter, and symbolization of consensus
may be mentioned among the reasons why differential responsibility
has a great advantage over too great equalization. On the negative

side it is crucial that any social system, the more so the more complex and larger it is, involves many interests and functions which in the nature of the case are distributive rather than central in relevance and are hence decentralized in operation. This means that persons and organizations which specialize in such functions, for example, economic production or simply family living, *cannot* to the same degree specialize in taking responsibility for public affairs.

As a very broad historical generalization it can be said that while in earlier civilizations (as distinguished from primitive societies) political responsibility has tended to be institutionalized in the hands of general upper classes or aristocracies, in modern western society at least the trend has been in the direction of its coming into the hands of groups with more or less of an occupational character, such as, "politicians" or civil and military "servants." There is no longer the presumption either that, by virtue of aristocratic status, disproportionate political influence and responsibility follows as a matter of course, or that the politically responsible, influential, or powerful would automatically control all important functions in the society. Of course imperatives of integration necessitate important relations between the responsible elements in different sectors of a society, but these are not of a simple character.

Differential responsibility in relation to collective goals seems to me to be the parallel in the political sphere of contract in the economic. Contract is, in proportion to the elaboration of the division of labor, the general institutional framework within which access to the factors of production and to markets for the disposal of products is regulated in a society; it is above all the framework which defines the relations of an organizational unit in the productive process to the structured social environment in which it operates. Similarly, differential responsibility is the general framework within which the rights and obligations of leadership with reference to collective goals are regulated in a society. Above all, it defines the relations to their social environment of the organizations specializing in performing this type of function in the society, the kinds of terms on which they may secure access to the necessary resources, and the kinds of relations they may es- tablish with the recipients of their services.

In the economic case, contract, as the most general institutional category, divides into two main branches or subtypes according to the two most fundamental types of resources employed in pro- duction, namely, social and nonsocial. The one branch, through the contract of employment, leads to the complex we speak of as institutions of occupational status and role, and regulates through them the utilization of human services in the productive process. The other, through the contract of investment, leads to the complex we call the institution of property, and regulates the utilization of nonhuman or nonsocial factors in production — of course, at various levels of economic generalization, from concrete materials and equipment to purely monetary resources.

I would like to suggest a conception of authority which defines it as parallel to one of the two subtypes of institutionalized dif- ferential responsibility, namely, employment and the occupational complex. From this point of view authority would be the complex of institutionalized rights to control the actions of members of the society with reference to their bearing on the attainment of col- lective goals. That the bearers of differential responsibility should have such rights — differing, of course, in kind and degree in different cases — is a necessary condition of fulfillment of the ex- pectations defining that responsibility. It goes back to the central point of integration of the collectivity through support of leader- ship. Authority thus is the institutionalization of given modes and levels of integration of the collectivity insofar as these are essential conditions of effective and legitimized collective action. It is the institutionalization of the rights of "leaders" to expect support from the members of the collectivity.

The second main branch or subtype of differential responsibility I would like to call responsibility for *regulation* of the activities of persons and collectivities with reference to their bearing on the public interest. This is parallel with the contract of investment and the institutional complex of property. I say parallel and not identical because the line of discrimination here is not that between the utilization of social (or human) and nonsocial resources, but that of the bearing of action on the attainment of collective goals as distinguished from activities which, though in accord and societal values, do not bear directly on political interests in this sense. Leadership, or politically responsible elements, must be in a position to influence such activities with respect to their bearing on the public interest, and implement institutional rules which define the requisite borderlines.[11] Because of the very great prominence of economic production in the activities of American society, it is with reference to this context that the concept of regulation has come to be most familiar; indeed, it is from economic production that its prototype has been taken for purposes of the present discussion. The distinction between authority and regulation is, at the societal level, essentially that between "public" and "private" spheres of interest.

As in the case of any other institution, a pattern of authority will be defined by reference to the four criteria outlined above: (1) legitimation in terms of the general values of the society; (2) status in the system of roles or collectivities to which it is applied; (3) the type of situation with which authority-bearers are expected to be faced; and (4) the sanctions which on the one hand are at their disposal, and on the other hand can be brought to bear by others in relation to their action.

The values of the society will define the main framework of attitudes toward the attainment of collective goals, the broad types of goals to which commitment is likely to be made, and the degree of legitimized "activism" with reference to such goals. Differential responsibility will then be the focus of the claim to authority as a condition of implementing that responsibility. But a third variable will be the type of situation in which authority is expected to be exercised; and finally, authority will differ according to the types of sanctions which are at the disposal of its holders, and the types

[11] There is a common ambiguity in the phrase "public interest" to which attention should be called. On the one hand it may refer to the interest of the social system in the sense of being in accord with the values of the system in relation to its situation — in this sense, for example, sound family life is "in the public interest." But this is, in a society like ours, a peculiarly "private" sphere, and severe limits are imposed on the rights of public authority to intervene in family affairs. The other meaning of public interest is the specifically political one, namely, having to do with the attainment of collective goals as such. It is in this latter sense that the concept is used here.

of counteraction with which they may be expected to have to cope, which are sanctions looked at from the obverse point of view. (This is the point at which questions concerning the use of coercive sanctions, particularly physical force, become relevant.)

MAX WEBER'S TYPES OF AUTHORITY

It seems to me that all four of these variables need to be taken into account in working out a general classification of types of authority. It is important to note that Max Weber's famous classification dealt with only one of them, namely the bearing of the general values of the society through the processes I have called those of legitimation. It may be worthwhile to try to state where Weber's three categories fit in terms of the present analytical scheme.

There is an important sense in which the concept of *traditional* authority constitutes the base line of Weber's analysis. This seems to me to be very nearly identical with what I have called diffuse differential responsibility, in a social system where differential responsibility in the political context has not been differentiated from generally superior status. Such authority exists, as Weber says, by virtue of a "traditional status." [12] The limits to this authority are not confined to a clearly defined context of political functions; within certain spheres there are clearly expected rights to act, and beyond these there is a diffuse sphere within which loyalty on a particularistic basis of generally superior status is expected. Though there is no formally defined administrative structure segregated from nonpolitical functions one may say that the limits of this loyalty are essentially those of acceptability or belongingness in the requisite collectivity. Barnard's well-known criterion applies here; that defiance of authority is essentially a bid to take over the responsibility of the agent of authority.[13] The outcome of successful resistance to such a bid is, if the defiance is persisted in, extrusion of the bidder from the collectivity — in extreme cases perhaps by execution.

Weber's other two types deviate from traditional authority in two directions. The rational-legal type is the consequence of a process of *differentiation* of political from nonpolitical functions in the

---

[12] *Theory of Social and Economic Organization*, p. 341.
[13] Chester I. Barnard, *The Functions of the Executive* (1938), ch. X.

social system. Authority then no longer rests in a diffusely superior status bearing differential responsibility but in a positively delineated set of powers or rights to exercise political responsibility in the social system. The focus of this functional differentiation or delineation is the concept of *office,* which is marked off from general social superiority in nonpolitical respects. The institution of office has this significance even though there is a realistic correlation between incumbency of office and the enjoyment of high status in other respects, such as lineage or wealth. Weber, it will be noted, does not distinguish between what have here been called authority and regulation, but throws them together as both legally regulated.

Charismatic authority deviates from traditional not by a further process of structural differentiation in the system, but by questioning the legitimacy of the traditional (that is, institutionalized) status-order. In some relevant aspects, the charismatic leader stands in explicit opposition to the traditional order; he sets his "personal" legitimation over against the institutionalized basis. But the claim is one in terms of legitimacy; as Weber says, acceptance of charismatic authority is treated by the leader as a matter of moral obligation.

If this analysis is acceptable, it can be concluded that Weber's classification is not one of types of legitimation in terms of different types of values, but on the one hand, of level of differentiation of the social system with reference to political function, and on the other, of stability of institutionalization of the value system in this respect. Variations which are a function of type of values, then, would be expected to be analytically independent of Weber's classification and could be applied to any of his three types. It would lead too far afield to attempt to work out here a classification of authority types in terms of values, and of the other three of the four variables outlined above, but this seems to be both an urgent and a feasible task for the further development of political sociology.

LAW AND INSTITUTIONS

The above discussion, and in particular the reference to Weber's category of rational-legal authority, raises the question of the relations of law in general to institutions in the sociological sense and to the institutionalization of authority in particular. My view

is that law, or legal process, is a set of mechanisms which operate
with respect to *all* categories of institutions in a society in which
law itself is institutionalized. It is not, in terms of content, specific
to any particular category of institutions. It does, however, have a
special relation to the political function in the society, since two
essential functions of a legal system, the definition of the scope of
jurisdiction and the authorization and implementation of sanctions,
inevitably involve political references.

Institutions, I have suggested, have primarily integrative functions
in social systems. But as normative patterns they do not operate
automatically — to suggest that they did would impute a kind of
animistic magic to them. To be legitimized they must be authoritatively interpreted with reference to more general canons of legitimacy. The mutual consistency of norms in a system requires
continual adjustment by action directly oriented to such problems,
since in terms of content the normative system is continually
changing. Furthermore, institutional norms must be applied in
detailed and particular situations, and the range of sanctions of
enforcement must be defined. In advanced societies, legal processes
are specially concerned with these functions.

Law is that aspect of the machinery for the definition and implementation of institutional norms which links legitimation
through authoritative interpretation with application and enforcement by political agency. Enforcing agencies are not in a strict
sense part of the legal system itself (considered as a subsystem of
social action, not of formulated rules) at all, but are part of the
political organization. Law enforcement is a political function. The
focus of the legal system is found in the courts which are interstitial
between political and nonpolitical systems in a sense parallel to
that in which political parties are interstitial between government
and the "public." The private legal profession is still another
interstitial structure which is even less "political" than are the
courts, mediating between the judicial processes and the interests
of clients.

Seen in these terms, the legal definition of the content and limits
of authority becomes an imperative necessity in a society where
functional differentiation has reached high levels. The effect of

such differentiation is, as noted, the creation of a whole complex of interests and structures which cannot be mainly concerned with the implementation of the collective goals of the social system as a whole, but in this frame of reference have various bases of legitimation as "private" spheres. The basis for this legitimation is of course the values held in common in the society, but the effect of this *must* be to limit the rights of public authority to "interfere" with these interests. The relative specification of the authority of persons and collectivities defined as carrying differential responsibility is a direct consequence of the institutionalization of obligations for the performance of nonpolitical functions in the society. The development of a legal system is thus a major requirement if the society is to reach levels of social differentiation where nonpolitical functions acquire, and can count on, institutionalized rights as well as obligations, in the performance of their jobs.[14]

For perspective it is important to be aware that law is only one of several mechanisms involved in the operation of institutional complexes in a complex society. Political processes also operate in this field since, in general, securing observance of institutional norms is taken to be a goal of the society. It is in this category that the law-enforcement functions of political bodies should be placed. But there are also very important processes which operate within institutional and legal frameworks, to be sure, but not directly as legal or as political process. Some of these involve relatively specialized and directly institutionalized processes as in the therapeutic treatment of illness, or some aspects of religion, education, and family functioning. These in turn shade over into "informal" mechanisms and processes. The sociologist tends to sum up both types of extralegal process as "mechanisms of social control."

THE GENERALIZATION OF INSTITUTIONAL PATTERNS

For the purposes of the present analysis attention has been focused on the total society. Authority has been treated as a political institution on this level and its relation to law stated in broad terms.

---

[14] Similar considerations of course apply to the importance of legal definition of other institutional pattern-complexes such as contract, property, employment, and many others.

The generalized analytical scheme employed, however, is not confined in its relevance to this level but is meant to be applicable to *any* social system. All social systems, that is, have integrative problems which are the focus of processes of institutionalization of values, and all social systems are differentiated to some extent with reference to the pursuit of collective goals. Hence it should follow that authority, or an institutional phenomenon cognate with it, should be a feature not only of the societies in their political aspect, but of all social systems. By definition, however, any social system other than a society is a subsystem of a society. Hence the question arises of the relation between the authority patterns on the highest societal level, that is, those defining its political structure in the sense in which we have discussed it, and on other levels.

The same general principles may be employed in approaching this question as have been used above. The values of a society operate not only at the most general level, but permeate its structure as a whole. Every subsystem has a value system of its own which is a differentiated and specialized version of the general value system, limited by the level and functions of the subsystem in the whole. It is an imperative of cultural integration that there should be a relative pattern-congruence at these different levels. But there must also be differentiation and specification appropriate to the particular subsystem.

When subvalues are institutionalized as such, they in turn legitimate subinstitutions which in turn are differentiated in relation to the structure and situation of the subsystem in question, and of the requisite categories of roles within it. Thus we would have variations in mode of legitimation, in the statuses of role-performers within the system, in their situations, and in the institutionalization of sanctions.

In these terms every subsystem within the society has its patterns of authority, because on its own level every subsystem has political functions and differential political responsibility. But these will differ for different types of subsystems within the society, by the various criteria by which authority-patterns can and do vary. One of these is the type of function of the subsystem in the larger society. Thus authority in a military organization under direct political control is naturally different from that in a business firm or in a university. A second basis of variation is the size and scope of the subsystem or collectivity. Thus a family not only has special functions but is a small group with a necessarily limited level of structural differentiation. Hence authority in it must be linked with the diffuse responsibility of the two adult members vis-à-vis their children, in a way which need not be the case in a more highly differentiated system. Degree of formalization of authority is linked to, but not identical with, degree of differentiation. In very large and highly differentiated private organizations there is not only control through the societal legal system, but there develops something very like a legal system for the organization as such.

When, therefore, the whole ramified structure of institutions in a society and its subsystems is looked at, it is a differentiated hierarchy of permissions, prescriptions, and prohibitions such that the higher level prescribes the limits within which the lower and more differentiated ones may operate. For any given subsystem the relation may be conveniently stated in terms of what is often referred to as the distinction between the "external" and the "internal" systems.[15] In its external relations, that is, those with other subsystems of the larger system, a subsystem or collectivity is subject to the institutionalized order of the system superordinate to it in the structural hierarchy. For example, a business firm is subject to laws of incorporation, contract, property, and employment in its operations in relation to other units through markets and the like. In its internal relations, within institutionalized limits, it can create its own order, pattern of authority, rules of property, and the like.

Internal relations are not, however, institutionalized only through the setting of limits to the range of private variability. There is also direct "authorization" of certain types of functions and hence requirements imposed on those who participate in them. A striking example is the generalization of the institution of incorporation in modern societies. The general point is that in many spheres where private agencies undertake socially significant functions in the context of large-scale organization which involves complex property relations and organization of personnel with many different types of competence, there is a strong tendency to adopt the

---

[15] Cf. G. C. Homans, *The Human Group* (1950), for a convenient delineation of this distinction.

corporate form. But this is essentially a delegation of public authority to a private group, which in exchange for the privileges of incorporation places it in a position of fiduciary responsibility for which it is publicly accountable. It is of course notable that extension of the corporate form beyond the governmental and ecclesiastical spheres on a considerable scale is a relatively recent thing.

AUTHORITY AND AUTHORIZATION

I have discussed authority in this paper as a phenomenon on the *institutional* level of the structure of social systems and carefully discriminated that from the level of collectivity functioning. In order to round out the picture I would like very briefly to indicate what seems to me to be the cognate concept for the operation of the collectivity as such. This is what I shall mean by *authorization*.

Authority, like other categories of institutionalization, has been defined here independently of any particular goals of the system though very definitely in relation to the goal-attainment function. Put a little differently, it is an essential prerequisite of the decision-making process in a social system, but not as such part of it. An institution is oriented to a general type or category of situation, decision-making to a specific situation.[16] By authorization, then, I mean that aspect of the process of collective decision-making by which organs or agencies of the collectivity in question, whose status is defined by a given type and extent of authority, are given permission to use this authority in particular situations with reference to particular goals. For purposes of defining the concept it is indifferent whether the process of authorization involves specification of goals or of measures to be taken to implement a goal. Further, systems may differ according to the degree to which and occasions on which authorization is necessary for various types of action.

A classic instance of what I mean here by authorization is one aspect of the function of the legislature relative to the executive in modern governments. Within limits the executive has authority to act in the light of the exigencies of the situation and to use his

[16] The relativity of the distinction is evident; it must be defined in terms of a definite system-reference.

authority over implementing agencies and the public to carry out his policy, independently of any decision-making process outside his own branch. But there are other areas in a system like ours, such as the assessment of new taxes, where specific legislative authorization is necessary before the executive action of revenue collection can take place. A military example may also be cited. A commander in the field generally has authority over the units under his command to order them into combat without their consent in the specific case. But he may still require authorization from a higher echelon, for example, the General Staff, before issuing a particular order of this sort.

In general usage, the word "authority" has been ambiguous on this point. Sometimes it has meant what is here called institutionalized authority to do certain *kinds* of things with or without specific authorizations, and sometimes it has meant permission or prescription to take specific action with reference to the exigencies of a specific situation. Whatever the terms chosen, it seems to me to be important to distinguish these two levels of reference in analyzing the functioning of social systems in pursuit of collective goals.

CONCLUSION

This paper has attempted, in an exceedingly brief compass, to canvass a range of related analytical problems in the theory of social systems which bear particularly on the definition and use of terms in the borderline area between political science and sociology. The most important general aims of the paper have been, first, to discriminate three important levels on which the analysis of social systems can be developed and, second, to locate more precisely than is sometimes done the *political* aspect of social-system function relative to others, notably the economic.

The three levels of reference for the analysis of social systems are values, institutions, and collectivities respectively. Values, it was suggested, define broad *directions* of orientation of the members of a system, independent of the specific content of system structure, situation or goals. Institutions are normative patterns defining categories of expected (prescribed, permitted, or prohibited) action on the part of persons situated in different statuses in the system, in different situations and commanding and subject to different sanctions. Collectivities, on the other hand, are concrete groups or organizations of persons in roles engaged in activities which have some sort of functional significance in the system of which they are parts.

It was also suggested that the political aspect of any social system concerned its organization and functioning with reference to the processes of facilitating and implementing the attainment of goals imputed to the system as a whole, that is, collective goals. In a differentiated society political action is concentrated in a complex of collectivities which we usually refer to as government, but is subject to control through a complex of institutionalized patterns. The generation of power and the formulation and implementation of collective goals and policies are the principal political functions.[17]

In this connection we suggest usages for three terms which are frequently employed in this general connection. First, the term *legitimation* may refer to the main link between values and their "spelling out" in the context of the institutional level of the regulation of action. An institutional pattern, that is, is legitimized in terms of the underlying values of the social system. Second, the term *authority* may be appropriately used to designate a particular *class of institutional patterns* of primary relevance to the regulation of political functions in a social system, namely, that where persons or offices bearing differential political responsibility (in a society as a whole or some subsystem of it) are held to be entitled to support or to promote certain types of integration of the system in relation to collective goals, that is, including the prescription and enforcement by sanctions of certain types of cooperation in promoting the goals and/or the prohibition of certain types of interference with such activity. Finally, third, the term *authorization* seems appropriate to designate the process by which, through decision-making within a collectivity, certain types of measures relative to particular situations and goals are permitted, prescribed, or enjoined which, without that decision process, would not be within the "authority" of the relevent agencies.

[17] The reader will remember the distinction between values and goals made at the beginning of the paper. The formulation of societal values is, in my terminology, *not* a political function.

It is furthest from the intention of this paper to be dogmatic about definitions of terms. Terminology in this area is not standardized and no one is entitled to legislate a particular usage. What is important is to take cognizance of substantive analytical problems of the order of those which have been reviewed, and in practice to avoid confusion between the different problems and levels of analysis.

13. Authority in Primitive Societies

E. ADAMSON HOEBEL

"The principle of authority comes into being from the beginnings of mankind . . . Political authority as we know it is indispensable even at primitive levels; we have defined it as the legally vested power to establish norms, to take decisions and to enforce them through the use of sanction by coercion." [1]

Upon acceptance of the general validity of Malinowski's observation, our task becomes one of examination of several questions. What are the situations in which authority is expressed? What varieties of authority are commonly manifest in different types of groups and societies? How is authority achieved or allocated? What are the discernible limits to the exercise of authority?

Authority, in its simplest terms, is here understood to mean the explicit capacity to direct the behavior of others. Authority is thus expressed in interpersonal relations; the quality of explicitness differentiates it from hidden or hypersubtle influence; and "to direct" means to alter or modify the behavior of others from the line of conduct they would presumably or possibly follow were the authority not exercised.

Malinowski referred the emergence of authority to the beginnings of mankind for the reason that it is observed to be a functionally universal component of organized social life among human beings. It is possible to go even further and take note of the fact that authority is very much in evidence among the infrahuman primates,

[1] B. Malinowski, *Freedom and Civilization* (1944), pp. 187–188, 248.

man's nearest relatives on the phylogenetic tree.[2] The reasons are clear enough. Man and the primates are the end-product of a long process of organic evolution leading to greater and greater adaptive variability on the part of individual members of the newer species. Capacity for random behavior that does not represent an instinctive adjustment between the organism and its environment has been enormously stepped up through elaboration of the nervous system and increasing generalization of the major motor organs of the body. Thus among human beings, as among no other creatures, has the range of potential behavior of adults been widened until its scope strikes us as approaching infinity.[3] The documentation of the forms in which the variety is expressed has been a major activity of anthropologists for more than a century.[4] Not only does the physiology of mankind make possible widely variable behavior; it also requires a long period of postnatal development before the maturing individual becomes capable of directing his behavior in ways that are not self-destructive or, at least, self-defeating. Thus authoritative control of infant and child behavior is an inherent necessity for continuance of the human species.[5] Finally, because human beings always live in groups cooperatively engaged in many activities, integration of the behavior of the component individuals is essential to effective group existence.[6] To achieve even minimal coordination of the activities of its members, each group finds itself faced by an *imperative of selection*. It must perforce fix upon a limited number of patterns for behavior, thereupon quite arbitrarily ruling out and suppressing a much larger corpus of possible patterns of behavior, so far as its membership is concerned. The resulting nexus of permissible patterns for behavior is what anthropologists have come to identify as the culture of a given society or intrasocietal group — its way of life. The imperative of selection

[2] Cf. E. A. Hooton, *Man's Poor Relations* (1944), for a comparative synopsis of the known behavior of primates.

[3] See J. P. Gillin, "Custom and the Range of Human Response," *Character and Personality*, 13:101–134 (1944).

[4] "Anthropology holds up a great mirror to man and lets him look at himself in his infinite variety" (C. Kluckhohn, *Mirror for Man*, 1949, p. 11).

[5] A biogenic approach to human socialization is ably developed by W. LaBarre in his recent book, *The Human Animal* (1955). For additional literature on the subject, see D. Haring, *Personality and Cultural Milieu* (1948).

[6] See D. Aberle, *et al.*, "The Functional Prerequisites of Society," *Ethics*, 60 (1950).

imposes an imperative of decision. In the growth of culture, many new behaviors do become established as permissible without explicit awareness of innovation. But again and again, innovation — which at the outset means deviation from established norms — is consciously weighed in terms of acceptability or unacceptability. Whenever this occurs, some members of the group will be found to be engaged in the process of determining what the behavior of others shall be. Authority is also exercised not only in the establishment and maintenance of norms, but in the initiation and coordination of activities from among norms that would otherwise remain dormant, so far as the immediate situation is concerned. For example, for the Siuai of Bougainville in the Solomon Islands, weeks of preparation led up to a great feast attended by eleven hundred visitors, an event of climactic excitement. When the day ended, an ordinary man said hopefully to the anthropologist, Douglas Oliver, "Now we shall rest. Now we can attend to our gardens."

Yet [writes Professor Oliver] early the next morning the wooden gongs boomed out again and they seemed louder than ever, probably because the noise was so unexpected. A few sleepy natives strolled in the direction of the club-house and heard Soŋi storm out: "Hiding in your house again; copulating day and night while there's work to be done! Why if it were left up to you, you would spend the rest of your lives smelling yesterday's pig.[7] But I tell you, yesterday's feast was nothing. The next one will really be big. Siham, I want you to arrange with Konnu for his largest pig; and you, Maimoi, go to Mokakaru and find a pig for Uremu; and — etc."[8]

The effective instruments of authority are sanctions — positive (rewarding) and negative (punishing).[9] Authority without sanctions is but an empty name. Any comprehensive study of authority in a society would necessarily require analysis of the total system of social control, the full inventory of the means utilized to induce conformity to behavioral norms, from child-training through explicit political and legal sanctions on the secondary level of relationships.

---

[7] That is, in reverie over the feast just completed.

[8] D. L. Oliver, A Solomon Island Society: Kinship and Leadership Among the Siuai of Bougainville (1955), p. 439.

[9] See A. R. Radcliffe-Brown, "Sanction, Social," Encyclopedia of the Social Sciences, vol. 13, pp. 531–534.

However, the focus of interest in this paper precludes immediate concern with all but the last of the levels of social control in primitive societies — authority in the application of political and legal sanctions.

Social organization comprises all the customary patterns of formalizing interpersonal and group relations within a society's culture. Political organization, from the viewpoint of the anthropologist, is most effectively conceived as that part of social organization which controls relations between groups within the society in terms of the societal whole; it also controls relations of the members of the society *qua* society in their contacts with other societies. Political organization, in this sense, is synonymous with State. Government is made up of more or less specialized personnel, occupying authoritative status in the system of political organization and performing the institutionalized roles that are linked to their special status.

It will be necessary, for the most part, to ignore tyrannical authority, that is, the exercise of coercive power resting on sheer might and unabashed ruthlessness, and to concentrate on authority internally created and accepted as right and good by those who are subject to its control. Such authority represents the more common type found among the primitive societies, at least.

Underlying every culture is a body of basic postulates implicit in the world view of the members of the society in question. These are broadly generalized propositions as to the nature of things and what is qualitatively desirable and what is not. Such postulates, which recent work in anthropological linguistics indicates are in part influenced by the very structure of the language spoken, set major goals for action, and as guides to selection of permissible lines of behavior, pattern the forms of political authority in those societies in which political behavior is an outgrowth of the indigenous social system and not a power structure imposed by outsiders.[10]

Those peoples who have the least complex cultures are surviving food-gatherers and simple hunters such as the Eskimos, Great Basin Shoshones (in the United States), the forest pygmies

[10] The relation of fundamental cultural postulates to jural postulates and the formulation of primitive law systems is developed in E. A. Hoebel, *The Law of Primitive Man: A Study in Comparative Legal Dynamics* (1954).

of Africa and Asia, the African Bushmen and Australian aborigines, all of whom live in regions of marginal subsistence.

If we consider the Eskimos as an example of the nature of political authority among the simplest types of societies, we find it lodges in two functionaries: the headman and the *angakok*, or shaman. The authority of the headman resides in his superior skill as a hunter, which is compounded of his outstanding energy, his technical proficiency, and a personality that evokes favorable responses from the members of his little community. As a hunter "he is first out on the ice in the morning." Experience has demonstrated that the times and places he chooses for the hunt bring consistently better returns of the meat upon which life in the Arctic so precariously hangs. The headman rarely commands or explicitly orders behavior. Rather, he leads by suggestion and example. The very terms by which the Eskimo identify him indicate the nature of his influence. Among the Baffin Island Eskimos, he is called *pimain*, "he who knows everything best"; among the Caribou Eskimos, he is known as *ihumitak*, "he who thinks"; and among the Unalit, *anaiyuhok*, "he to whom all listen."

The *angakok* wields authority in his sphere because he has entered into a personal relationship with supernatural beings whose activities also directly influence the survival of the community. Individual sinning (the violation of cultural tabus) drives the sea mammals to shun the local territory. The *angakok* is the inquisitor who determines who has sinned and how, and he can order penance or even banishment of sinful persons. The secular authority of the headman is amorphous; the supernaturally derived authority of the *angakok* is explicitly coercive.

Among the Shoshones, the headman of the local group is called *tekniwup*, "good talk thrown out to the people." Like the Eskimo authority, he knows best. He is counselor to his little band of followers; he gives no orders, renders no judicial decisions. As one of my Comanche informants said of the Comanche *tekniwup*, "I hardly know how to tell about him. He didn't have anything to do, except to hold the band together." Among the Shoshones and Comanches, in contrast to the Eskimos, the medicine man exercised little coercive power except through illegal sorcery. As we move through all the simple, nomadic food-gathering peoples, we find the pattern is essentially the same. Authority rests on an intimate and superior knowledge of how best to exploit the meagre resources of the local ecology. It is diffuse in nature, ambiguous, and altruistic — rarely, if ever, domineering or tyrannical. The beginnings of political authority are modest and egalitarian.

The societies just discussed are small and unsegmented. That is, they normally include populations numbering no more than one or two hundred persons; they have no internal groupings other than primary families and extended kindred. Societies that have a sufficiently developed technology, coupled with reasonably adequate resources, expand their population aggregates to include several thousand individuals among whom is always found a greater or lesser degree of internal specialization. Among cultures on this level, a greater degree of variation in configuration is also notable. To illustrate, let us look at the Plains Indians, a Melanesian society, the Pueblos of New Mexico, and certain peoples of Africa.

Four kinds of prowess were valued among the nomadic buffalo hunters of our Western Plains midway in the nineteenth century. The first of these was military, the second was peaceful altruism, the third lay in supernaturalism and the fourth was the accumulation of wealth in horses. Authority was vested in those who achieved distinction in the first two areas. The introduction of the horse and the gun to the Indians of the Plains, combined with the migratory movements of tribes set underway by European settlement and imperialistic rivalries in the eastern woodlands, provided the basis for a florescent elaboration of a war complex among the Plains Indians.[11] The males of each tribe were ranked according to their performances on a carefully graded scale of deeds of valor in the face of the enemy. The topmost among those who had won a place well up on the scale were recognized as war chiefs. In the less developed tribes, peripheral to the western margins of the plains, the explicit authority of such leaders was limited to such raiding parties as were organized and led by a given chief. For the duration of a raid his word was absolute for those who had accepted his leadership through joining his war party. But upon occasion of an enemy attack on a home village,

[11] M. B. Smith, "The War Complex of the Plains Indians," *American Philosophical Society, Proceedings*, 28:425–464 (1937).

the war chiefs exercised no particular authority, since all the males fought, each according to his enthusiasm. Among most of the Plains Indian tribes, the warriors were organized into military societies — men's clubs with distinctive ceremonies, songs, and dances, who also exercised police and judicial functions in the maintenance of order in the camp and during the communal buffalo hunt.[12] Their authority stemmed directly from prowess in the highly valued skills of arms. But in no sense was their authority one of sheer might, for the situations in which they acted were limited in number, and the ways in which they acted were channeled by definitely established patterns of due process. Among the Cheyennes, Last Bull was deposed as chief of the Fox Soldiers for persistent irregularity in overexercise of his authority. Even more impressive is the fact that among virtually all North American tribes the powers of decision-making for the band or tribe was vested in a council of civil, or peace, chiefs as against the war chiefs. The peace chiefs of the Plains tribes were headmen of the Eskimo or Shoshone type with stepped-up powers. Although as individuals these men may have had praiseworthy records as warriors, their authority as chiefs derived from their distinction as wisemen of peaceable demeanor who were generous in their largesse. They could also be individually notable for the quality of their medicine (supernatural powers derived from visions), but medicine power was not in this group of cultures a major basis for political authority.

In Melanesia, the counters by means of which men rate their prestige status are commonly, albeit not exclusively, those of exchange manipulation (success in headhunting may go along with it). The Siuai of Bougainville, already mentioned, serve very well to exemplify the pattern. As reported by Professor Oliver, "The principal *goals* motivating behavior referable to this system (sociopolitical rank) are renown and the power that accompanies it, and the most important *activities* carried out directly in pursuit of these goals are: acquisition of negotiable capital in excess of amounts

---

[12] R. H. Lowie, *The Origin of the State* (1927), pp. 76–107; and "Property Rights and Coercive Powers of Plains Indian Military Societies," *Journal of Political and Legal Sociology,* 1:59–71 (1943). See also K. N. Llewellyn and E. A. Hoebel, *The Cheyenne Way* (1941), ch. 5.

required for subsistence and other kinship system purposes; construction and maintenance of club-houses, and manufacture of wooden slit gongs; and that part of feast-giving specifically related to acquiring renown." [13] The negotiable capital is in the form of pots, pigs, and shell money. Club-houses, which stand along the trail, are established as lounging spots where all comers among the adult males are fed, where the proprietor's slit gongs are kept, and where the personal guardian spirit of the owner resides. The building of a club-house requires the skilled services of gangs of men who must be sumptuously fed. To achieve this requires great manipulatory skill in organizing the labor of numbers of people. The greatest effort, however, goes into "out-doing" feasts for rival leaders, feasts that are very similar to the well-known potlatches on the Northwest Coast of North America. The ingredients that make a Siuai *mumi* (leader) are said to be ambition, skill, industry, and goodness. A man is believed to be born with ambition or without: its presence is believed to be detected early in life, and the child who is believed to have it may be financially backed by his kinsmen in getting a start towards leadership. Skill means technical knowledge plus the ability to put it effectively to use. The ability to accumulate capital is a special skill. Industry means endless effort; some Siuai admit that even if they had the ambition and skills, "the work of becoming a leader is too difficult — never any rest from planning, negotiating, working, and supervising." Goodness means all those attributes we have noted for the Plains Indian peace chief and the headman among food-gatherers: "generosity," "cooperativeness," "geniality," and "decency" — honesty in his transactions.

In the past, *mumis* also organized war parties and head-taking expeditions to exact revenge from those who had affronted one or another of their followers, or to test the relative strength of another *mumi*. In recent years, however, the authority of the *mumi* rests on his wealth-manipulating abilities. His local community is small, and questions of general policy, aside from organizing the renown-giving activities in whose glory the community basks, do not seem to be large. The coercive powers of the *mumi*, since the Australian Administration has arrogated a monopoly of physical

[13] Oliver, p. 456.

coercion to itself, rest on the sensitivity of other men to his words of praise and disparagement. The *mumi* may also fine his followers for inadequate performance. Their reward is "identification" with him in his reputation as it is built up and spreads beyond the home district.

The concentration of concern with feasts and gong-resounding ceremonies, built upon pig and shell-money exchange, that characterizes so much of Melanesian chieftainship has led some earlier writers to observe that authority in this part of the primitive world is "ceremonial" rather than "political." This misses the point. Authority is the organizing force for group endeavor. The endeavor may focus on one or more of a variety of goals. If the chief means is ceremonial feasting and private club-houses, then indeed political leadership may be largely confined to activities in such areas.

Returning to the United States for our next example, we see a type of culture in which political authority derives almost entirely from religious sanctity and position in a priestly hierarchy. The pueblos of central and eastern New Mexico are dominated in their organization by a series of secret religious fraternities upon whose ritual performances the well-being of the entire society is dependent. Power depends upon mastery of esoteric ritual and knowledge through long years of apprenticeship in the lower ranks of priesthood. Material wealth is irrelevant; a man has what his gardens produce; there is no significant system of economic exchange; no competitive feast-giving; war has not been a major activity for some centuries. The supreme head of the village-state is an ineffably sacred priest-chief, called the *nahia,* "the Mother," the living embodiment of the culture-founding goddess of mythological times. Although he ought not to be troubled by dispute and decision-making, when appealed to, Nahia's word is absolute and final. His sanction is mystic, for he more than any other knows best how to preserve the intricate balance of the universe. On lesser levels, the heads of the various societies collectively share the same quality, and so form the tribal council under the direction of an officer called by the name of one of the mythological Twin War Gods, if the problem to be decided is primarily sacred in character, or under the direction of a more noticeably temporal officer, the "governor," if the matters in issue are essentially secular. Note that a distinction between religious and political would be invalid here, for by the nature of Pueblo culture all matters religious concern the entire pueblo and are therefore political. The sanctions exercised by these authorities range from scourging with a cat-o'-nine-tails through incarceration to death.

The several societies thus far referred to are small in size. The chief variable is in the differential weighting of basic values as it affects the allocation of authority. Societies made up of larger populations manifest additional principles of organization with concomitant variation in principles of authority.

Africa[14] confronts us with a number of primitive societies whose populations run into the hundreds of thousands and even several million. Some of these are segmented into kinship groups, but lack hierarchical distinctions or centralized political authority. The kinship groups are unilateral aggregations of kinsmen, called lineages. Lineages exist on a number of levels: that is, a major clan (or lineage) may include two or more sublineages, etc. Each settlement characteristically has a headman, who is the most effective member of the dominant lineage in the settlement, effectiveness being determined by his qualities of good sense and forcefulness tempered by consideration for the sensibilities of his lineage mates. Political organization exists in the mechanisms for maintaining equilibrium between the numerous settlements and lineages — with the headmen serving as spokesmen and crystallizers of policy for their own lineages in relation to others. The ultimate restraint is the inconvenience of feud if common agreement cannot be reached in the settlement of conflicts of interest between the members of different lineages. Ritual functionaries backed by possession of supernatural authority may also function in the enforcing of settlement of disputes. Space precludes detailed examination of the authority system in a given decentralized, segmented society, although excellent accounts are available.[15]

Perhaps enough has been said to set the contrast to the centralized

[14] See M. Fortes and E. E. Evans-Pritchard, eds., *African Political Systems* (1940).
[15] On the Nuer of the Sudan, see E. E. Evans-Pritchard, *The Nuer: A Description of the Modes of Livelihood and Political Institutions of a Nilotic People* (1940), and P. P. Howell, *A Manual of Nuer Law* (1954); on the Tallensi, see M. Fortes, *The Web of Kinship Among the Tallensi* (1949).

system also found in Africa. In such systems the structure is definitely pyramidal. At the core, lineage organization with lineage ancestors and lineage headman usually exists as before. The essential difference lies in the fact that *a* lineage or *a* clan has become established as dominant, and its headman is also chief or king for all other subordinate lineages or clans within the tribe. The dominance appears generally to have been established by military superiority and is consistently maintained by means of a liege-lord relation of personal allegiance of subchief to supreme chief. The subchief is commonly selected by his lineage or clan but must be confirmed by the paramount chief to whom he owes allegiance. He is chosen, in the first instance, as kin or local group headman but functions simultaneously as a village or district agent of the superior chief. Quite consistently in Africa (and indeed in Indonesia and elsewhere among primitive agriculturalists) the king has "title" to the land as the viceroy of the ancestors, who though bodily dead, are alive in spirit. He controls the land, its fruitfulness and prosperity, albeit delegating its distribution and use to the lower order of chiefs, and through them to the people. But through such control he possesses ultimate authority over all things, for he represents the collectivity of ancestors not of his lineage alone but of the entire tribe. If his control extends to conquered tribes, then of course his control rests directly on superior force. Thus, even at home, his sacred authority is usually buttressed by an ultimate power to impose the death penalty according to the patterns and processes set in the tribal culture.[16]

Because the African states of the order under consideration have been built through military dominance, during their formative stages military genius is the prime requisite to chiefdom, as in the cases of Shaka of the Zulus and Osai Tutu of the Ashantis. Yet these men also exhibited great organizational skill and personal charisma. In the stable African state generalship is largely delegated to lesser chiefs, while the paramount king devotes his time and major attention to legal administration, ceremonial ritual on behalf

[16] See, for example, R. S. Rattray, *Ashanti Law and Constitution* (1929); K. A. Busia, *The Position of the Chief in the Modern Political System of Ashanti: A Study of the Influence of Contemporary Social Changes on Ashanti Political Institutions* (1951).

of his kingdom, and the supervision of his legion subchiefs. In 1939 Basutoland, in the Bechuanaland Protectorate of southern Africa, was ruled (leaving aside the British Colonial Office) by 1,006 headmen under 316 subchiefs, who were under eighteen chiefs and one paramount chief, or king.[17] In addition, such system provides for a host of special court and other administrative functionaries such as treasurers, spokesmen, drummers, umbrella bearers, and (in the case of the Ashanti) even a keeper of the royal umbilical cord.

To sum up all the variations on authority in primitive socio-political systems in a limited paper is quite impossible. Only the major features have been sketched here. In essence they are: Authority is implicitly essential to biological and cultural survival. It begins in child-training. Human communities contain more than a single conjugal family, and even where these include distant kindred, two or more recognized kinship groups are always found within a society. Political authority exists when there are powers of decision controlling the behavior of these subgroups in relation to each other, or where such powers are exercised to control behavior of members of other societies. Among the simplest societies political authority is diffuse and ambiguous, though recognized. What does exist is highly personalized and achieved through performance rather than ascribed to inherited status. Authority rests on hunting skill, general wisdom, or specialization in supernaturalism. Although not discussed in this chapter, authority among the Australian aborigines (and the Andaman Islanders) rests largely on seniority among the males. Elsewhere, prestige and associated authority flow from success in military endeavor, economic prowess, religious leadership, or such other foci of cultural interests as are set in the basic value system underlying the culture.

In the large segmented societies such as are exemplified in primitive Africa, authority in the decentralized type of systems is in the hands of lineage and clan headmen; in the centralized states it is ordered in a hierarchy of headmen representing kinship groups or villages, but deriving their power from the paramount chief as well. The power of the central authority, in particular, is always

[17] I. Schapera, *Government and Politics in Tribal Societies* (1956), p. 42.

multiphasal in its magico-religious, military, economic, charismatic, and kinship aspects. Among complex primitive societies polygynous marriages prevail for those well up in the authority structure. Absolute hereditary succession does not occur, for under these conditions a choice may be made from among the numerous aspiring sons or nephews (depending on whether the descent system is patrilineal or matrilineal) who are legitimate heirs to the deceased ruler. Thus personal qualifications remain an important operative factor, although increasing institutionalization of office, which is corollary to increasing complexity of society, steps up transpersonalization of authority as an element of bureaucracy.

Resistance to authority, along with its acceptance, is implicit in all social relations. This is a special subject worthy of full attention in its own right. The reader who wishes to familiarize himself with some recent anthropological thinking on this phase of the question will find stimulus in Professor Max Gluckman's lectures on *Custom and Conflict in Africa*.[18]

[18] M. Gluckman, *Custom and Conflict in Africa* (1955), especially ch. II, "The Frailty in Authority."